TODAY'S RAILWAYS
REVIEW
OF THE YEAR

VOLUME
3

DAVID CARTER
PETER FOX

▲The May timetable included the dropping of the weekday through service between Portsmouth and Plymouth, to the annoyance of many passengers (and the Royal Navy). Weekend services remained, however, this view showing 50045 'Achilles' storming along the single-track section of main line between Yeovil Junction and Crewkerne with the 09.05 Brighton–Plymouth. The date is 15th July.

Tom Clift

▼The Princess Royal Stanier Pacifics were once fairly regular performers on the North Wales Coast route. 1989 saw a welcome return of the Class to their old stamping ground when 'PRINCESS ELIZABETH' made several sorties from Crewe to Holyhead. In glorious sunny weather No. 6201 makes a fine sight as it hurries towards Pemnmaenmawr with the outward leg of the North Wales Coast Express on 3rd September.

Hugh Ballantyne

CONTENTS

Edited by David Carter and Peter Fox.

Written by David Carter, Peter Fox, David Brown, Maxwell H. Fowler, Brian Garvin, Paul Jackson, Kevin Lane, Les Nixon, Paul Shannon and Neil Webster.

Published by Platform 5 Publishing Ltd., Lydgate House, Lydgate Lane, Sheffield, S10 5FH.

Typesetting by Nicolette Williamson.

Printed by Loxley Brothers Ltd., Aizlewood Road, Sheffield, S8 0YS.

ISBN 1 872524 08 7

Further copies of this book may be obtained from Platform 5 Publishing Ltd. at the address shown above. Please enclose 10% of purchase price (UK) or 20% (abroad) to cover postage and packing.

Volume 1 (1987) and Volume 2 (1988) are still available at a price of £11.95 each plus postage and packing.

Title page: Class 20s 20061+20093 pilot Class 47/4 No. 47444 at Waitby, near Kirkby Stephen, with the 08.25 Leeds–Carlisle service on 25th November. The Class 20s were provided to attract modern traction enthusiasts to travel on the trains, and were a great success. Other unusual classes were used as pilots on other Saturdays.   *Hugh Ballantyne*

A busy scene at Settle Junction on 11th March: 47488 with the 12.40 Carlisle–Leeds passes 20075 and 20023 heading 6V39 07.36 Mossend–Margam steel coil train, the latter diverted via the 'Little' North Western because of WCML engineering work.   *Paul Shannon*

From the Publisher

This third volume of Today's Railways Review of the Year covers the most important events of the 1989 for British Rail, London Underground, light rail transit, railway preservation, Channel Tunnel and European railways. The last section of the book contains a comprehensive Diary with over 700 entries, a valuable reference work.

The volume is published four months earlier in the year than volume 2 was and we hope to be earlier still next year. People interested in railways had no shortage of good news magazines in 1989 to keep in touch with month-to-month events, even though quality of reporting seemed inversely related to the frequency of publication. However, by analysing a year's news in one book, all clearly-divided into topics, we hope that readers will be able to put the numerous developments in context. We hope you enjoy reading it!

We would like to thank all contributors and photographers and the following organisations:
British Rail (British Railways Board, BR Property Board, Network SouthEast, InterCity, Railfreight, ScotRail, Western Region, London Midland Region, Southern Region, Anglia Region, Eastern Region); Department of Transport; NUR; ASLEF; Eurotunnel; London Underground Ltd.; Docklands Light Railway; Transport 2000; Railway Development Society; NS (special thanks); SNCF; BAA plc; Metro; Merseytravel; Greater Manchester PTE; South Yorkshire PTE; Tyne & Wear PTE; Strathclyde PTE; West Midlands PTE; 202 Squadron, RAF Manston; GEC Alsthom; Shell UK; London Regional Passengers Committee; the TUCCs; Robbins-Markham Joint Venture; Nottingham Development Enterprise; Bournemouth Evening Echo.

Least helpful, in terms of information provided, was the Eastern Region press office at York, ironically Platform 5's 'home' region.

DAVID CARTER (Editor)

PETER FOX (Publisher and Editor)

TODAY'S RAILWAYS REVIEW OF THE YEAR VOLUME 4

We welcome good quality photographs of major news and developments. Due to the sheer volume of contributions in previous years, we have decided that any photographs submitted for Volume 4 of no newsworthiness will simply be returned immediately. We will be sending precise details of our requirements later in the year to those photographers on our files; to receive these details, please contact the publisher for an application form.

All photographs should have your name and a caption written on the back. The caption should include details as to why the photograph is newsworthy. Also, please ensure that captions are not written on the back of light areas of prints, e.g. sky, as these can show through during the computerised scanning process.

▼One set of vacuum-braked Mark 2 stock was painted in LNER tourist green and cream livery (every coach being named) for use on the summer 10.46 Dingwall–Kyle of Lochalsh loco-hauled service and return. 37417 heads the Kyle-bound train at Portnacloich on 1st June. The last coach is an ex-Class 101 DMU vehicle, now an observation car No. 6300 'Hebridean'. *Les Nixon*

Britain's Railways in 1989

In May, the country reflected on ten years of Conservative government. In 1979, the Advanced Passenger Train and track repair arrears were news. Sir Peter Parker (BR Chairman), Ray Buckton (of ASLEF), Sid Weighell (of the NUR) were the personalities. In 1989, overcrowding and the Channel Tunnel (and high-speed link) were in the news. Sir Robert Reid, Neil Milligan and Jimmy Knapp respectively, were in the limelight. There had been a revival in rail's fortunes, this occurring despite government policy rather than because of it. Road traffic had also increased by 40% over the decade. The prime minister never hid her dislike of railways: in her view they are big, nationalised unaccountable and unionised. The answer: privatisation.

It was left to the new transport secretary Cecil Parkinson to postpone moves towards BR's privatisation. All the options, consultants had discovered (at great expense), led to problems – some of which were clearly at odds with the governments new 'green' pretentions. Critics argued that privatisation is not needed: BR is the most cost-effective railway in Europe; it has not worked in the past; it would make any (future) national transport planning difficult; it would permit asset-stripping of valuable city centre sites. The Central Transport Consultative Committee had also listed five 'essential guards' to protect passengers if BR is privatised: grants for 'socially necessary' lines; continuing protection for passengers against line closures; the benefits to passengers of BR being a single network to be preserved if the network is split into separate companies; a body to prevent a monopoly position being abused, including the ability to control fares, monitor quality and possibly to act as a safety agency; passengers to continue to have recourse to an independent statutory council able to deal with grievances.

The new secretary of state for transport carried on where his predecessor left off, cynically described by Neil Kinnock as "Paul Channon with a chin." There were, however, growing signs of a rift between the Department of Transport (DTp) and the Department of Environment. Chris Patten, secretary of state of the latter described the DTp's road traffic forecasts as an "unacceptable option."

▲ The most spectacular and famous viaduct on the Settle & Carlisle line was devoid of track on 15th October whilst repairs took place, so guaranteeing the line's immediate future.   *Les Nixon*

NUR general secretary Jimmy Knapp attacked the government's policy on railway investment: "Good communications are not an optional extra to be provided when market forces decide. The government certainly avoided the distinction between using public money for claimed record investment and giving BR permission to invest its own money, raised from ticket sales, asset sales, or borrowed at interest.

Vandalism remained a problem, with British Transport Police often the unsung heroes trying to prevent it, through, for example the continued operation of 'Q' trains. The derailment of an Oxford–Paddington express in August highlighted the problem. The debris – sleepers, old rail lengths, etc. – that some of BR's civil engineers leave on linesides was criticised as an invitation to vandals. Vandalism is not confined to the UK. During 1989, EEC countries (plus Austria and Switzerland) set up an intelligence network (with UIC support) to combat the scourge of graffiti vandalism. Fare evasion also remained a strain on BR's resources.

Two more serious accidents, at Purley and Bellgrove (Glasgow), were caused by trains passing signals at red – and so intensifying the debate on railway safety. In contrast, the spectacular Settle & Carlisle was reprieved after the six-year battle to save it.

BR ANNUAL REPORT

Against a background of reduced government support (aimed solely at Provincial and Network SouthEast), the Group had an operating surplus of £107 million. This became a surplus of £304 million after income from property sales and other items were added. Bob Reid praises greater staff productivity and greater private-sector involvement, particularly in train catering and privately-owned freight rolling stock and facilities. Mentioning the government's privatisation studies he warns that there is a long way to go before a proper return on assets employed is attained; BR's long-term future depended on efficiency and safety.

● **INTERCITY** In its first year as a fully commercial business, InterCity turned an operating loss into a profit of £57.4 million against a background of buoyant demand. Out of the quality of service objectives set for InterCity, the greatest improvement was in the frequency of carriage cleaning, interior and exterior.

● **NETWORK SOUTHEAST** The business sector almost halved its call on government support during 1988/9 making an operational loss, before government grant of £137.7 million. Enquiry bureaux became more efficient at answering calls but carriage cleaning standards deteriorated and load factors (degree of overcrowding) exceeded targets.

● **PROVINCIAL** Passenger miles increased by 9% and earnings by 6% in real terms. An operating loss of £465.5 million was made before government grant. The target for service provision (at least 98.5% of services to run) was exceeded. Punctuality failed to improve much on the previous year but carriage cleaning showed a marked improvement.

● **RAILFREIGHT** The business sector increased its operating surplus to £69.4 million. Having had no government support for over a decade and now split into sub-sectors such as Railfreight Coal, Railfreight Metals and Railfreight Petroleum, its performance was very commendable.

● **PARCELS** A £12.4 million loss on a gross income of £125.5 million was made. This reflected the loss of newspaper traffic in 1988. Red Star continued its rapid growth in a very competitive market and the future of the £46 million Post Office contract was secured for the next five years. The appointment of 11 Post Office contract managers and 40 area Red Star managers with direct reporting lines showed the sector's commitment to its future.

On the personnel front, the size of the labour force was further reduced and the move towards performance-related and business sector-related pay continued. Generally, a more attractive career and promotion structure was being aimed at.

Again, property sales and letting produced a huge contribution to BR finances. The BR Property Board produced no less than £335 million. Office, retail and leisure developments were numerous and there was a particularly large growth in rental income from station trading. Notable sources of income were from Mercury Communications (whose cable routes are often alongside key rail routes) and from London station developments; on the latter the pace of development is due to increase still further. Apart from the obvious environmental improvements, the income from the 500-plus refurbished arches completed by 1989 was also welcome.

One interesting point emerged on land sales: closed lines were no longer a major feature of the Board's redundant assets. From an original 11,000 miles of closed lines there were only 852 miles remaining, half of which were in hand for sale. (This could, however, cause problems for future rail re-openings – ed).

BR CORPORATE PLAN 1989

BR Corporate Plan 1989 was published in December, the sixth since 1983. Over the next three years government support to BR will continue to fall. The key target is that, by 1992/93 Provincial will be the only business sector to receive a Public Service Obligation grant. The level of grant required is expected to be reduced to £345 million. By then, the non-supported sectors of InterCity, Freight, and Parcels will have to make profits of £95 million, £50 million and £9 million respectively (at current prices). Plans should be drawn up by 1990 for Network SouthEast to achieve a real return on assets employed and, by 1995/96, a commercial rate of return.

Although the External Financing Limit (set by the Treasury for the sum of the PSO grant and outside borrowing in any one year) will not change much, investment will rise sharply. This will come from internal sources, mainly fares and property income, and rising productivity.(As has occurred since 1980, fares will probably have to rise faster than inflation).

Of the £4.9 billion of new investment planned most (52.5%) will be spent on new traction and rolling stock. 30.4% will be invested in infrastructure and the remainder in stations and terminals. Network SouthEast will continue to invest particularly heavily.

For Railfreight, the Channel Tunnel and the privitisation of the electricity supply industry will have profound effects but planning for these changes is well-advanced.

Within the broad financial objectives, the Board would have to: produce a plan for bulk freight which will achieve a minimum of 8% return on assets by 1994/5; carry out further research into the relationship between cost and quality of services; examine the case for 'bustitution' where necessary; study Provincial fares and marketing, including exploitation of scenic routes and joint ventures with the private sector.

The 1989 Corporate Plan depends upon 2.9% annual growth in consumer spending, an optimistic figure. As some 92% of the Board's proposed investment is forecast to be funded internally there could be problems ahead.

Cecil Parkinson – the new secretary of state for transport

The son of a railwayman, Cecil Parkinson first became a Member of Parliament in 1970. Since then he has held four Cabinet posts before becoming secretary of state for transport, another Cabinet position. His previous jobs never involved having to do serious battle over a departmental budget. Transport would involve charged negotiations against the Treasury.

Despite Cecil Parkinson's past roles as a member of the Falklands 'War Cabinet', party chairman, architect of the City's 'Big Bang', of British Telecom and electricity privatisation, transport will still be a challenge. He was fortunate in having as his deputy Michael Portillo, reckoned by his officials to be the most able minister they have ever worked with; Parkinson and Portillo had worked together before at the Department of Trade and Industry.

Cecil Parkinson's main skill is presentation of policy. He has ambition

too. The Economist magazine (29/07/89) said of the reshuffle: "Mr Parkinson had a mixed reshuffle. Transport ... was below his ambitions. But if he can make a success of the preparatory work laid by Mr Paul Channon (who, despite his awful public image, was admired by his top officials), he may yet inherit the Treasury."

By the end of the year he was also defending the reductions in BR's subsidy: "Government commitment to public transport should not be measured by the level of subsidy. People are prepared to pay if they get a decent service. You don't need to bribe them to use it."

The Replacement of Sir Robert Reid

Bob Reid, 55 and chief executive of Shell UK was appointed BR chairman Sir Bob Reid's replacement on 6th December. This followed months of uncertainty for British Rail and embarrassment for the government.

The job description had not sounded inviting. For an annual salary of £93,000 – low by private-sector standards – the new chairman would face a disgruntled workforce and the wrath of commuters and occasional travellers alike. His actions would be constrained by government demands to reduce subsidies. Ultimately, he might have to organise the break-up of his own industry through privatisation.

There was a dearth of internal candidates. Jim O'Brien retired in April, aged 54. Derek Fowler one of the two vice chairmen decided to take early retirement. On 21st September Cecil Parkinson accepted the resignation of Reid's most obvious successor, David Kirby, 56, the other vice chairman.

Cecil Parkinson appointed a leading City firm of head-hunters. Many names appeared in the newspapers but most regarded the salary as derisory. It was rumoured that the salary was being reviewed.

After approaching some 20 possible candidates Bob Reid was appointed his namesake's successor. On becoming chairman in October 1990 he will earn £200,000 a year. Thirty five years with Shell, he has worked his way up through the ranks. In his five years at the top he has re-organised Shell UK from a bureaucratic company to an efficient and highly profitable one. The consensus was that BR was lucky to have such a forward-looking, capable and personable new chairman.

Both the Reids are Scots but there the similarities end. Sir Bob Reid has been chairman since 1983 after replacing the enthusiastic and extrovert Sir Peter Parker. He has a reputation as a shrewd administrator and maintains a low-key public image. Bob Reid 2 as he is being called will be much more visible.

On appointment Reid said: "I want the trains to run on time, to be safe, to give a good service, and to improve morale. If I achieve that, I don't really give a damn who gets the credit for it."

▲ Electrification work on Network SouthEast's Cambridge–King's Lynn line started in early summer. The line has a catchment area of about 200,000 people, far less than around the Edinburgh–Dundee–Aberdeen InterCity/Provincial/Railfreight-sponsored line which is to stay diesel-operated to the chagrin of campaigners. Here, 20043 and 20069 take the electrification train across the Fens on 18th August.   *Michael J. Collins*

A SUMMER OF STRIKES

The seeds of the 1989 rail strike were sown in November 1988 when BR announced that national pay bargaining would end and be replaced by five business sector bargaining units. Greater flexibility and regrading of clerical, depot, station and permanent way staff was sought. These changes followed BR's success in negotiating greater flexibility in 1987, changes which included the Trainman concept and performance-related pay.

In December 1988 several newspapers reported that the government had ordered BR to pay a maximum of 7% in the coming wage round, a pay norm established for nationalised industries. Ministers denied interference.

Storm clouds had been gathering for longer. Staff morale was low: poor pay led to skill shortages and a deteriorating service (e.g. train cancellations); it also led to excessive hours worked. Some staff saw the public service aims, covering, broadly, the 1950s to the 1970s, as conflicting with the new commercial reality of the 1980s. It was alleged that the more recent 'authoritarian attitude' of management, under pressure to meet financial targets, was the cause of the break-up of the 'railway family'.

Many BR managers knew that an offer above 7% was necessary to 'buy off' restrictive practices and offset inflation that was edging towards 8.5% in spring 1989. Like other businesses, BR was caught out by the state of the economy – a slowdown of consumer demand, (caused by high interest rates), so reducing revenue.

With pay on the railways being relatively low, press stories of huge executive pay rises elsewhere in industry and commerce did not help. The government made little attempt to discourage such increases. Despite extra payments to rail workers in the South East introduced by BR in January, staff in this 'overheated' part of the country were especially unhappy about pay.

The rail strikes by the NUR and ASLEF on BR caused severe road congestion but, with each strike, commuters and travellers adapted. By July many people were on holiday anyway. London's streets, in particular, were not much more congested on strike days than usual. The government eased parking restrictions and part of Hyde Park, for example, was turned into a car-park. Despite the press branding the hot summer months as the 'summer of discontent' due to strikes elsewhere, people seemed to cope; bigger problems were only encountered abroad – French air traffic control technicians were on strike!

The degree to which the rail unions enjoyed public support surprised the Board. Not until the biggest union, the NUR, rejected BR's improved offer did opinion change.

At the end of the strike Sir Robert Reid said: "There are no victors, there are only victims." The improved pay offer cost BR a total of £160 million, £50 million more than planned. In return the unions gave a commitment to negotiations on bargaining machinery with a February 1990 deadline.

The unions had successfully flexed their muscles whilst appearing reasonable. Jimmy Knapp, general secretary of the NUR, judged the mood of his members well. His communication skills were not perfect: "British Rail stabbed us in the back by blowing the talks out of the water before they even got off the ground." But he stood up to condemnation from the prime minister who could not hide her contempt for his union: "These people are there to serve the public, but they don't." Her chancellor threatened investment cuts, her employment secretary threatened removal of the right to strike. The general secretary and his executive knew that these were empty threats. In his last few weeks as transport secretary, Paul Channon remarked: "How quickly some people forget the lessons they learned just a few years ago."

The legitimacy of the strikes was in no doubt with most members voting. The NUR was more worried about the abolition of national bargaining than ASLEF and the TSSA, both single-skill unions. All three unions achieved pay rises comparable with other settlements in late summer and at least a say in future bargaining procedure.

With the ASLEF/NUR/LUL dispute relations between unions and employer never seemed to reach the depths of the dispute on BR. After numerous strikes, official and unofficial, and much talking a similar pay settlement was reached with agreement on payments for one-man-operated trains. London Underground withdrew its 'Action Stations' proposals for modification before presenting them to the NUR again, with some posts certainly to be filled by competition rather than seniority.

THE COMPETITIVE SITUATION

Railways cannot be seen in isolation so here are the main trends of 1989 on the ferries, airlines and in the motor industry (cars, coaches and HGVs).

Ferries

Fearing the opening of the Channel Tunnel, ferry companies were investing. Rationalisation of routes (e.g. Folkestone–Calais, Newhaven–Dieppe) to concentrate on core routes (e.g. Dover (Western Docks) –Calais) was being considered. Olau Line introduced the biggest car ferry ever to operate from Britain as part of a £117 million plan to re-equip its Sheerness–Vlissingen route. Their two new ships have cost £60 million to build, the rest of the investment going on new port facilities. Up to 1,600 passengers, 575 cars (or 118 HGVs) can be carried on each, an example of the move towards 'super ferries' to trim operating costs. Hoverspeed will introduce a high-speed catamaran on the Portsmouth–Cherbourg route.

In December, the government vetoed an application by P & O Ferries and Sealink to pool their Channel fleets. After a Monopolies and Mergers Commission inquiry, Nicholas Ridley, trade and industry secretary, stated that pooling could not be allowed so far in advance of the Tunnel's opening.

Despite rough or cancelled crossings, leisurely journey times and often poor standards of service and comfort, the ferries had carried over 20 million passengers across the Channel by 31st December. Unfortunately for passengers, the Channel's third and most innovative carrier, Brittany Ferries, only operated from Portsmouth, Poole and Plymouth, leaving the Straits of Dover P & O/Sealink-controlled.

Latest forecasts indicate a 57% average switch of cross-Channel car passengers to Eurotunnel's shuttle in 1993, or in only 42 months' time.

The declining importance of Weymouth as a ferry terminal was highlighted by British Channel Island Ferries' switch of Channel Island sailings from Weymouth and Portsmouth to Poole – with important implications for rail passenger flows to the three. A special bus service links Poole station to the ferry terminal.

Cars

Car ownership continued to rise. The real cost of motoring continuing its steady fall (hours work required to run a car) during the 1980s. The romantic notion of the 'open road' – despite what car advertisements might tell you – became rarer.

The motor industry spent large amounts on persuading people that it cared about the environment. Saab and Volvo showed their cars in woodland settings with copylines emphasising that catalytic converters reduce acid rain. Although helpful devices, advertising claims made for three-way catalytic converters were high: Audi explained that 'as engine exhaust pass through at around 300°C, these precious metals convert nitrogen oxides, unburnt hydro-carbons and deadly carbon monoxide into harmless nitrogen, water and carbon dioxide ... the stuff that makes fizzy drinks fizzy.' (Carbon dioxide is also widely regarded as a contributor to global warming).Most cars pump out four times their own weight in carbon dioxide each year. Road vehicles in Britain produce over 100 million tonnes of carbon dioxide per year; rail transport produces 2 million tonnes. Catalytic converters are also expensive, often fail to work properly due to poor maintenance and short journey lengths (the necessary temperature not being reached). They also increase carbon dioxide emissions as they impede the flow of exhaust making the engine run less efficiently. Lean-burn technology is not fully compatible with catalytic converters!

Lean-burn technology (which can reduce carbon dioxide emissions) is still at an early stage. Unfortunately, the motor industry's main marketing weapon in 1989 was not fuel economy but paint colour; should your sales representative be in an 'executive' colour (moonrock or oxblood, for example) or a green colour car? The best ray of hope was the EEC's £827 million 'Prometheus' project to increase car efficiency with 17 car manufacturers backing the programme.

By contrast, railways use far less energy per passenger or per tonne of freight. For the majority of the network that is not yet electrified, it should be pointed out that the diesel engine, although not environmentally perfect, is inherently 'lean-burn'.

Research was well-advanced on dashboard-mounted radio data navigation systems for cars to beat traffic congestion. Cynics pointed out that, once available, these systems would simply advise everyone to drive down the same back alley!

During 1989 unleaded petrol consumption increased from 3% to 29% of sales, a welcome start.

With memories of petrol crises fading, the motor industry continued to grow. 600,000 jobs depend directly or indirectly on the motor industry.

As the 1980s came to an end the car – for long a symbol of wealth, personal identity and freedom – had begun to be seen as a problem. Whereas the decade was regarded as one of growing personal independence, the nineties were being heralded as a decade of interdependence. There was growing concern about the impact of one mode of travel, here the car, on other individuals, on other modes of transport and on the environment. People began to realise that the use of the car had increased to a point where it must be restricted, particularly in cities.

▲On the thirtieth anniversary of the opening of the M1 motorway, 90024 heads a Wolverhampton–London Euston service past Whilton, south of Kilsby Tunnel. The date is the 30th March. Later in the year Chris Rea's single 'The Road to Hell' (from the best-selling album of the same name) became the first chart song to deal with road congestion, Rea singing about his experiences on those other notorious motorways, the M4 and M25. Perhaps Cecil Parkinson should sing along to the chorus: "This ain't no upwardly-mobile freeway. Oh no, this is the road to hell."   *John B. Gosling*

Buses/Coaches

In March, Nigel Lawson, chancellor of the exchequer, delivered his Budget speech. He increased the duty on Britain's 72,000 PSVs in an attempt to make them "cover their track costs." For example the annual road tax on coaches with over 60 seats would rise from £100 to £450. (On car road tax, he resisted calls for higher taxes on bigger-engined cars).

Inter city coaches' punctuality fell due to increasing road congestion. On a more local level bus deregulation caused rapid change in the form of bankruptcies, company sales, takeovers and animosity between rivals. Research published during 1989 showed that 10% of bus passenger miles had disappeared since deregulation. In a few areas local rail services benefited from a switch from relatively infrequent or unreliable bus services.

Heavy Goods Vehicles

1989 continued the trend during the 1980s for fewer, heavier lorries. There was a more widespread use of 38 tonne vehicles and of contract distribution (which tends to allow a more intensive and efficient use of vehicles). Of importance to Railfreight, the government bowed to EEC pressure to allow 40 tonne vehicles on Britain's roads, albeit from 1999.

Airlines

Led by small, innovative and more personal airlines like Capital Airlines, domestic air services continued to expand. Competition on certain domestic air routes, combined with British Rail's recent above-inflation annual fare increases, has resulted in a rapid closing of the gap between air and rail fares; in some case rail travel is more expensive.

Announcements made during the year pointed to particularly rapid developments of Glasgow (at the expense of Prestwick) and Cardiff airports. In the South East, Stansted and Southampton airports will grow quickly.

In December, European transport ministers agreed to liberalise European air travel by removing bilateral tariff agreements between airlines. Airlines will be free to charge whatever economy fare they like, provided at least one of the countries involved approve. This total fare freedom will come into effect on 1st January 1993, six months before the opening of the Channel Tunnel. In the meantime fare zones will be introduced allowing airlines to cut ticket prices to as low as 30% of the standard economy tariff. British Rail International, before and after the opening of the Channel Tunnel, will be up against increasingly competitive airlines. BR also gets a three-year breathing space from the continued protection by foreign governments of their national carriers, keeping fares high.

ROADS

In May the government launched its 'Roads for Prosperity' White Paper. Spending on trunk roads will double to £12 billion over 10 years. Behind the plans lay new traffic forecasts, announced the same day: total traffic was forecast to increase by between 83% and 142% by the year 2025, compared with 1988.The new programme aimed to add over 2,700 miles of new or widened roads to the trunk road network. Mr Channon defended the emphasis on road investment: "The scope for railways to take the strain is limited. A 50% increase in passenger carrying by train would reduce road traffic by only 5%." Included was the £960 million conversion of the M1 to eight lanes. (In contrast, electrification of the rest of the Midland Main Line (Bedford–Sheffield) would cost £160 million).

Environmental organisations responded by launching 'Roads to Ruin'. They estimated that just parking all the new cars forecast will need an area larger than Berkshire.

The government wanted to see greater private-sector involvement in trunk road construction and operation to supplement public works. Private bidders were therefore sought for the design, building, finance and operation of a pilot £300 million 36-mile motorway north of Birmingham. Only three companies submitted bids. The reasons included alarm at Eurotunnel's cost overruns and a feeling that the £12 billion trunk roads programme would provide enough work.

By the end of 1989 plans for encouraging private motorways by simplifying and changing road building procedure had largely been destroyed by the weight of legislation scheduled for the new session of Parliament and lack of interest. The publicly-financed roads programme was also in trouble due to construction inflation. The cost of the planned one-mile Limehouse link road in Docklands (not in the programme) rose by 650% in a year to £300 million. Similarly, a 6 km section of the M66 (part of the Manchester outer ring road project costing £300 million) opened in 1989 at a cost of £60 million.

In July a report on the M25 was published. Consultants had suggested that up to dual five lanes may be needed. Initially, extra capacity might come about through reduced width layouts (i.e. narrower lanes). An outer 'orbital network' 10–25 km outside the M25 might be needed.

The Confederation of British Industry published its 'Trade Routes to the Future' report. It urged a doubling of spending on new roads and railways. £21 billion had to be spent to meet the challenge of 1992.

It was plain that there would be no immediate switch from heavy spending on roads. Mr Parkinson kept emphasising the need of a balance between modes of transport. The so-called 'roads lobby' – based loosely around the powerful British Road Federation – meanwhile maintained its pressure for no retreat from the huge 'Roads for Prosperity' programme. The simple fact that traffic increases to fill extra road space clearly had not struck home; suppressed demand for road space is almost infinite.

CONGESTION

Congestion causes pollution, noise, frustration and expense for car and coach passengers and freight haulage companies alike. The growing use of 'just in time' delivery systems to shops and factories would, as demand for roadspace exceeded supply, increasingly become 'just too late'! Road congestion costs £15 billion per year the CBI said.

Transport sclerosis in and around London focused politicians' minds and several measures were introduced or proposed to improve traffic flow, more of which in a moment. No longer being considered was large-scale road building, due to the political cost of homes being demolished and a worsened environment. A £4 billion 16-mile motorway under the Thames from Chiswick to Docklands promoted by Costains aroused little more than polite interest. Even the Adam Smith Institute (in its 'Traffic in the Cities' report) said that – apart from the removal of localised bottlenecks – there was no longer a case for massive new road building in cities.More light rail schemes and a greater use of private minibuses were suggested.

Questioned on greater subsidies to public transport to reduce London's road congestion, Cecil Parkinson said that: "It is the politics of the madhouse to subsidise fares still further at a time when London Transport already has more passengers than it can cope with." His predecessor Paul Channon had taken the same line emphasising a balanced investment strategy to expand capacity and remove bottlenecks on BR, the Underground and the road network: only a balanced approach would ensure a choice of transport modes for travellers.

The government launched various initiatives aimed at 'traffic calming' and 'civilising the car' – such as improved signposting and a campaign against illegal parking. Other schemes mooted by backbenchers and the Opposition included various forms of road pricing and licencing to enter city centre zones. Pay-roll-based public transport levies and mandatory employers' contributions to employees' commuting fares, as is practised in France, were also mentioned.

In December, BBC TV screened one of its 'Despatches' programmes, a documentary about European road congestion. One strange but symbolic statistic emerged: currently, European car production exceeds the European birth rate.

▲Class 141105 in Metro (West Yorkshire PTE) livery operating a Huddersfield–Sheffield service prepares to call at Dodworth shortly before its official re-opening on 15th May. Dodworth is in the South Yorkshire PTA area three stations south of the boundary with the West Yorkshire PTA area.   *Les Nixon*

▼Metro, the operating side of the West Yorkshire PTA, has a high-profile publicity and marketing division, each line in the area being promoted separately with timetables and literature widely-distributed. Partly as a result, passenger demand is high and overcrowding a major problem. Here, chairman of the PTA Michael Simmons opens Berry Brow station on the 9th October.   *Metro*

BR Network

During 1989, the total BR route mileage did not change much. There were a number of freight route closures, but there were also some re-openings to offset these. Significant lines completely closed were Stoke-on-Trent–Caldon Low, Appleby–Warcop and Wymondham–Dereham–North Elmham. On the positive side, Walsall–Hednesford and Airdrie–Drumgelloch were re-opened for passenger traffic.

SETTLE & CARLISLE DECISION

Two months after an All-Party group of MPs was formed to defend the line, Britain's longest-running railway closure saga ended on 11th April with the government's announcement that BR would not be allowed to close the 72½-mile route which crosses some of the most spectacular scenery in Britain.

During the previous month the line had again proved useful as a diversionary route over all four weekends due to engineering work between Preston and Penrith on the West Coast Main Line. The Blackfield–Hellifield line, also saved from threatened closure, was used for the diversion as well.

The 1970s and 1980s had seen the transfer of London/Nottingham–Glasgow expresses to the WCML (later withdrawn completely) and the gradual reduction in services on the line. BR's inflation of costs associated with the line – from maintenance to fuel to crewing costs – and the denial until 1983 of any closure plan led to the accusation of "closure by stealth." The line's revenue, however, began to rise under the management of Mr Ron Cotton, the innovative project manager appointed to oversee the closure of the line.

By 1989 the line was the jewel in Provincial's crown and use had risen fivefold compared with 1983. Support for retention came from action groups, councils, and users, whether privately or through the TUCC, MPs and others.

The secretary of state for transport gave two principle reasons for his decision: evidence of hardship and the line's importance to the local economy; changes to the line's costs and revenues. On the cost side, independent consultants had revised downwards the cost of repairing Ribblehead Viaduct. Revenues were buoyant due to improved marketing, publicity over the closure and the re-opening of intermediate stations, so opening up more of the surrounding countryside to walkers, cyclists and, of course, providing new journey opportunities for locals. English Heritage, local authorities and the Rural Development Commission were also offering new grants totalling £1.6 million. The Settle & Carlisle line was the first refusal of a railway closure since the Conservative government came to power in 1979.

For the future the government wanted to see greater private-sector involvement, improved marketing, increased tourist-use of the line and, in certain instances, higher fares. By October £600,000 was being spent repairing the deck of Ribblehead Viaduct and other structures on the line. Shortly afterwards, service trains piloted by unusual diesel locomotives were being run to attract the modern traction enthusiast, a long overdue move.

Mr Channon's April statement concluded: "I look to all who have promised to support the line to work together to ensure that it has a successful future and so that the case for closure will not re-emerge."

The decision not to close the last great navvy-built line was a borderline one and its timing was unexpected. Cynics pointed to the series of transport disasters that had co-incided with Mr Channon's tenure of the top job at the Department of Transport – Lockerbie, Kegworth (M1), Clapham, Purley and Glasgow; they suggested that the Settle & Carlisle line's reprieve was a much-needed popular move. The real reason for the reprieve was probably that inferred by James Towler in his book

'The Battle for the Settle & Carlisle'. Since the closure of the line was first proposed in 1983, new local services had been introduced, the users of which had not been able to object to the closure, as the services were not in existence at that time. Although the TUCCs had called for additional evidence from such users, it was clear that the procedure of the Transport Act 1962 had not been followed, and that in the event of a ministerial decision to close, high court action would ensue which would result in the whole closure procedure having to be restarted. As the proceedings had by then taken over six years and attracted a record 22,150 objections, it had become clear that there was no prospect of the BRB being able to close the line in the forseeable future anyway. By the end of the year plans had been announced to spend another £2.5 million on Ribblehead Viaduct in 1990 (mainly on arches and piers) and £1.5 million a year for the next five years on repairs to the other 10 viaducts, 14 tunnels and 325 bridges along the route. The very damp Blea Moor Tunnel will receive particular attention.

Temporary speed restrictions will be removed over time, services improved and stations at Settle, Appleby and Kirkby Stephen refurbished, in the long-term a restored northbound platform at Ribblehead. Campaigners continued to press for new services, including the return of Midland Line–Glasgow trains, and regular services on the Blackburn–Hellifield line.

INVERNESS BRIDGE COLLAPSE

On 7th February all five central arches of the Ness Viaduct at Inverness were swept away by flood waters. Only the track and cabling bridged the 110 metre gap. The Highlands had experienced torrential rain and there had been serious flooding at Kingussie on the main line from Perth.

Ninety minutes before the initial collapse 37415 had hauled the early morning Inverness–Invergordon Speedlink over the bridge.

The 1862-built bridge had been examined each year, including less frequent underwater examinations by engineering divers. The prompt decision to replace the bridge was welcomed as some were quick to say that BR would use the collapse as an excuse to close the Kyle of Localsh line and Far North line. The cost of the new bridge would, in money terms at least, greatly exceed the £13,500 cost of building the original!

ScotRail's operation to maintain timetabled rail services by bussing passengers between Inverness and Dingwall is covered in the 'Provincial' section of the book. Construction of the new bridge started in August. A steel girder was chosen which would rest on the old stone abutments and two new concrete piers in the river itself. The original land arches were left intact.

CLOSURE PROPOSALS

Two significant closure proposals to surface during 1989 affected Lincolnshire. The first one was that of the line from Trent East Jn. (Gainsborough) to Wrawby Jn. (Barnetby). This was the former main line of the Manchester, Sheffield and Lincolnshire Railway and the fastest route from Sheffield to South Humberside. At present the line offers infrequent, awkwardly-timed services, bad connections and has not been marketed at all. Public hearings had been arranged by the two TUCCs concerned (North East and Eastern England), but the whole procedure was halted when another closure proposal was announced, that of Doncaster (Black Carr Jn.) to Gainsborough (Trent West Jn.). This had been cited by BR as an alternative route in BR's closure notice for the Gainsborough–Barnetby line!

Three weeks after the Doncaster–Gainsborough proposal was announced, it was rescinded, following protests from Lincolnshire County Council which argued that cost cutting and improved marketing could save the line.

The Gainsborough–Barnetby proposal had been billed as a test case for bus substitution, but the replacement bus service proposed was totally inadequate, taking twice as long as the train. The year ended with no action on this proposal – still on the books but suspended – a sorry state of affairs.

The TUCCs produced 32 arguments for retention of the line in summary of private objections raised. BR managed to answer 'no comment' to almost a third of them, including the points that 'savings made by the closure would be minimal; small-scale bus substitution has been discredited in the recent Monopolies and Mergers report and that a major housing development was proposed for Northorpe which is on the line.

STATIONS OPENED OR RE-OPENED (RO)

03/04 Tutbury & Hatton (RO) – Crewe–Derby
10/04 Cannock (RO) – Walsall–Hednesford
10/04 Hednesford (RO) – Walsall–Hednesford
10/04 Landywood (RO) – Walsall–Hednesford
17/04 Bloxwich (RO) – Walsall–Hednesford
15/05 Airbles – Coatbridge Central–Glasgow Central
15/05 Dodworth (RO) – Barnsley–Huddersfield
15/05 Drumgelloch – Airdrie–Drumgelloch (Strathclyde)
15/05 Greenfaulds – Glasgow Queen Street–Cumbernauld
15/05 Islip (RO) – Oxford–Bicester Town
15/05 Milliken Park – Ayr–Glasgow Central
15/05 Stepps – Glasgow Queen Street–Cumbernauld
15/05 Yate (RO) – Bristol Parkway–Gloucester
29/07 Llanrwst – Blaenau Ffestiniog–Llandudno Junction
09/10 Berry Brow (RO) – Barnsley–Huddersfield

STATIONS CLOSED OR CLOSED FOR REDEVELOPMENT (RD)

24/11 Rosyth Dockyard – Inverkeithing–Rosyth Dockyard (Fife)
30/10 Mansion House (RD) – Circle/District Lines (LUL)

STATIONS RENAMED

16/05 Shaw to Shaw & Crompton – Manchester Victoria–Rochdale
29/07 Llanrwst to Llanrwst North – Blaeunau Ffestiniog–Llandudno Junction
02/10 Magdalen Road to Watlington – Ely–King's Lynn
24/10 Surrey Docks to Surrey Quays – East London Line (LUL)

SEASONAL USE OF STATIONS

23/07 to 03/09 Ironbridge Gorge – Madeley Jn. (Telford, Shropshire)–Coalbrookdale
19/03 to 01/10 Stanhope – Bishop Auckland–Stanhope (County Durham)
25/06 to 01/10 Sugar Loaf Halt – Central Wales Line
23/07 to 10/09 Trawsfynydd – Blaenau Ffestiniog–Trawsfynydd (Gwynedd)

SEASONAL PASSENGER USE OF LINES

Bishop Auckland–Stanhope
Madeley Jn.–Ironbridge Gorge
Blaenau Ffestiniog–Trawsfynydd

LINES CLOSED

20/01 North Elmham–Dereham (Norfolk)
09/02 Stoke-on-Trent (Stoke Jn.)–Leek Brook Jn. (Staffordshire)
09/02 Leek Brook Jn.–Caldon Low (Staffordshire)
31/03 Appleby West Jn.–Appleby North Jn. (Cumbria)
31/03 Appleby North Jn.–Warcop Sidings (Cumbria)
30/06 Wymondham Jn.–Dereham (Norfolk)
27/08 Darnall West Jn.–Attercliffe Jn. (South Yorkshire)
01/11 Merthyr Vale Colliery–Merthyr Vale, Black Lion Crossing (Mid Glamorgan)
31/12 Carbis Wharf–Bugle, Goonbarrow Jn. (Cornwall)

LINES REPRIEVED FOLLOWING CLOSURE NOTICES

11/04 Settle Junction–Petteril Bridge Junction, Carlisle (North Yorks/Cumbria)
09/05 Henley-in-Arden–Bearley Junction (Warwickshire)
28/07 Black Carr Jn. (Doncaster)–Gainsborough Trent West Jn. (South Yorks/Lincolnshire)

STATIONS REPRIEVED FOLLOWING CLOSURE NOTICES

Settle, Horton-in-Ribblesdale, Ribblehead, Dent, Garsdale, Kirkby Stephen, Appleby. Langwathby, Lazonby, Armathwaite, Wootton Wawen.

LINES CLOSED TEMPORARILY

07/02 Rose Street Jn. Inverness–Muir of Ord

▲The Ness Viaduct at Inverness is seen almost three months after its collapse. Note some track lying in the river and the rubble from one of the central piers. The date is 28th April.   *Max Fowler*

LINES RE-OPENED FOLLOWING TEMPORARY CLOSURE

25/09 Goole–Gilberdyke Jn. (Humberside)

LINES RE-OPENED FOR PASSENGERS (P) AND/OR FREIGHT (F)

23/01 Rutherglen West Jn.–Rutherglen North Jn., Glasgow (PF)
10/04 Walsall–Hednesford (PF) (West Midlands/Staffordshire)
15/05 Airdrie–Drumgelloch (P)
15/05 Thornton South Jn.–Thornton West Jn. (PF) (Fife)
29/10 Craigentinny Jn.–Powderhall, Edinburgh (F)

LINES RE-OPENED FOR TRIAL (T) OR SHORT-TERM (ST) PASSENGER USE

15/05 Wigan [L & Y]–Wigan [L & NW] connection (T)
02/10 Channelsea Jn.–Temple Mills East Jn.–Copper Mills Jn. (ST) (Greater London)
02/10 Tottenham South Jn.–Tottenham East Jn. (ST) (Greater London)
02/10 South Tottenham West Jn.–Seven Sisters Jn. (ST) (Greater London)
02/10 Kensal Green Jn.–Willesden Jn. Low Level (ST) (Greater London)

MAJOR TRACK AND/OR SIGNALLING WORK (COMPLETED)

Stansted; Durham (completed); Newcastle; Huddersfield (completed); Warrington Central (completed); Swinton; Liverpool Street (completed); Chester (completed); York.

ROUTE ELECTRIFIED AND ENERGISED

Doncaster (Arksey)–York (Skelton Jn.)

MAJOR STATION EXPANSION, RE-BUILDING OR REFURBISHMENT (COMPLETED)

Reading (completed); Marylebone; Liverpool Street; Charing Cross; Cannon Street; Fenchurch Street; Cardiff Queen Street (completed); Manchester Piccadilly; Scarborough (completed).

ROUTES SOLD TO THE PRIVATE SECTOR

Aberystwyth–Devil's Bridge – Vale of Rheidol line

▼47348 is at the head of the demolition train at Darnall East Curve, Sheffield, on 4th July. The view is from Attercliffe Junction.   *M.A. King*

RAIL–AIR LINKS

The Bill, deposited in November 1988, for the Paddington–Heathrow rail link was rejected by a House of Lords select committee on environmental grounds; plans would have to be modified. With fast rail–air links in place, Paris, Frankfurt, Amsterdam, Düsseldorf, Genève, Zürich and Brussels airports for instance are years ahead of Heathrow which should have its rail–air link by May 1994, eventual parliamentary approval permitting.

The 'Heathrow Express' joint venture will cost £235 million, £190 million or 80% of which will be funded by Heathrow Airport Ltd., a wholly-owned subsidiary of BAA plc; the rest will be funded by BR's Network SouthEast.

Plans are for a 15-minute frequency service using 100 mph HAL-owned and maintained EMUs giving a 16-minute journey time, or 20 minutes from Paddington to Terminal 4. Services will be offered 18 hours a day. Between six and seven million passengers a year are expected, most making use of the main station serving terminals 1, 2 and 3.

The branch will leave the WR main line just west of Hayes and Harlington station, at Stockley. Environmental modifications put forward by the end of 1989 included two-metre-high walls to reduce noise, more tunneling and more natural screening. The Stockley flyover's highest point is surrounded by warehouses, not homes.

On 10th July it was decided that Manchester Airport, the third busiest airport in Britain (and the 16th in the world) should get a rail link. Paul Channon sanctioned the construction of a £25 million passenger line to Manchester Airport. BR will pay 55% of the cost with the rest coming from Greater Manchester PTE. There will be a short spur from the existing Manchester–Wilmslow line between Heald Green and Styal. It will open in 1993 when a second £557 million passenger terminal is due to open at the airport. The platforms will be initially designed for six-coach trains but there will be room for expansion to 13-coach trains.

Moves to have an airport spur constructed from the nearby freight-only Vale of Glamorgan line near Cardiff were quashed by the government as unviable.

►A model of the proposed Stockley flyover junction just west of Hayes where the branch to Heathrow diverges. Two of the 13-strong fleet of Heathrow Airport Limited's 25 kV EMUs are shown. After their 100 mph sprint from Paddington the EMUs will slow to 45 mph for the branch. Note the high walls to reduce noise. The 'Down' loco-hauled passenger train (pulling 'International' coaches?) and the 'Down' freight are both travelling 'wrong' line – on the Up Main and Up Relief respectively!   *BAA plc*

▼An aerial view of the new terminal under construction at Stansted Airport. The dotted lines indicate the alignment of the tunnel which runs from a point west of the airport under the main runway and apron before emerging and running through a wide curve into the station. The inadequate terminal currently used will not be rail-saved as its role will change to become a General Aviation Terminal.   *BAA plc*

Locomotives & Coaching Stock

Most developments in the field of traction & rolling stock are given under the headings of the individual BR sectors. Details are given in this section of more general developments.

LOCOMOTIVES

Class 03. Only five of this once 230-strong class were still in service at the beginning of 1989, three based at Birkenhead North Depot for use on the nearby Dock lines and as depot pilots, and two with specially reduced height cabs based at Ryde for use on Departmental trains on the Isle of Wight. The Birkenhead Docks duties were withdrawn from 10th March. The depot pilot turn was handed over to a Class 08 and this rendered the only surviving mainland machines surplus and they were removed to Chester depot for store at the end of that month, pending possible sale for industrial use or preservation. 03170, overhauled at Swindon as recently as February 1986, found a new home almost immediately, being moved to Longsight depot on 27th April prior to sale to Otis Euro Trans Rail at Salford and during the latter part of the year green liveried 03162 (D2162) was purchased by Wirral Borough Council, who agreed to loan it to the Llangollen Railway. 03073 remained at Chester depot at the year end, together with 03084, 03158 and 03189 stored at March being the only BR owned members of this class still extant on the mainland.

Class 08. 449 strong at the beginning of 1989, this class suffered one addition and eight withdrawals during the year, far fewer than for any year in the recent past. The addition was the return to capital stock of 08600, which had been in Departmental service since January 1979, carrying the number 97800 since June of that year. With the repair shop at Slade Green depot being closed for conversion to the depot for the forthcoming 'Networker' EMUS, this loco was reallocated to Chart Leacon, where it has now regained its former number.

The withdrawals comprised two of the 13 remaining vacuum braked only members of the class (08202 & 08769), which had become surplus to requirements with the continued demise of vacuum braked coal traffic in South Wales and a few dual and air braked examples, several for sale to industrial users. In this latter category 08650 passed to Foster Yeoman Ltd. at Merehead, 08669 to Trafford Park Estates Ltd at Manchester, and 08846 to BREL (1988) Ltd. at their Derby Litchurch Lane works. The remaining withdrawals comprised locomotives which had become accident damaged or were considered to be beyond economic repair. 08463 & 08763 fell into this latter category, whilst 08785 suffered collision damage at Alexandra Dock Junction, Newport in the early part of the year.

Overhauls of the class continued during the year, with 32 members of the class appearing from BREL Crewe, BRML Eastleigh, RFS Industries Doncaster and RFS Industries Kilnhurst. This latter will carry out the work previously done at RFS Doncaster, the Kilnhurst premises previously having been owned by locomotive builders and repairers Thomas Hill. BRML Eastleigh no longer undertakes Class 08 overhaul work, 08940 being the last of this type to be dealt with there in February 1989.

Class 09. This class still remains the only one of the pre-1975 classes fully intact, albeit with one member in Departmental service. At the start of the year all but three of the class were based on the Southern Region, with the others on the Western.By the end of the year two examples had been transferred to Tinsley depot on the Eastern Region for specific use on a trip working where the 27 mph maximum speed would be beneficial due to the amount of main line running, these being replaced on the Southern Region by Class 08s.

Class 31. Scheduled overhauls have ceased on Class 31/1 locomotives, although some unclassified work is still authorised. Nineteen of the sub class were withdrawn during

1989, with several more being saved by the Provincial Sector's DMU difficulties causing continued use of 31/4s on Provincial duties rather than Departmental turns, thus causing 31/1s to be retained for these latter duties. Overhauls to Class 31/4 continue at BRML Doncaster, with a total of 21 locomotives being dealt with in 1989. Most of these appeared in the BR General grey livery, despite being ETH fitted locomotives, and only late in the year was 31423 outshopped painted in the BR Mainline livery more appropriate to many of the duties of the class. Sole Class 31/4 to be withdrawn was 31443, which suffered fire damage at Tallington in the middle of the year.

Class 33. Heavy withdrawals of this class had originally been expected to occur during 1989, but buoyant Channel Tunnel construction traffic meant that not only were a number of the class reprieved but also a limited overhaul programme was sanctioned at BRML Eastleigh.

Class 37. The end of the Class 37 refurbishing programme came during the year with the outshopping of 37719 from BREL Crewe in March. This also heralded the end of Class 37 classified repairs at this location, with work now being carried out at BRML depots at Doncaster and Springburn, and at Plymouth Laira depot.

The Class 37/0 locomotives numbered in the 373xx series were all renumbered during the year to make this latter sequence clear of all locomotives other than those of genuine Class 37/3s. The locos allocated to Motherwell for Metals sub-sector traffic reverted to their original TOPS numbers in the 37/0 series, but those locos whose original numbers lay within the 373xx series were allocated vacant numbers in the 372xx series formerly occupied by locomotives now converted to Class 37/4. Four Class 37/3 locomotives reverted to standard Class 37/0 configuration as their re-geared bogies were removed as spares for the refurbished locomotives, a shortage arising due to the destruction of a number of bogies by collisions.

Three members of the Class were withdrawn during the year. First to go was 37062, withdrawn on 13th March after suffering damage in a 27th February collision at Warrington. One week later 37113 was condemned at BRML Doncaster due to poor overall body condition, but was later reprieved and given a CEM overhaul after inspection of 37260 in early August following fire damage showed this loco to be in a worse condition.

Class 43. Repainting of the fleet of HST power cars into InterCity 'Swallow' livery continued throughout the year at CEM overhauls undertaken at Bristol Bath Road and Neville Hill depots. As cars were overhauled their nameplates were removed as it had been decreed that the previous style of nameplates did not match the revised livery. The nameplates applied to newly named repainted cars (So far no car has received new style nameplates to replace removed plates) most definitely did match the livery – to such a degree that the nameplates are almost invisible in 90% of lighting conditions. This of course defeats the object of naming!

Class 47. A net 12 locomotives were withdrawn during the year, 8 Class 47/0 and 4 Class 47/4. Of these 47008 had not been overhauled for almost 8 years at the time of its withdrawal, and this and 47012/101/110/124/428 all had the now 'Non-standard' Brush TG160-60 Mk. 4 Main Generator Equipment. No locomotives fitted with this type of generator are currently being overhauled. 47411 is of course one of the prototype batch and is therefore also non standard. 47469/542 both were withdrawn as a result of collision damage, 47143/203 due to poor general condition and 47198 due to fire damage.

Class 50. The expected heavy inroads into this Class expected for 1989 did not occur, mainly due to the late DMU deliveries and other difficulties of the Provincial Sector. This meant that the planned 47/7 cascade to Network South East did not occur in as great a quantity as had been anticipated (only two locos coming south) and as a result Waterloo to Exeter and Paddington to Oxford workings remained in the hands of Class 50s. A net three locomotives were withdrawn during the year, 50025 due to severe derailment damage, 50012 due to power unit defects and 50039 due to general run down condition. 50040 was withdrawn in December, but reinstated almost immediately and finished the year in stored status.

Class 81. Five locomotives were withdrawn during the year, leaving only six survivors at the year end. Of these, two (81002/4) are engaged solely on e.c.s. movements to and from London Euston and are restricted to 40 mph, and one (81010) is stored.

Class 83. The last two members of this class still in service were withdrawn during March. 83009/12 were replaced on Euston e.c.s. duties by 81002/4, and ended the year as part of the long line of withdrawn electric locomotives at Crewe ETD.

HAULED COACHING STOCK

49 new Mark 4 coaches were placed into service during 1989, whilst a net total of 115 Mark 1s and 28 Mark 2s were withdrawn. Four reinstated coaches are of interest – they were for steam locmotive driver training on the Fort William–Mallaig section! The withdrawn coaches were mainly compartment types released by deliveries of new DMUs and EMUs.

36 Mark 2D open firsts were converted to TSO with a mixed unidirectional/facing seat arrangement and renumbered in the 62xx series. Conversely, one Mark 2F SO was reinstated to FO and gained its old number, 3403.

DIESEL MULTIPLE UNITS

94 new DMU vehicles were delivered during 1989, almost all being used to replace previously loco-hauled services. On the other hand, a net total of 261 old DMU vehicles were withdrawn. It is not difficult, therefore, to understand the reason for the overcrowding and cancellation of trains in the Provincial sector! Notable withdrawals were the last of the Class 120 Swindon Cross-Country units and the Class 111 half-powered vehicles which were numbered in the 78xxx series.

ELECTRIC MULTIPLE UNITS

Excluding the Isle of Wight, 320 new EMU vehicles were delivered during 1989, whilst 217 were withdrawn. In addition, a large number of Class 302 and 438 cars were out of use but not withdrawn. The main withdrawals were of Classes 302, 303, 311 and 438.

▶▲ Class 45 finally became extinct from traffic during 1989. One locomotive, 45106, had been retained for operating InterCity specials, but met with its end due to a fire at Hendon whilst working the 07.12 Derby-St. Pancras service. 45128 was selected as a replacement celebrity for no apparent reason other than the fact that it was dumped at Tinsley depot itself rather than with the majority of others in the nearby secondary yard, where many of the locos were known to be in better condition and had been overhauled much more recently. It was hardly surprising therefore to find after load bank testing that 45128 was in need of a Main Generator change, something which sponsors InterCity were unwilling to pay for, and so the whole project was dropped and the class fell into oblivion. 45128 is seen at Doncaster awaiting tyre turning alongside the withdrawn 47342.
G.W. Morrison

▶▲ A brake fault resulted in all Class 90 locomotives being taken out of service on 16th August. However, steps were soon taken to rectify this situation and locos were gradually released for traffic over the next few days. 90013/24/6 are seen awaiting attention at the rear of Willesden TMD on 20th August with 87028 'Lord President' also visible. *Brian Morrison*

▶ Class 120s finally finished service in Scotland in October 1989. Glasgow Queen Street is the location for this shot of 120 532 on a Falkirk Grahamston working. Note the Class 101 centre car. *Maxwell H. Fowler*

Channel Tunnel Progress

THE BUILDING OF THE CHANNEL TUNNEL

The year did not start well with the Channel Tunnel project claiming its first fatality, caused by a waste train going out of control. By October, a total of four men had died in accidents.

By the end of March boring was exceeding target rates for the first time. On the British side the service tunnel was over 7 km out to sea. Just as things were looking better, Eurotunnel announced that opening of the tunnel would be delayed by a month to 15th June 1993. TML, the contractors, would receive a £100 million bonus if the Tunnel was completed by the new date.

Determined to attract media attention to more positive news, large numbers of press were invited to Coquelles in April where the French shuttle terminal was being built. A boring machine named 'Virginie' completed the 3.25 km service tunnel from Sangatte on the coast as the crowds looked on. At the same time the 600-metre service tunnel from Holywell Coombe under Castle Hill to the terminal area at Cheriton, Folkestone, was completed despite difficult conditions.

When Eurotunnel first 'went public' in November 1987 the entire project was costed at £4.8 billion. By April 1989 the figure for completion was £5.4 billion. At first there was little alarm at the cost overruns, their being almost expected. City analysts knew that the 1987 prospectus had only contained rough estimates of cost drawn heavily from cost estimates of the aborted 1975 Channel Tunnel project. Eurotunnel shares continued to rise in value to £11.54 each in June after which they fell rapidly with mounting concern about the project's finances.

A maximum of £6 billion had been arranged, £1 billion from shareholders and £5 billion from a syndicate of world banks. By agreement, the banks' money was paid only as work progressed and on the evidence that the project was on target. By July that was no longer the case. There was a growing divide between Eurotunnel, Transmanche-Link (the contractors, a group of 10 British and French construction companies) and the banks. The latter were legally permitted at this stage to withdraw support for the project but chose not to.

Towards the end of July Eurotunnel was starting talks with the banks about increased loan facilities above the £6 billion in loans and capital already arranged. Meanwhile directors pointed out that tunnelling was making good progress with 27 km in total completed.

Eurotunnel was claiming that about £7.2 billion would be needed to complete the tunnel and were blaming TML for the cost overruns. TML were estimating £7.6 billion and the banks fearing that, at worst, £8 billion might be needed.

One of the reasons for mounting costs was 'construction inflation', exacarbated by the many projects being undertaken in the South East of England – Canary Wharf, Broadgate, etc. Materials and labour costs were rising rapidly at above-inflation rates.

TML's management was widely regarded to be unsuitable for the job with some key personnel coming from the inappropriate backgrounds. The management structure was also relatively inefficient. Until May general disillusionment with management decision-making process had caused many resignations from TML. On the appointment of a highly-respected American, Jack Lemley, as new chief executive things slowly improved.

One of the other reasons for disagreements between Eurotunnel and TML was the constantly-rising specification of the tunnel and terminals. This was mainly improved safety measures in the light of accidents such as King's Cross. The

◄Alastair Morton, co-chairman of Eurotunnel became an increasingly controversial figure. Aged 51, his enthusiasm, dilligence and powers of persuasion were useful for Eurotunnel. Fluent in French, he has developed a close working relationship with André Bénard, his French counterpart.
Eurotunnel

Intergovernmental Commission, a body set up by the governments of Britain and France was responsible for setting most of the strict (and expensive) safety standards.

There was a growing distrust between Eurotunnel and TML and a feeling that more people were monitoring than digging. At the heart of the dispute was Eurotunnel's Project Implementation Division (PID) which monitors TLM's progress. Its staff had increased to 350 by the autumn – increasing labour costs for Eurotunnel and for TML (competing for experienced staff with similar skills). TML staff had to respond to the output of the PID also increasing the contractor's costs; generally there was a duplication of work.

By October the arguments were becoming even more heated. Analysts said that Eurotunnel was demanding a top specification Channel Tunnel, regardless of cost. The contractor was simply working to a minimum standard to meet (rising) contract specifications and trying to charge more for it – simply maximising profits. Morton wished TML had come up with a realistic price at the start of construction and was now laying the blame squarely with the contractors. Did they, he asks, "sufficiently think out what is involved in equipping a tunnel?" … "No, they did not."

Some observers were saying that the crisis could be solved by a merger between the two parties. By December, however a Setec/Atkins (independent consulting engineers) report recommended that TML was not eligible for the extra £500 million to complete the 'lump-sum' part of the contract – the terminal and tunnel fitting out. The consultants had "supported in general terms" the revised estimate of £7 billion to build the Channel Tunnel. Negotiations continued with the banks for extra loan facilities and the Eurotunnel share price began to recover after months of falling due to uncertainty. Agreement was made more certain by a decision to downgrade running speeds through the Tunnel which would decrease revenue for Eurotunnel (by cutting capacity), but also reduce costs – the main saving coming from a reduced number of piston-effect relief cross-ducts (which prevent pressuré building up in front of the huge shuttle trains).

One month earlier a huge crowd had watched the official completion of the 7.9 km service tunnel from Holywell Coombe under Sugarloaf Hill to Shakespeare Cliff. The Howden TBM, therefore, had completed the British landward service tunnel drive. By the end of December almost one third (48 km out of 150 km) of all tunnelling associated with the Channel Tunnel project had been completed at a cost of £1.85 billion. Two under-land service tunnels and the French south running tunnel between Sangatte and Bessingue (Coquelles) were complete. By the end of the year all the tunnel boring machines were in operation and work commenced or completed on all under-land and under-sea sections of the tunnel.

Cheriton terminal will not be such a mar on the landscape: Eurotunnel, alongside local councils and conservation groups agreed to restore and manage chalk grassland between Dover, Folkestone and Etchinghill. However, Chris Patten, environment secretary, and Cecil Parkinson approved a new A20 road linking Dover to the Channel Tunnel entrance near Folkestone. The road will run 200 yards from Shakespeare Cliff through unspoilt coastal downland. Opponents of the scheme had suggested a more expensive but less environmentally damaging upgrading of the existing A20, which would have included a tunnel under Dover's Western Heights.

▲One of the two Markham marine drive running tunnel TBMs for the Channel Tunnel seen at the company's Chesterfield factory shortly before being disassembled for transport to Folkestone. The TBMs are the result of a Robbins-Markham joint venture. Markham have produced the concrete segment erectors and back-up conveyors (for spoil), Robbins (USA) the cutter head (seen above), drive, shield and grippers. Each machine must drive a minimum of 25 km through chalky marls. *Markham & Co. Ltd.*

CHANNEL TUNNEL TRAIN ORDERS

Two major orders were placed in 1989: for the Cheriton–Coquelles shuttle trains and for the 'Three Capitals' high-speed trains to serve London, Paris, Brussels, and beyond.

On 26th July Transmanche-Link (TML), the group contracted to design, construct and commission the Channel Tunnel, placed a £600 million order for the initial rolling stock for shuttle trains, this cost being considerably more than Eurotunnel had been expecting.

Brush Electrical Machines Ltd., a subsidiary of Hawker Siddeley, which in turn is part of the Euroshuttle Consortium secured the contract to build 40 Bo–Bo–Bo electric locomotives to haul the trains. The Swiss company Asea Brown Boveri, also in the five-nation consortium, will co-operate with their design and construction. The other members will construct 252 'tourist wagons'. They are Bombardier Inc. of Canada, ANF Industrie of France and BN Constructions Ferroviairies et Metalliques of Belgium. In total, Euroshuttle Consortium secured £350 million of orders.

The rest of TML's order went to an Italian consortium of Breda Construzioni Ferroviarie, in conjunction with Fiat Ferroviaria to build 252 wagons to carry HGVs and their drivers.

Each locomotive will cost about £1.9 million with one at each end of the train. The drivers' cabs will be air-conditioned and pressurised. The locomotives will weigh 128 tons and have a continuous rating of 7,500 hp. If problems arise, this power is sufficient to start the 2,250-ton train on the maximum 1 in 90 gradient, as well as the other 'dead' locomotive. On shuttle trains passengers will not be segregated from vehicles.

RFS Industries at Doncaster produced a special wagon body to test concepts for bogies to be used on shuttle trains. The wagon can simulate the different loadings to be experienced. Fiat, Kawasaki, ABG and MAN bogies were subjected to some complex stress and ride tests during the year.

In December contracts were signed for the construction of 30 'Three Capitals' high-speed trains to work Channel Tunnel passenger services from June 1993 between London and Paris/ Brussels.

This Transmanche Super Train Group's 'lead company' is the ubiquitous GEC Alsthom. The consortium building the new trains is under the supervision of the 1987-formed International Project Group to define technical and commercial specifications of proposed trains and monitor their development on behalf of the parent companies (BR/SNCF/SNCB/ NMBS).

Industrial design features will be the product of an international consortium.

BR's share of the contract is almost 47%, equivalent to 14 of the 30 trainsets with 13 for SNCF and three for SNCB. The fleet will be jointly-owned and operated but divided nationally for deployment and maintenance.

The trains will be 393 metres long and in 2 + 18 formation. There will be 794 seats of which almost three quarters will be standard class. Maximum speed (to be actually used on the TGV-Nord line) will be 300 km/h. The power cars will be able to collect power from: 25 kV ac; 3000 V dc (SNCB overhead); 750 V dc (BR Southern Region 3rd rail).

CHANNEL TUNNEL POLITICS

All year there were calls to upgrade rail (and road) links from the Tunnel to the Regions, especially the London bottleneck. Transport 2000 and others urged cost-benefit analyses of Tunnel-related rail investments to ensure that regional and environmental factors are considered.

The Great Central Railway Group proposed building a £1 billion railway from Ashford to Rugby via Tonbridge and Redhill. South of Rugby part of the Great Central Railway's trackbed would be used again. Terminals – for passengers and freight – would be at Ashford. Beaconsfield and Rugby. The plans were backed by Eurotunnel.

In August agreement was reached over on-train customs checks. Approval was given for mobile customs teams to question and search passengers on moving trains operating services from provincial cities to Paris/ Brussels. For services starting or ending at Waterloo there would be standard customs facilities near the platforms, however.

In the face of growing criticism of government doggedness over a high-speed rail link to the Tunnel, Michael Portillo attacked what he saw as long-held assumptions about State-support of transport services in a speech in November. Citing private-sector involvement in the City and Beckton extensions of the Docklands Light Railway, the Manchester Metrolink and various road schemes, his main example concerned the Channel Tunnel and link. "Eurorail will share in the funding, the risks and the rewards. For the first time since 1948, the private sector will be participating in providing main line rail services in Britain."

On 14th December BR launched 'International Rail Services for the United Kingdom'. The plan was produced in accordance with Section 40 of the Channel Tunnel Act 1987 and prepared after regional consultations.

Section 42 of the same Act said that the Board had a duty to operate its international services on a fully commercial basis – providing a rate of return at or above that required. It was stated firmly by Sir Robert Reid that profitable, not necessarily desirable, trains would be operated. Trains serving the Regions were no exception.

The Board announced that up to 80 passenger trains (40 each way) and 54 freight trains (27 each way) would operate through the Tunnel. Over 70% of the international freight traffic would begin or end its journey beyond London. BR expected to carry some 13 million passengers and over 6 million tonnes of freight on international services in the early years of Tunnel operations.

There would be 15 passenger trains daily in each direction between London and Paris and a similar service between London and Brussels.

There would be two trains a day in each direction from East Coast Main Line destinations to the Continent, one from Edinburgh and Leeds to Paris each morning with the portions combining at Peterborough with a similar service to Brussels. On the West Coast Main Line there would also be two trains a day in each direction, one from Manchester and Birmingham to Paris with the portions combining at Rugby with a similar service to Brussels. The return service would be in the evening in each case.

Driving cabs would be incorporated at the mid-points of the 18-coach trains, these units therefore having a different specification to the standard London–Paris/Brussels inter-capital trains.

Current studies indicated that Plymouth/Swansea–Bristol–Paris/ Brussels, Edinburgh–Newcastle–Darlington–York–Doncaster–Paris/Brussels, and Glasgow–Carlisle–Lancaster–Preston–Crewe–Paris/Brussels night trains would be viable, one train in each direction. The Brussels section of each train could continue on to Amsterdam or Köln. Seating and sleeping accommodation would be provided. Night services from London to more distant destinations such as southern France were also being investigated.

Motorail services and plans for the upgrading of stations at Ashford, Fréthun (near Calais) and Lille – including expanded car parking facilities – were also mentioned.

The plans for international train services from beyond London were not greeted with enthusiasm, it being pointed out that the 30% of passengers coming from beyond London will be badly served. Responding, BR argued that the number of seats available from the North would be more than the combined capacity of airlines flying from northern airports to Paris and Brussels.

The document also included a graph drawn up in association with Coopers and Lybrand. It suggested that with the Lille–Brussels high-speed line opening in 1995 and high-speed links to London, Köln and Amsterdam opening in 1998, rail travel could then represent: 80% of the daytime rail/air travel market between London and Paris; 77% of that between London and Brussels; and about 58% of that between London and Köln/Amsterdam.

Plans for Railfreight Distribution's (RfD) operation of international freight services were also detailed. Against a background of increasing trade with EEC countries, particularly France, West Germany, the Low Countries and Italy, RfD would offer much faster journey times for both international freight (using demountable, or 'swap', bodies) and trainload flows. The latter could be to distribution terminals or to private sidings. The likely demise of customs clearance of EEC freight after 1992 would also speed traffic flows.

There would be up to 12 regional freight centres (for intermodal and conventional wagon rail-head activities) and three train operating centres – at Doncaster, Crewe and Wembley – where traffic from more than one terminal would be combined for its onward journey to mainland Europe. For some bulk traffics, steel for example, consolidation would often not be necessary.

RfD would continue to look at new intermodal and conventional wagon designs to ensure that the smaller profile of the BR loading gauge would not hinder the development of through freight services.

The West London line would be upgraded and the route between Redhill and Tonbridge electrified.

Finally, the Parcels Sector would offer a new service with same-day delivery to Paris and Brussels (using parcels space on international passenger trains). An overnight service also serving more distant locations would also be available.

◄South Darenth near Swanley was the venue for a protest meeting over BR's proposed high-speed rail link on 11th March. Do the residents realise that congestion and noise from road traffic without relief from the construction of a new line will disturb them rather more? Mobile demonstration vans fitted with loudspeakers and playing 'recordings of TGVs at speed' led some Kent residents to believe that high-speed trains were as 'almost as loud as Concorde'!
Rodney Lissenden

HIGH-SPEED RAIL LINK TO THE CHANNEL TUNNEL

In France the TGV-Amiens group intensified its efforts to have the TGV Nord line diverted away from Lille towards the Picardy capital. French enthusiasm, nerve, and vision continued to contrast with British dithering over a high speed link to the Channel Tunnel to supplement existing tracks.

The TGV Nord, it was revealed, might have even higher line speeds than the TGV Atlantique line. In accordance with long-standing plans to redevelop the area to the east of Paris, the scale of the French plan to make Paris Europe's transport hub became clear. The TGV Nord would link in with the TGV-Sud Est and TGV Atlantique via a by-pass line east of Paris. It will link an expanded Charles de Gaulle airport, a new town called Marne-la-Vallee, the £1.3 billion Eurodisneyland site and the new science city south of Paris. These plans were included in the proposed European high-speed network covered in the 'European Scene'.

On 8th March British Rail revealed the preferred alignment of the proposed high-speed link to the Channel Tunnel. Responding to environmentalists' pressure, the route chosen was underground from King's Cross through Warwick Gardens (Peckham) to Swanley, Ashford and the Tunnel, a total distance of 68 miles. Overall, 23 miles are in tunnel, 16 miles run alongside existing railway and 14 follow the alignment of the M20 motorway. Only 15 miles is new surface route. The maximum line speed is 140 mph. With the rejection of routes 1, 3 and 4, BR's modified route 2 featured considerable tunnelling around London and Ashford, widespread use of cuttings and reliance on existing transport corridors. Maidstone and Ashford will have international stations, the former called Mid-Kent Parkway.

BR also announced that it will pay compensation to residents wishing to move if their property is within a 240 metre-wide corridor along the route. Compensation for noise would also be available.

At the same time BR announced that it would be inviting private-sector consortia (who had already gone through a pre-qualification phase) to tender for the construction and possible ownership of the rail link.

BR also rejected two alternative high-speed rail link schemes, RACHEL and TALIS. Both involved a more northerly route from Stratford in the East of London, through industrial Essex, under the Thames and through North Kent towards Ashford. RACHEL (Rainham to the Channel Tunnel) was put forward as a cost-effective 'grand design' in the French manner to further regenerate the East End and link with upgraded rail services up the Lea Valley to Stansted airport, Cambridge (science city) and the East Coast Main Line. There could be a spur from Stratford to King's Cross. TALIS (Thames Alternative Link International System) also advocated the use of undeveloped parts of south Essex for part of the route, after leaving existing BR tracks.

Six consortia expressed initial interest in the high-speed line.

One of these was a powerful Anglo-American group employing the authors of RACHEL and TALIS. Nine industrial, financial and construction companies were in the group alongwith MCA which was thinking of building a Universal Studios theme park at Rainham Marshes on the new line. The £3.4 billion route was familiar: Stratford–Rainham–Tilbury–Ashford–Channel Tunnel.

As the summer went on rumours began to fly about the escalating cost of the link – possibly £3.5 billion due to construction price inflation and the environmental safeguards stipulated.

In the Commons, one Conservative MP suggested that many people in Kent thought that taxpayers' money should play a part in environmental protection. Michael Portillo was adamant: "Ports and airports are expected to be environmentally acceptable, yet no government subsidies are available for that purpose."

On 14th September BR announced final alterations to the link with some further environmental concessions. Costs at Swanley, for example, would be increased by up to £20 million by extending the London tunnel to the east of the M25 thereby saving the Green belt between Swanley and Swanley Village.

There were now only two consortia in the running: the P & O Group/British Airports proposal advocating Stratford; the Trafalgar House/British Insulated Callender's Cables proposal advocating King's Cross.

On 13th October Cecil Parkinson finally knocked the idea of Stratford as a terminal on the head. There had been little political support for Stratford with its inadequate A13 road link and Central Line transport connections; there was a feeling that the Underground line, despite its £750 million modernisation, would not have been able to cope.

On the 1st November, M. Michel Walrave of the SNCF suggested that, if the British government will not help with a proper Channel Tunnel rail link, France might have to – by allowing BR a bigger share of the eventual proceeds.

Indecision led to criticism from unexpected places. On 31st October the Daily Telegraph editorial said: "Where decisions have to be taken affecting the future pattern of the nation, it behoves ministers to grasp the nettle and not to place the onus on commercial organisations, whether in the public or private sector." The Observer agreed: "To expect BR to act as a commercial entity … while still in public ownership, subject to government diktat,is official folly."

On 3rd November British Rail chose the Trafalgar House/BICC consortium, 'Eurorail', as it private sector partner to develop and operate the link. BR and Eurorail decided to delay the Parliamentary Bill for the authority to build the line until November 1990. BR also announced the possibility of an additional international station at Swanley and that new negotiations had started with the SNCF over the division of receipts for international services "in relation to the emerging cost of the new rail link." In the Commons Cecil Parkinson welcomed the "sensible" delay. Kent County Council complained about plans for Swanley on planning, Green Belt and highway grounds.

During November Eurorail maintained that forecast revenue would not support the £1.3 billion cost of the 18 mile King's Cross–Swanley tunnel and other environmental measures forced by the government.Despite the fact that the government has a large amount of prestige riding on the success of the whole Channel Tunnel project, it was made plain that no financial assistance would be available, as was stipulated in the Channel Tunnel Act (1987), Section 42(3). It certainly was not that ministers failed to realise the scale of the environmental measures involved. Cecil Parkinson had said: "It is now proposed to put so much of the route in tunnels that BR will have to move more earth for it than Eurotunnel will shift for the tunnel under the sea."

On 5th November, about 4,000 protestors against BR's plans for a high-speed rail link, supported by some Kent and south east London MPs, marched along Whitehall and into Trafalgar

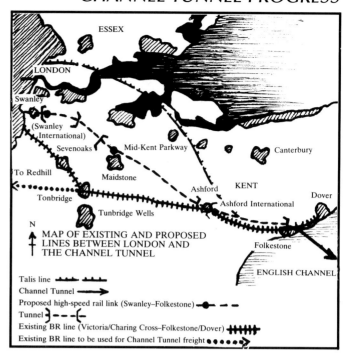

MAP OF EXISTING AND PROPOSED LINES BETWEEN LONDON AND THE CHANNEL TUNNEL

Talis line
Channel Tunnel
Proposed high-speed rail link (Swanley–Folkestone)
Tunnel
Existing BR line (Victoria/Charing Cross–Folkestone/Dover)
Existing BR line to be used for Channel Tunnel freight

Square.

At a rail users groups conference on 11th November it was pointed out that: "An important part of the cost-benefit case for building the M20 is the saving of life by transferring traffic from the dangerous A20. But BR is explicitly forbidden to count the saving of life through transfer of people from the A20/M20 to a new high-speed railway."

On 21st November the Queen's Speech which outlined the government's agenda for the new parliamentary session failed to even mention transport. Neil Kinnock, leader of the Opposition, launched a stinging attack on the government in response, and criticises the lack of investment in a high-speed rail link through Kent.

By December it was clear that BR and Eurorail would be taking a step-by-step approach to the link. For the Swanley–King's Cross section, upgraded existing above-ground BR tracks (via an enlarged Snow Hill tunnel) became the plan – so dramatically cutting costs. Tunnelling under south east London was deemed too expensive and would require obtrusive ventilation shafts every mile or so.

Two of Japan's leading providers of project finance, Industrial Bank of Japan and Sumitomo Trust were appointed as co-lead banks alongside Barclays by Eurorail. By delaying the parliamentary Bill, BR was able to give Eurorail's advisers, led by Kleinwart Benson, the merchant bank, more time to arrange loans.

By confirming the intention to site the new London terminal at King's Cross, the BR/Eurorail joint venture gave new impetus to the London Regional Consortium's redevelopment of the station and surrounds.

BR pressed on with plans to upgrade its existing lines in readiness for 1993, the year of the Tunnel's opening. On 27th November it deposited its Number 3 Bill in Parliament seeking powers for railway works at the proposed Ashford International station and expansion of capacity at Headcorn, Borough Green and Otford. Also included in the Bill was the West Hamstead 'chord' in north London which will link King's Cross to the West Coast Main Line.

After seeing what had happened to the high-speed line, on 29th November BR warned of the consequences of Parliament postponing consideration of the King's Cross Railway Bill by one year. Introduction of some services such as through trains from Scotland, the North and the Midlands to the Continent would be delayed by more than two years.

Throughout the year BR reminded Kent commuters that their trains might one day also use the high-speed line; Ashford–London times, for example, could be halved.

CHANNEL TUNNEL PROGRESS

▶The Cheriton terminal site is seen from the west looking towards the English Channel. Part of Folkestone is on the right. The site covers 140 hectares. Just visible are the portals leading to the tunnel itself. Three tunnels, each of just over 50 km in length, form the 'Channel Tunnel'. This is the biggest construction project in Europe and is matched in world terms only by an international airport being built offshore at Osaka, Japan. The photograph was taken at the end of the year. *Eurotunnel*

▼Passengers and most freight travelling to and from the North will travel via the West London Line which is to be electrified and improved. It certainly needs both! Class 47 No. 47616 passes Lilley Bridge, Kensington with the 07.18 Manchester–Brighton on 2nd September. *Les Nixon*

▲Until, and if, the new high-speed line is built this will be the congested and slow link between London (Waterloo) and the Channel Tunnel. Although signalling and some track layouts are being upgraded, the investment involved is negligible compared with French spending on their TGV Nord line. 73201 'Broadlands' rattles along the main line past Paddock Wood with a 'Royal Highlander' special train on 29th March. *Rodney Lissenden*

DEVELOPMENTS AT KING'S CROSS

The North's frustration towards the London/Kent bottleneck was symbolised by the King's Cross scheme which was the key to fast international services. Without King's Cross the alternative would be the perennial circuitous journey via Kensington Olympia adding at the very least 30 minutes to international journey times.

After announcing its choice of King's Cross as its second London terminal (after Waterloo), British Rail lobbied intensively for its redevelopment. With direct links to the North, five Underground lines and connections with Thameslink there was no comparison with the Stratford alternative being put forward by some private consortia. Although the focus of business activity had been shifting eastwards in London, Stratford was too far east.

On 6th May BR revealed its plans to transform King's Cross and St. Pancras stations. The Board lodged an application with Camden council for outline planning consent to develop a 110,000 sq. ft. passenger concourse to link the two stations and to the new sub-surface platforms. BR stressed that the new building will match the splendour of the King's Cross and St. Pancras train sheds and the Midland Hotel, all Grade 1 listed buildings. The plans did require the demolition of the Great Northern Hotel. The architects, Foster Associates, would aim for 'elegant simplicity'.

Two days later the King's Cross Railway Bill – powers to build the sub-surface international and expanded Thameslink platforms and railway works associated with it – got its second reading in the Commons by 211 votes to 41.

On 16th October the London Regeneration Consortium (consisting of the National Freight Corporation, Rosehaugh and Stanhope Properties), developers of the 134 acre site, put forward revised plans after discussions with Camden council, English Heritage and other bodies. This involved more parkland (34 acres), less office space (6.5 million sq. ft.) and more residential space (1,660 homes). The amount of shopping space (300,000 sq. ft.) and leisure and community space was unchanged at 300,000 and 360,000 sq. ft. respectively. The development of the area would help to fund construction of the new international station, the chief reason for BR's keenness for the King's Cross site.

InterCity

The major announcment of importance for InterCity was that at long last the sector had actually turned in an operating profit – £57.4 million, as compared with an operating loss of of £86.2 million for 1987/88. This was no mean feat and reflects well on the policies of InterCity's director, John Prideaux.

THE WAY FORWARD FOR INTERCITY

In May Dr. Prideaux gave an important lecture to the Royal Society of Arts. He said that the business had clear targets and know how to achieve them. More specifically, for 1989/90 assets must at least show a 2% return on a full current cost accounting basis. The means are:

●Market research: for example "the typical InterCity passenger is not an established businessman, but a girl in her early 20s visiting a friend at the weekend."

●Quality: speed; comfort; cleanliness; service (partly through the appointment of senior conductors); 'product identity' (livery, styling, lettering, brochure, map and timetable design).

●Efficiency: controlling demand by ticket-type; controlling overcrowding by reservation rules; organisational and operational efficiency (for example, transferring HSTs between routes).

●Effective marketing: he cited the introduction of airline-style APEX tickets in Scotland, a range extended in January – the pre-booked and discounted tickets applied from more Scottish stations to London (and other destinations such as Manchester and Birmingham).

●Attractively-timed services including a greater use of regular interval timetables.

EAST COAST MAIN LINE ELECTRIFICATION

Electrification of the East Coast Main Line progressed well. In September the first electric-hauled passenger train ran into York, appropriately a charter train carrying delegates to a conference on electrification! Class 91s began operating certain London King's Cross–Leeds trains in March (14 months early) being matched with the first rake of Mark 4 stock in October.

Work proceeded on the £1.8 million electrification of the 3.2 km line between Leeds and Neville Hill Depot. The central trainshed at York station, Durham Viaduct and the Royal Border Bridge at Berwick-upon-Tweed were locations for new 'low-profile' overhead line equipment (OHLE) designed by Ove Arup and Partners.

York's new signalling control centre took over control of its central section of track stretching from Dringhouses to Skelton Junction (north of York Station). The centre features Solid State Interlocking and an Integrated Electronic Control Centre.

Major trackwork associated with the project continued at York and Newcastle with work at the former completed by May. At Edinburgh the south bore of the twin Calton tunnels was relined, with enough clearance for OHLE.

▼The new timetable saw InterCity services to Bradford using Forster Square station instead of Interchange. 31462 is ready to haul 91002 together with its train of HST stock back to Leeds on the evening of 26th May. *David Rodgers*

The new Reading station concourse (see p. 28) *T.N. Bowden*

MARK 4 COACHES ENTER SERVICE

On 20th September, InterCity's new coaches, the Mark 4s were shown off to the media with a press run from London King's Cross to Leeds and back and a presentation in Leeds Town Hall. The brandname 'INTERCITY 225' is being used to describe the new trains for the East Coast Main Line which consist of a Class 91 locomotive, 9 or 10 Mark 4 coaches and a Mark 4 driving van trailer (DVT). The '225' refers to the design speed of these trains and is in km/h. The '225' of the InterCity 125 brandname for the HSTs was of course in miles/h. The Mk 4 coaches were then infiltrated gradually into King's Cross–Leeds diagrams.

There are three basic types of Mark 4 coach, first, standard and catering. To confuse staff and enthusiasts alike, first class coaches are lettered 'PO' – 'Pullman Open', second (sorry – standard) class coaches are lettered 'TO' – 'Tourist Open' and the catering vehicles which are restaurant buffet firsts are lettered 'SV' – 'service vehicle'. Tightlock couplings are fitted, but end coaches must have drophead buckeyes to enable connection to Class 91 locomotives with the buckeye on other locomotives with a conventional screw coupling. There are three variants of standard class coach, the standard type, the end type (lettered 'TOE') and the disabled type (lettered 'TOD'). The standard variant has 74 seats with two toilets at one end, one of which is longer than the other to accommodate a fold-down baby-changing table. The disabled version has one large disabled person's toilet and only 72 seats plus, of course, space for a wheelchair at the end of the saloon.

One of the main aims of the Mark 4 coach designer has been to eliminate the 'narrow-bodied airliner' look of a long thin tube. This is achieved by the use of full-height smoked glass partitions and works very well in the first class vehicle. In the standard class vehicles there are only three of these in total and thus the effect is not so good. The overall impression of the interiors of these vehicles was that of a marked improvement over the Mark 3.

Other features of the Mark 4 are a body profile which slopes inwards markedly towards the cantrail (to accommodate the

▲▲◀Mark 4 open first 11206 at Leeds on the media run of 20th September.
John Augustson

▲◀The restful interior of the Mark 4 open first. Note the concealed main lighting and the smoked glass partitions which help to break up the saloon into smaller areas.
Peter Fox

◀The interior of the standard class vehicle. Note the change in seat colour when changing from a smoking to a non-smoking area.
Peter Fox

▲ The power operated sliding plug door.
Peter Fox

▼ The push button-operated interior doors.
Peter Fox

▲ The kitchen in the restaurant-buffet first.
Peter Fox

possibility of tilt), sliding plug doors, vestibule doors operated by a push button and bogies designed by the Swiss firm SIG. Unfortunately, the curving performance of these bogies is not up to standard and further work is obviously required.

▼ The centre of the first class coach has a 'chicane' where the seating layout reverses from 2+1 to 1+2. _Peter Fox_

▼ A rake of Mark 4s with DVT 82201 at the front forms the 13.10 Leeds–London King's Cross at Bridge Jn. (Doncaster) on 11th October. 91001 'Swallow' is pushing from the rear.
M.A. King

OTHER ELECTRIFICATION PROJECTS

Authority for the £12.25 million electrification of Edinburgh–Carstairs was given.

In April the Midland Main Line strategy Report was published, a document produced by consultants on behalf of Derbyshire, Leicestershire, Northamptonshire and Nottinghamshire County Councils, together with Sheffield City Council. The consultants, who used rather dubious assumptions e.g. that new stock would be required and that there would be plenty of work elsewhere for the displaced HSTs, analysed four options (on a cost-benefit basis) for the line: immediate electrification – at a cost of about £800,000 a mile – and upgrading to 125 mph running speeds where practicable gave the best return (over 7%). London–Sheffield times would be reduced to one hour 50 minutes. (Soon after the report was published, the Treasury raised the required rate of return to 8%). Interim measures to further improve the line's performance would include new Parkway station near Trent South Junction and Kegworth, principally to serve the expanding East Midlands Airport. A reassessment of station stops south of Leicester by InterCity trains was recommended. The report's strangest suggestion was that Grimsby and Lincoln InterCity trains should travel via Nottingham to London St. Pancras instead of down the East Coast Main Line.

SERVICE CHANGES

On the Midland Main Line signalling, track and operating improvements led to a welcome average 10% reduction in journey times with average Sheffield–London journey times reduced to 142 minutes, the southbound 'Master Cutler' taking 130 minutes. An hourly St. Pancras–Sheffield and St. Pancras–Nottingham InterCity service was not introduced until the start of the October timetable with the transfer of another HST set from the East Coast Main Line.

On the West Coast Main Line the most symbolic change was the restoration of a competitive sub-5 hour timing for the 10.30 Euston–Glasgow 'Royal Scot' and 09.40 southbound departure. The former was faster: 4 hours 53. Manchester, Liverpool, Blackpool and Lancaster services saw greater capacity, as did those to the West Midlands.

On InterCity's Cross Country routes the higgeldy-piggeldy nature of the timetable was continued, causing pathing problems for regular-interval services on other routes. Timings remained pedestrian on certain parts of the key NE-SW axis, particularly Birmingham–Bristol. However, minor alterations were made to relieve overcrowding on several more leisure-orientated services, an important source of revenue on this route. Also, although no substitute for a re-introduced InterCity service via the Settle & Carlisle, the 'Cornishman' HST started and ended its journey at Glasgow Queen Street, travelling via Edinburgh; this gave one direct train between Derby/Sheffield and Glasgow.

A new 15.25 Newcastle–Cardiff filled a major southbound gap in the timetable; the stock for this service came from an extension of the Plymouth–York 'Armada' to Newcastle.

After two years of worsening travel opportunities on the Liverpool–South West services, retimings and extensions were introduced to improve matters. A new Chippenham–Bath–Bristol Temple Meads–Birmingham Manchester service was introduced to fill a gap in the timetable.

Changes to InterCity services on Western Region included a new Pullman service. With the success of the much-vaunted 'Red Dragon Pullman', the 08.00 Paddington–Swansea and 11.36 return were upgraded to the 'St. David Pullman'.

SLEEPING CAR SERVICES

Sleeper services between London and Fort William were routed via Glasgow Central (instead of Glasgow Queen Street) making valuable savings in journey time. By the end of the year a rake of nine sleeping cars (SLEP) were stored at MoD Bicester as 'out of use', a depressing sight.

CATERING

Quality of service remained patchy. The Central Transport Users Consultative Committee estimated that 3% of advertised catering facilities were cancelled. The May timetable gave little indication of catering quality or buffet opening hours. Standard class ticket-holders remained unsure as to whether there would be enough room in the restaurant car to enjoy a full meal. Its failings well-publicised, BR dropped the brand name 'Cuisine 2000', the cook-chill catering operation.

On a more positive note, the range and quality of InterCity On Board Services' sandwiches improved and standards of catering stayed high on Pullman services.

ADVERTISING

A success story for InterCity was the succession of awards won for advertising, itself far slicker than the early 1980s; long gone were the days of 'This is the Age of the Train' and backwards-running HSTs!

The new professionalism started in 1987/88 with 'Sentimental Journey', an InterCity advert that played on the romance and glamour of long-distance rail travel. Imaginative photography of trains speeding through countryside was used, and at stations like Penzance, York, Crewe and Edinburgh.

'Concerto' first appeared at the end of 1988 but was screened most in 1989. It cost £400,000 to make and was aimed to circumvent the public's apparent dislike of 'British Rail' by playing on its love of 'Britain's Railways', an important distinction. The advert, which appeared in 90- and 150-second versions, proved popular. It opened with an aerial shot of an overnight mail train and uses the theme from the GPO Film Unit's 1935 film 'Night Mail'. After the first stanza of Auden's verse commentary, the actor Tom Courtney takes over. Aerial shots of InterCity (and Provincial and Railfreight) trains are shown, most in attractive or dramatic locations. Hugh Hudson directed the commercial, Vangelis the music, the team famous for 'Chariots of Fire'. At the advertising world's equivalent of the Oscar ceremony, the Golden Break Awards, the award for best photography went to 'Concerto'.

At the same award ceremony, BR's 'Relax' advert was 1989 outright winner. It showed a boy playing chess with an old man on an InterCity train and used an American blues soundtrack and special effects. It aimed to contrast refined, quietly-efficient InterCity train travel with congested roads and, probably, cramped domestic airlines. This advert also received recognition at other award ceremonies.

LONG-DISTANCE COMMUTING

Commuters travelling daily to London from places like Bristol, Stafford, Grantham and Norwich faced big fare rises (up to 15%), something the national newspapers were quick to report. Comparisons were instantly made with fares paid by long-distance season ticket holders in France, roughly half of those in Britain. Not mentioned were the relatively low fares per mile paid (certainly compared with Network SouthEast passengers, often travelling in less comfortable surroundings). John Prideaux stressed that long-distance commuters only generate 5.5% of the sector's revenue and are too "vociferous and privileged."

SILVER STANDARD

After the success of 'Silver Standard' on Liverpool–London Euston trains, the concept was extended to Manchester–London Euston services.

CAPTIVE AUDIENCE

As motorists fumed in the normal peak-hour crawl on the M25 they could not help looking up to the airship hired by InterCity to fly over the entire length of the motorway during December. In huge lettering on each side was written: 'InterCity – 750 trains a day'.

►Class 91-hauled electric services to Leeds started in March with Mark 4 carriages starting to appear in October. 91003 heads a London King's Cross–Leeds service on 14th October. A HST power car pushes the train (of Mark 3 coaches) from the rear.
Les Nixon

▼With the delivery continuing of Mark 3 DVTs and their rapid commissioning, full fixed-formation working commenced on the WCML. 82121 approaches Linslade Tunnel at the head of the 13.48 Birmingham New Street–London Euston on 11th August. 90016 is at the rear. *Chris Wilson*

▼▼Class 90 locomotives Nos. 90026–90036 were painted in 'mainline' livery. On 30th September 90027 is in charge of the 13.30 London Euston–Lancaster service at Winwick South. *Paul Senior*

▲◄33021 and 33022 depart from Wellingborough bound for Leicester on the 'InterCity Diesel Day' held on 21st May (see Diary section). *A.J. Woof*

▲Following the Traincrew Agreement of 1988 InterCity introduced the grade of senior train conductor. The aim was to increase customer contact and care as well as carrying out guards' former duties. Ken Garvock, based at Newcastle, sports the smart uniform in this view. The personal organiser is intended to carry timetable information, a calculator, note pad, promotional literature. etc. *BR InterCity*

◄As part of the general re-routing of services at Manchester (see Provincial section), 47639 takes the Windsor Link at Ordsall Lane Jn. with the 16.23 Manchester Piccadilly–Glasgow/Edinburgh on 15th May. *Paul Shannon*

▼In March conversion started of certain Class 47/4s into the 478xx number series. With extended fuel capacity their use is concentrated on long-distance InterCity services. By December, 45 locomotives had been converted. 47804 (formerly 47591) blasts out of Southampton on 23rd August with the 13-coach 10.40 Poole–Glasgow/Edinburgh 'Wessex Scot'. *G.F. Gillham*

NEW LOOK AT YORK AND DURHAM

▲York station and environs were subjects of much track modernisation, the project being completed in 1989. The view here shows the central shed with middle road removed, new overbridge and catenary installed. The date is 13th February.
Colin Boocock

▲▶The new Vultron departure indicator on the main 'Up' platform is shown, behind it 43093 at the rear of the 15.02 'Aberdonian' to London King's Cross (photographed on the same day).
Colin Boocock

▶Following the first revenue-earning electric working to York, 91003 departs on its return journey to London King's Cross with the 09.31 charter service (see text). The date is 23rd September.
B.J. Nicolle

▼Durham Viaduct had ballast changed, track renewed and special unobtrusive OHLE installed during the first half of the year. Trackwork and the platform layout at Durham station were also modernised. During March, a 10-day closure of the viaduct involved all ECML trains being diverted over the Leamside route; British Transport Police successfully detered vandalism on this notorious stretch of line so avoiding disruption to services. A London King's Cross–Edinburgh HST crosses the famous viaduct on 24th July, the new wiring in situ.
Michael J. Collins

INTERCITY DIVERSIONS

▲47447 heads the 10.30 London Euston–Glasgow Central at Birkett on the Settle & Carlisle line, this diversion taking place on 25th March.
A.J. Woof

◄With the diversion of West Coast Main Line services over the S & C during weekends in March, a shuttle service was operated between Carlisle and Lancaster on 4th and 11th March. Class 31/4 No. 31413 is having little difficulty pulling the three-coach 11.44 Carlisle–Lancaster at Low Gill on 11th March. *Les Nixon*

◄▼During the early part of 1989, InterCity trains running between Preston and Wigan were diverted via Lostock and Crows Nest Junction on Sundays. To avoid run-round operations pairs of Class 20s were used. Here, 20052 and 20004 climb away from Hindley towards Crows Nest Jn. with the 10.00 London Euston–Preston on 12th February, the last day of these movements. 47517 is at the rear to lead the train on to Preston away from Lostock. *A.J. Woof*

▲▲►Summer Sundays produced several diversions of London Paddington/Poole/Brighton to Manchester/Liverpool/Wolverhampton/Glasgow/Edinburgh trains over the Costwold line. 47574 runs down grade from Chipping Campden towards Honeybourne with the 09.30 Brighton–Glasgow/Edinburgh on 6th August. *Geoff Bannister*

▲►With the temporary closure of the south tunnel at Haymarket, West Coast Main Line trains were routed via the Edinburgh suburban line to arrive at Waverley from the east. 47006 heads the 06.57 Coventry–Edinburgh through Slateford station on 10th October.
Michael McGowan

►Due to modernisation of signalling between Huntingdon and Peterborough on the ECML, trains were diverted at Hitchin via Ely to Peterborough over four weekends in October. Amidst ancient trackwork and signalling (shortly to be modernised) at Ely, 47466 heads 'dead' 91008 and HST power car No. 43068 with the 09.15 London King's Cross–Leeds on 15th October. *Ian Cowley*

▲For several weekends after Easter, East Coast Main Line trains between Newcastle and Edinburgh were diverted via Carlisle and Carstairs. 43195 and 43194 propel a diverted London King's Cross–Edinburgh train at How Mill on the Tyne Valley line on 8th April.

J. Brian Carter

WESTERN REGION CHANGES

▲Severe overcrowding on morning HST services to London Paddington led to the introduction of additional loco-hauled trains from Bristol at 07.26 and 09.03. Here, 47603 heads the 09.03 Bristol Temple Meads–London Paddington at Fox's Wood, near Keynsham, on 22nd June. *John Chalcraft*

◀After 12 years' service on the line, Class 50s were replaced by Class 47-hauled trains on the Cotswold line. On Sunday 14th May 50036 'Victorious' leads the 16.15 Hereford–London Paddington at Norton Bridge Junction, Worcester. The signal box and associated semaphore signals were due for replacement with MAS later in the year.
Andrew Bannister

▼An aerial view and a view of part of the concourse of the new £20 million Reading station complex, opened by the Queen on 4th April. The station boasts an improved ticket office and more shops in the new 'Brunel Arcade'. An office complex – 'Apex Plaza' – is linked to the station. There is also a well-designed 1,600 space multi-storey car park, retail warehousing and a new Post Office sorting facility. The new building is at right angles to the original Great Western station building which is to be preserved.
BR InterCity/Brian Morrison

Network SouthEast

1989 was a year of consolidation for Network SouthEast, which celebrated its third anniversary on Saturday 10th June by holding a 'Network Day', with the usual reduced-fare rover tickets. Financially, NSE's policy of encouraging off-peak traffic reduced its operating deficit to £141 million in the year ending March 1990. However, by the end of the year growth was levelling off due to the rise in interest rates etc. and it was announced by Cecil Parkinson that, as part of a new three-year financial plan, NSE would be required to be self-supporting by 1992–3.

The year saw no improvement from 1988 as far as staffing was concerned, with continuing crew shortages (particularly in the suburban area) still causing an unacceptable level of cancellations. The one-day strikes during June and July probably hit NSE harder than the other sectors. Following these, a programme of initiatives aimed at restoring public confidence, coined 'Operation Recovery' was put in hand, the main customer incentives being a one third reduction in the price of Day Returns and Travelcards and 'Thirteen months for the Price of Twelve' for Network Cards renewed before the end of October.

The Central London Rail Study was published, a joint venture by Network SouthEast, London Regional Transport and the Department of Transport. As a priority, a new East–West link to main line standards was recommended as urgent to relieve overcrowding on both NSE and LUL lines. However, the new secretary of state for transport had a similar commercially-minded attitude towards new rail projects as his predecessors, without enough consideration of the social benefits to be gained, and authorisation of the link, which would connect the Paddington/Marylebone suburban lines to those out of Liverpool Street, was delayed for a year 'for further studies'! A Bill for the construction of this much-needed new link might be deposited in Parliament in November 1990.

On 3rd October, NSE director Chris Green made a speech to the Railway Study Association. Passenger business, he said, had risen 25% since 1983, and 468,000 people used NSE services into central London every day. The largest of BR's business sectors, £1.4 billion will be spent over the next five years to improve quality and raise capacity. Suburban car-parking space will be increased by a third to 100,000 by 2001.

The reduction in subsidy to NSE would be met by new technology (especially 'Networker' trains), strong marketing and high quality, the latter covering reliability, punctuality, information provision and cleanliness. A new senior quality manager has already been appointed.

In the drive to meet financial targets, Mr Green wants to see:
- A further growth in leisure and off-peak travel.
- Greater provision for increased non-central London commuting ('trans-suburb').
- More Driver-Only Operation of trains.
- Better signalling, including the elimination of all semaphore signalling by 1995.

On the quality front, poor reliability was mainly caused by staffing problems. Better pay, grading, greater flexibility (and variety) and the 'elimination of boring jobs' would help improve matters.

On cleanliness of trains Mr Green cited the particularly bad graffiti problem in Kent. The new route management system – plus a meeting with the New York City Transit Authority to see how it has tackled the craze – has enabled a better co-ordinated campaign to eradicate the scribbles. (Why has this decision to act taken so long? – ed.)

Finally, for strategic planning, a station for Dunstable (population 50,000) and a direct rail link to Luton Airport were among Chris Green's priorities.

LINE MANAGEMENT

The main development on Network SouthEast during the year was probably the introduction of 'line management' coincident with the start of the summer timetable in May, giving each line (or group of lines) within each sub-sector a specific identity, and a responsible commercial manager. Apart from leading to a hopeful increase in staff morale, this should also enable problems besetting a particular service to be identified and dealt with more quickly. Managers will have greater responsibility for budgets, timetables, local marketing, local investment and staffing levels. Continuing the policy of providing identification symbols started with 'Thameslink' the year before, the trains on each route have been given a name and a badge (ranging from the clever through the mundane to the plain idiotic!), these also appearing on timetables and other literature. Where the lines form a discrete network, such as the Chiltern and Great Northern lines, this is fine, but with the interworking of stock on Southern and Anglia Regions, it is a bit odd to see 'Marsh Link' at Oxted, or 'Portsmouth Express' at Reading! During the year, NSE stripes at last became more common than blue/grey on the sector's rolling stock, and these spread for the first time even to Southern Region 'EPB'(Class 415/416) stock!

INFRASTRUCTURE

Steady progress with infrastructure improvements continued in 1989. A new station was provided at Islip (on the Oxford–Bicester North line re-opened the previous year). An impressive new structure was completed at Guildford, while work continued on major building projects in conjunction with lucrative office development, such as at Liverpool Street, Charing Cross and Cannon Street. Signalling developments included the inauguration of driver only operation (DOO) on South London Lines suburban routes, with mirrors, CCTV cameras and video monitors appearing on platforms. Similar work was progressing on South Western Lines from Waterloo, as part of the Waterloo Area Resignalling Project (WARS).

TICKETING

Ticketing developments included the renaming of the London area 'Capitalcard' to 'Travelcard'; the zones were renumbered from 1 to 5, and there were minor changes in validity. The Network Saver became the Network 'Awaybreak' ticket, again with minor validity changes from its predecessor. Many new ticket machines were introduced during the year, some taking banknotes, in an effort to cut down queues at ticket offices.

ROLLING STOCK

Deliveries of new Class 321 4-car EMUs from York Works continued speedily throughout 1989, including the units for Northampton Line services, with an improved and enlarged first class section. Four orders for new rolling stock were placed during the year. These included 26 new Class '319' units, ostensibly to replace vehicles destroyed in the Clapham and Purley accidents, but in reality to provide increased services on the 'Thameslink' routes. Two orders for Class 165 'Network Turbo' DMUs were placed, for the Chiltern and Thames lines respectively, and the first batch of Class 465 EMUs were authorised – these two latter types are dealt with in the appropriate section. The total number of vehicles ordered was 752, at a cost of £433.3 million.

▲ Track re-modelling taking place at Liverpool Street on 25th March. Apart from this weekend total shutdown, the station has continued its £125 million five-year redevelopment whilst handling over 180,000 passengers per day. Shown here are some of the western-side platforms with part of the huge Rosehaugh Stanhope/BR Broadgate complex taking shape above. Eventually, 16 out of the 18 platforms will be full-length – capable of taking 12-coach trains. Liverpool Street's redevelopment is being financed by the Broadgate project.

Dr Iain C. Scotchman

▲▶ 'The Victory Arch' at Waterloo was floodlit for the first time in 1989. The date is 8th December. *Colin J. Marsden*

▼ After experiments on the BR network at Upwey (Dorset), Weybridge (Surrey), and following successes on the Docklands Light Railway and Singapore Mass Transit system, a 9 km stretch of single line between Botley and Fareham was equipped with aluminium extrusion third rail. This rail has a steel rail insert on the upper surface. Aluminium rail conducts electricity better than steel rail, so reducing substation requirements. It is also easier to handle. This view was taken just north of the old Knowle Hospital station and is looking towards Fareham. The date is 23rd September. *Mervyn Turvey*

▼▶ £4 million is being spent on Chiltern Line station improvements, most on Marylebone which handles about 17,000 passengers per day. Work is still in progress in this December view of the concourse, now terazzo-covered. Platforms are being lengthened and paved. The £50 million Total Route Modernisation of the line includes new MAS signalling controlled by an Integrated Electronic Control Centre at Marylebone. *Network SouthEast*

▲Civil engineering work on a major realignment of the 'Thameslink' route from Blackfriars to Farringdon (reopened in 1988) commenced in 1989. A major part of the project is the construction of a new subsurface station, named 'St Pauls Thameslink', on the new alignment to replace Holborn Viaduct terminus. On 3rd November, 319 058 was photographed passing the construction site between Holborn and Blackfriars with the 10.11 Cricklewood–Sevenoaks service; the new alignment will descend into the box tunnel centre-right in the picture. Holborn Viaduct (or at least, its two remaining platforms) just survived 1989 and was due to close in early 1990.   *Brian Morrison*

▶The only station on NSE to be re-opened during 1989 was at Islip, on the Oxford–Bicester line, itself brought back to life the previous year. Passenger services recommenced from the start of the summer timetable on 13th May, when Class 101 DMU L207 leading L400 were photographed running into the station with the inaugural train for Bicester. The original station closed on 30th December 1967.   *Martin Loader*

▼The major Network station rebuilding completed during 1989 was undoubtably Guildford. The formal opening ceremony to mark completion of the £8 million scheme took place on Friday 8th December, and was performed by the Bishop of Guildford who arrived in the cab of an electric train. Apart from the impressive new station building, features to note include completely retiled and re-edged platforms, completely new platform canopies covering a far greater area than previously, and refurbished footbridge and subway. The result is a station worthy of the city, and an enormous improvement on the shambles which preceded it. This view, looking towards London, was taken on the day of the official opening.   *Brian Morrison*

NEW AND IMPROVED SERVICES

A number of new routings and accelerations took place on NSE services from the commencement of the May 1989 timetable, particularly on the Southern Region. Apart from those illustrated below, they included the introduction of a half-hourly service on the Hastings via Tonbridge line (electrified in 1986) and extension of the off-peak Waterloo–Hounslow–Woking service to Guildford. An hourly fast service from King's Cross to Cambridge was inaugurated, completing the journey in less than one hour. Owing to traffic growth on the Great Northern outer suburban lines, a half-hourly service was introduced as far as Huntington from October, utilising Class 317s released from the Northampton line by the introduction of new 321/4s.

◀A minor adjustment to 'Thameslink' services saw the hourly off-peak Cricklewood–Petts Wood–Orpington service extended down the main line to Sevenoaks. This calls at all stations, in place of the former Charing Cross–Tunbridge Wells trains, which are now extended to Hastings to give a half-hourly service on that route. Emerging from autumnal fog at Sevenoaks on 6th December is 319 046, arriving with the 11.11 from Cricklewood. A resignalling scheme for the Kent Coast main line, announced on 23rd November, will make Sevenoaks signal box (left background), redundant – the whole route will be controlled from a new signalling centre at Ashford. *Chris Wilson*

▲On the Waterloo–Portsmouth 'direct' line via Guildford and Haslemere, the hourly off-peak fast service was accelerated to do the journey in 102 minutes, mainly by omitting the Woking stop. For this new 'Portsmouth Express' service, 12 refurbished '4 Cig' (Class 421/4) EMUs were given minor electrical modifications to give them improved acceleration. Externally, they could be identified by some rather ugly black trim on the cab ends, as on 1823 seen here leading units 2307 and 1824 over Port Creek with the 09.08 Portsmouth Harbour–Waterloo service on 20th September. *Chris Wilson*

◀Five of the seven '4 Bep' (Class 412) buffet car EMUs on the Portsmouth line were rebogied for the new service. Mark 6 motor bogies recovered from withdrawn 'Rep' units have replaced the Mark 4s originally fitted, while the original 'Commonwealth' trailer bogies have been replaced by the B5 (SR) type. Approaching Hilsea, 2304 leads 'Cig' 1817 with the 10.20 Waterloo–Portsmouth Harbour on 24th September. *David Brown*

▲ Ramsgate fast services were rerouted from May, being diverted from their traditional route at Chislehurst to run via Swanley to Ashford, calling only at Maidstone East. Cynics could surmise that this was to clear paths for International trains to run via Tonbridge when the Channel Tunnel finally opens! The inaugural service was worked by two 4 Ceps, led by 1620, unusually smart in NSE stripes and sporting a most impressive headboard. The train is seen here at Maidstone East.   *Brian Beer*

NORTH LONDON LINK IMPROVEMENTS

►From the start of the October timetable, the 'North London Link' third-rail electrified line from Richmond to North Woolwich became part of the 'North London Lines' network also including the Euston–Watford local service and associated connections. The major improvement was the introduction of Class 313 sliding-door EMUs, already used on the Watford line and a huge improvement on what had gone before. Based at Bletchley, this special fleet was increased from 16 to 20 to cover the extra duties, all members being equipped with extra pick-up shoes (compared with the GN units) to cope with the somewhat indifferently-aligned conductor rail on these routes. Following a notably successful refurbishment at Brondesbury Park, plans were announced to refurbish or rebuild all the stations along the line, to 'new designs that blend with the local environment and are attractive to everyone who uses the line'. A Gala Day was held on the line on Saturday 7th October; 313 017 stands at North Woolwich after arriving with an additional special service which had conveyed invited guests AND ordinary passengers!

Alex Dasi-Sutton

►The 313s superseded SR Class 416/3 2 EPB units, built in 1959 and introduced to the line in 1985 as part of service improvements carried out then. Running into a deceptively leafy Finchley Road, 6330 forms a Richmond –North Woolwich service on 1st August. Far from being withdrawn however, these EMUs continue in traffic on South London Lines services, including the writer's regular 18.21 Victoria–Dorking!   *Kevin Lane*

LINE LOGOS & LIVERIES

A full list of 1989 Line names is listed below.
Thames (arms of Oxford colleges)
Chiltern (Chiltern Hills)
North London Lines (colours of former Harlequin Line symbol)
Northampton Line ('barge-art' rendering of Grand Union)
Thameslink (City skyline)
Great Northern Line (King's Cross station)
Anglia Electrics (applied to 315 and 321 EMUs on Great Eastern) (badge of Anglia Regiment)
London Tilbury and Southend (Thames barge)
Kent Link (Greenwich)
Kent Coast (badge of Cinque ports)
South London Lines (Crystal Palace)
Sussex Coast (Brighton Pavilion)
Marsh Link (Ashford–Hastings, applied to some Class 203 and 205)
Oxted Line
South Western Lines (Victory Arch, Waterloo)
Waterloo and City
Island Line (Isle of Wight) (outline of island)
Wessex Electrics (applied to 431, 438 and 442 units). (Heraldic helmet)
West of England (Waterloo–Exeter, applied to NSSX and NSSA Class 50 locos and stock) (arms of Exeter)
North Downs Line (badge of Tonbridge)
Portsmouth Express (applied to 421/4 and 412 EMUs working Waterloo–Portsmouth Harbour fast services. (HMS Victory)

▲Definitely the largest, and arguably one of the finest badge designs is that applied to 'EPB' stock on 'Kent Link' suburban services; it is a shame that it adorns some of the grottiest rolling stock on NSE. Newly in NSE livery for 1989, facelifted Class 415/4 EMU 5486 stands at Charing Cross on 6th December, waiting to depart with the 14.48 to Gravesend. The new ambience of the platforms of this busy London terminus, now being buried under a 14-storey Laing office development, can be seen in this view. *Chris Wilson*

Logos: *Brian Morrison/NSE*

Although the various lines were given their new identities from May, not all the logos were ready, and on some routes rolling stock did not receive them until September/October, including 'Kent Link' and 'Sussex Coast'. The design of certain other logos was changed during the year following a less-than-successful first attempt; for example the original 'South Western Lines' logo depicted the Victory Arch at Waterloo, completely unknown to the majority of customers: it was changed (on '455' EMUs at least) to a new logo, showing Windsor Castle, later in the year. Similarly 'Uckfield Line', carried on the line's DEMUs became 'Oxted Line'; it is however ironic that Oxted line services to East Grinstead are formed of electric units displaying 'South London Lines' or 'Sussex Coast'! With the introduction of Class 313 units to the Richmond–North Woolwich line, 'North London Lines' branding was introduced to these units working this and the Euston–Watford Junction local service, replacing 'Harlequin Line' introduced the previous year. While some of these changes were sensible and necessary, perhaps the original planning could have been better – money could have been saved too! Some of the symbols were produced in a version on a grey background for use on stock retaining blue/grey colours, but some of these also found their way onto NSE-liveried vehicles!

A decision was made at the start of 1989 to paint all but the shortest-lived stock on NSE in the red, white and blue striped paint scheme. Stock appearing in this livery for the first time included Classes 104, 415/4, 415/6, 415/7, 416/2, 416/3, 416/4, and 455/9. Later in the year, it was decided to omit the 'Network SouthEast' branding from suburban units with large numbers of doors – these therefore have no external identification of ownership at all. Locomotives of Classes 47 and 50 began to be outshopped in the darker blue NSE livery; this included former Railfreight sector 50149 'Defiance', which returned to its former identity of 50049 for use on the Waterloo–Exeter line during March. Although the BR corporate double-arrow symbol has been omitted from coaches in NSE livery for some time, the last Class 50s to be repainted during 1989 now also lacked these; instead a 'West of England' Line badge was applied.

NETWORKER DEVELOPMENTS

During 1989, the first 'Networker' multiple units for NSE routes were authorised. Orders were placed for two fleets of Class 165 'Network Turbo' DMUs, 77 vehicles for the Chiltern Line due late 1991 and 163 vehicles for the Thames Line (Paddington Suburban) due 1992. These will be in 2- or 3-coach formations, with 23 m bodyshells, and will be built by BREL, with Perkins diesel engines. The first batch of the new Class 465 750V dc third-rail inner-suburban units for Kent Link services were also ordered, where they will replace very outdated and down-at-heel EPBs, hopefully from late 1991. As a start, 100 four-car units will be built at a cost of £257 million, half by BREL and half by GEC-Alstholm (formerly Metro-Cammell). Design-wise, these new trains will closely follow the mock-up displayed at Victoria in December 1987, with plug-doors, dot matrix destination displays internally and externally, aluminium bodyshells and (in the electric version) three-phase drive to half the train's axles. While these new trains will no doubt be an advance on what has gone before, eulogies from the transport secretary that they will be the 'best commuter train in Europe' rather invite scepticism!

▶Various systems for the 'Networkers' are being tested out on SR Class 455 EMU 5824, which at the beginning of the year was fitted with electronic dot-matrix displays, automatically operated via a two-figure code from a keypad in the cab. Those externally seemed to work quite satisfactorily, but those inside were never seen in operation by this writer, although apparently they were in use finally by the year end, following a certain amount of 'head-scratching' by staff from RTC Derby! With headcode on the left and destination display on the right, 5824 stands at London Bridge on 29th April. Unfortunately, in spite of appearances, this train is going nowhere – it is merely parked for the weekend!   *Chris Wilson*

▶The 'Networker' testbed EMU fitted with Brush Three-Phase ac traction motors, converted from former Class 210 DEMU vehicles and hitherto working on the SR as unit 457 001, was marshalled with a pantograph trailer from 313 034 at Derby RTC during October. The unit, renumbered 316 999, is now the electrical prototype for the projected Class 331 EMU for LT&S services. It was sent to Anglia Region for testing under 25 kV ac catenary, and is seen in Colchester sidings shortly after arrival on 8th November. Until the end of the year, it was engaged on runs on the Colchester–Clacton line.
                    Michael J Collins

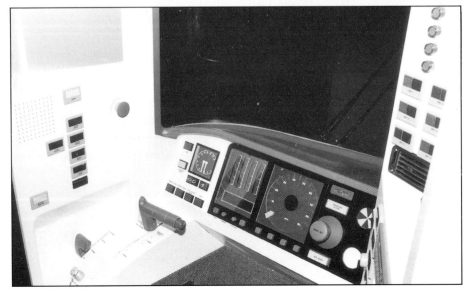

▲ The mock-up for the first express version of the 'Networker', the Class 471 for Kent Coast services, was unveiled to Press and Public on Wednesday 6th December, and was on display at London Victoria for comment by customers for three days. It will be the first 'Networker' variant to have a gangwayed front end, and the success of the designers' efforts can be judged in this view. Class 471 will also be the first of the breed to have a 100 mph capability. Present plans envisage the first 45 4-coach units to enter service in 1992/93, with a final fleet size of around 200 units; they will replace the 4 Ceps and various other stock presently in service.   *Colin Marsden*

◄Internally, the mock-up consisted of a pair of standard Class saloons, with two first Class compartments between. It is rather sad to see (and somewhat cynical of the designers) that the same design of standard class seating has been used as in the inner-suburban Class 465. Not only that, but one of the two saloons has 3 + 2 seating, surely too cramped for the Dover–Victoria journey? First class seating is similar to that in the Class 442 'Wessex Electrics', six-seat compartments with curtains and illuminated buttons for individual reading lamps. This view shows the standard class saloon with 2 + 2 seating; note also the full carpeting, concealed lighting and the ubiquitous Edward Pond murals. In the vestibule the mock-up includes tip-up seats, a telephone and space for a catering trolley. Lights are fitted above all exterior doors to illuminate the steps and immediate platform area.
David Brown

◄ The Class 471 mock-up also included a driver's cab. The main new feature here was the combined push/pull power and brake control, incorporated for the first time on a BR EMU.   *Colin Marsden*

ROLLING STOCK DEVELOPMENTS

▲ Electric locomotive-hauled services from Liverpool Street to Cambridge ceased from May 1989, the Cambridge trains going over to Class 321 EMUs and the few remaining Kings Lynn through trains to Class 47 haulage. On 23rd February, 86223 'Norwich Union' speeds southwards through Broxbourne in charge of the 11.05 ex Cambridge. Incidentally, the one NSE-allocated Class 86, 86401 'Northampton' was returned to the InterCity sector from 1st January 1990.   *Chris Wilson*

▼ Laira-based Class 50 locomotives from the NSSA pool took over the haulage of all Waterloo–Exeter line services, including the Waterloo–Salisbury semifasts, from May. The latter were previously in the hands of Class 33/1 + 4 TC push-pull formations. To cover this, the pool was increased from 13 to 20 locomotives. Although dedicated rakes of refurbished Mark 2A/B/C coaching stock were due to be used on all these trains, there were shortages throughout the rest of the year. To alleviate this, the SR 'boat set' (mainly formed of Mark 2C compartment firsts) was split up and used in the 5-coach Salisbury rakes when not in use for its intended purpose. However, when it was being utilised, there was no choice but to form trains of 4 TC trailer units, officially superseded when workings with Class 33/1 locomotives ceased. As the Class 50s are not fitted for push/pull operation, the TCs could only be used as hauled stock, and special brake hose extensions were necessary. An example of an almost daily occurance until the end of the year, 50018 'Warspite' hauls units 8021 and 8001 away from Clapham Junction, forming the 16.15 Waterloo–Salisbury service on 19th August. Note the unseasonal fitting of snowploughs on the locomotive!   *David Brown*

▲ The first of the new 25 kV ac electric units of sub-Class 321/4, for use on Northampton Line outer-suburban services out of Euston, was officially handed over at BREL York Carriage Works on 3rd July. By the end of the year 321 401–443 were in traffic, and they had displaced all the 317/1s working on the line to the Great Northern. This new type differs from the earlier 'Anglia Electrics' of Class 321/3 in having a larger first class section with much better seating, and more legroom in standard class. The bodyshell of the DTC reverted to the 319 driving trailer design with one small and one large window behind the cab (rather than two medium sized ones), and this vehicle is leading as 321 422 passes Doncaster with a test run prior to delivery on 20th September improved first class seats (similar to those in the Class 442 'Wessex Electrics') and wider seat spacing are also being retrospectively fitted to the earlier Anglia Region units following customer comment.   *Les Nixon*

◄ Also unveiled at York on 3rd July was a Class 321 Driving Trailer temporarily painted in the proposed BAA/NSE livery for the five Class 322 'Stansted Express' EMUs, due for delivery in mid-1990. From May 1991, these will provide a half-hourly shuttle between London Liverpool Street and Stanstead Airport using the new link under construction during 1989.   *B.J. Nicolle*

▲The Class 321/4s replaced Class 317s on semi-fast services out of Euston. On 10th July, 321 403 is seen leaving Euston with the 10.26 to Milton Keynes Central, whilst Class 317/0 No. 317 332 lurks in the background forming the 10.52 for Birmingham New Street. *Brian Morrison*

► At the start of 1989, NSE was in the middle of a six-month trial of Class 47/4 on the Waterloo–Exeter line, where it was proposed that they would replace the not-particularly-reliable Class 50s on the route. In the event, the Class 47s proved no more reliable than the 50s when used on this service and is was decided to retain the 50s in the short term, until new stock was introduced. The three 47/4s used for the test were 47473, 47547 and 47587; here 47547 passes under Battledown flyover (near Worting Junction) with the 11.10 Waterloo–Exeter service on 18th March.
Rodney Lissenden

►Although Class 33/1 + Class 438 (4 TC) combinations had been ousted from the Bournemouth–Weymouth route the year before, they continued to be used on the Waterloo–Salisbury semifast trains (leaving Waterloo at 10 minutes past even hours off-peak) until the start of the Summer 1989 timetable. On the last Saturday of such operations, 13th May, 33111 passes Winchfield, complete with appropriate commemorative headboard, leading the 14.10 Waterloo–Salisbury. In spite of their official displacement, such formations continued to appear sporadically on the Salisbury line, as well as on sundry other services, throughout the summer of 1989. *Alex Dasi-Sutton*

ON THE 'KENNY BELLE'

▲ The 'Kenny Belle' peak-hour Clapham Junction–Kensington Olympia shuttle was formed of a Class 73 Electro-diesel locomotive pulling or pushing a Class 438 4 TC trailer unit through the summer of 1989, replacing the SR DEMUs and WR DMMUs previously used. On the evening of 20th June, 73130 'City of Portsmouth' was in use, seen here passing Earls Court propelling its TC towards Clapham Junction. Although quite luxurious for such a short journey from the passengers' point of view, operationally these arrangements were not a success. In particular, the EDL, working on diesel power, could not provide heating or lighting when pushing, and for a short period during September a loco was provided for BOTH ENDS of the train, rather a waste of resources! Following this, a Class 33/1 diesel was used for a few weeks, after which the service reverted to a 2-car DMU.   *John S. Whiteley*

▼ For a few weeks Old Oak Common-based Class 104 twin-unit L701 (53479 + 53437), resplendent in NSE stripes, was an unprecedented sight at Clapham Junction on the 'Kenny Belle', particularly as it was generally berthed in the carriage sidings there during the day. On 6th December, it was photographed waiting to depart with the 16.50 to Kensington Olmypia. By the end of the year, a dedicated Metro-Cammell Class 101 unit, numbered L200, was provided for the service.   *Chris Wilson*

◄ Southern Region Class 438 4 TC Driving Trailer Standard 76327 was modified at Eastleigh early in the year, and ran through the summer as part of unit 8028, on such diverse workings as Waterloo–Southampton stoppers and Saturday Weymouth–Bristol trains. Here it seen entering Basingstoke on 26th August propelled by 33116, forming the 16.25 from Basingstoke. Externally, the standard SR GRP gangwayed cab end was modified by the addition of a central headlamp and marker-light clusters under the cable-recesses, while the leading half of the vehicle was fitted with tinted glass windows with 'hopper' ventilators. Internally, the original 2+2 seating was replaced by modern 319-style seats with removable covers in a 3+2 formation, somewhat more tightly packed in. Different panelling and floor covering types were fitted in each half of the vehicle. When empty, the ambience was reasonable, but packed when full, the effect was claustrophobic. Not being equipped with any form of heating, this (thankfully) unique coach was taken out of service in the autumn.

A C Smallbone

► Following an inspection by Department of Transport officials it was decreed that, owing to limited clearances, only stock fitted with limited-opening windows would be able to work on the Oxted line from May. This is somewhat odd considering that full width Mark 1 stock has been working on the route since the mid 1950s! Anyway, the entire Brighton allocation of Class 423 4 Vep EMUs, and all Selhurst-based DEMUs had to have their door droplights hurredly modified to open only a short way, while those which had to open fully (due to external locks only) were equipped with window bars. The remaining Class 416/3 2 EPBs not already so modified for North London Link workings were also fitted wirth 'zoo' bars. Since May, all London–East Grinstead electric trains were due to be formed of Veps and EPBs thus fitted. The bars over the corridor droplights of Vep 3442 may clearly be seen as it passes over the River Arun near Ford with the 16.25 Brighton–Portsmouth Harbour on 13th August, far from the Oxted line! *Chris Wilson*

► After so much time and effort went into designing them (?), the cab ends of the Class 442 'Wessex Electrics' were sadly disfigured by removal of the jumper cable recess covers during January. This followed an incident at Bournemouth depot when one fell off onto a fitter's foot (fortunately without injury), and they seem unlikely to be refitted. Showing clearly the gaping holes beneath the cab windscreens, 2402 stands at Winchester on 7th April. Motor Buffet Brake 62938 has just been named 'County of Hampshire' to commemorate the Centenary of the County Council. Note also the new station nameboard on the up platform. During the year, work was completed in equipping all the motor coaches in these units with a bar-lounge area, replacing half the van space. *Mervyn Turvey*

▲ The first three of eight 'new' Class 483 two-car EMUs for the Isle of Wight were delivered during 1989, the first arriving on the Island during July, some months later than originally intended. Purchased from London Regional Transport the year before (see 'Todays Railways' volume 2), the ex-1938 EHO tube stock vehicles were found to be in a somewhat worse condition than BR engineers had envisaged, and thus rebuilding took longer than expected. Following testing, unit 001 was used for an inaugural special on 13th July, conveying various senior members on NSE management, local dignitaries etc from Ryde Pier Head to Brading to celebrate the introduction of the new trains, and is seen here at its destination, waiting to return to Ryde. Incidentally, while the special was running, the 'normal' 20-minute interval service on the line had to be suspended, being covered by Southern Vectis buses! Although the banner on the now-redundant Brading station footbridge reads 'The New Island Trains are Here', the Island Line's normal customers (be they locals or holidaymakers) had to wait until 7th October before they could sample the new stock, other than on the odd Ryde Pier shuttle shortly after delivery in July. *Colin Marsden*

◀▲ The refurbishment work on the ex-1938 tube stock vehicles, carried out at BRML Eastleigh Works, is extensive. Internally, virtually all surfaces have been replaced with new panelling, woodwork has been polished up and seats re-upholstered in 'blue blaze 1' NSE moquette. Electrically, new fluorescent strip-lighting has been installed, as well as passenger door-control with illuminated 'open' and 'close' buttons. The work has been carried out to an extremely high standard and is commemorated on small brass plaques. This view shows the interior of car 121 from unit 483 001. *Brian Morrison*

◀ After delivery under their own power from Eastleigh to Fratton Depot via Woking, the Class 483 car bodies were loaded individually onto low-loader lorries for shipment across the Solent on the Ryde–Fishbourne car ferry. The bogies were carried separately, and reunited with their bodies in the former Merstone bay platform at Sandown, the area around being specially cleared and road access provided. Unit 003 went over to the Island on 27th September, and in this view car 223 is about to be off-loaded by crane. *Chris Wilson*

▲ Following rebuilding, the units made several runs on the mainland for commisioning and driver training purposes. 483 002, formed of vehicles 122 and 222, made a number of trips on the Portsmouth 'direct' line, and is seen here approaching Haslemere with a test run from Fratton on Sunday 24th September. The NSE livery applied includes the new lighter shade of grey (already seen on Classes 321 and 442), and sits extremely well on these 52-year old trains, which certainly do not now look their age. *David Brown*

DEPARTMENTAL DEVELOPMENTS

▶ The Southern Region's diesel-electric sandite unit 1066 (officially 066), formed of narrow-bodied 6S vehicles, was repainted into NSE stripes at Selhurst in July 1989, the only ex-Hastings line DEMU vehicles to be so treated. Following a visit to Cardiff Cathays for the installation of AWS equipment, the unit was used for sandite spreading duties during the autumn 'leaf-fall' season on the Oxted line, and is seen here on one such working passing Hever en route for Uckfield on 10th November. The semaphore signalling seen in this view was eventually replaced in the first week of 1990, some months late! *Rodney Lissenden*

▶ Another vehicle modified for sandite spreading is ADB 977579, which finally entered service in time for the autumn, having been under conversion from an SR ex-'Tyneside' 2 EPB driving trailer in Selhurst Repair shop for more than two years! Designed for working with Class 319 EMUs north of the Thames, the alterations required have been fairly drastic. The cab end has been shaved of the normal SR embellishments and fitted with standard light units, while both ends have been fitted with fully-automatic 'tightlock' couplers. Internally, standard 319 cab equipment has been fitted, and a diesel generator is installed to provide heat and light, and to operate the sandite pump. Following a rather secretive test run to Bedford and back the previous week, this peculiar vehicle is seen inside Selhurst Cleaning Shed on Saturday 19th August. It was in regular use between Selhurst and Bedford through the autumn, and a second similar vehicle based at Hornsey for use with Great Northern Line 317s was ready by the end of the year.

David Brown

▲1989 marked the centenary of lines from Shenfield to Southend Victoria and Southminster. A 40-minute service was provided on the Southminster branch with green EMUs 302 200 and 306 017 on the weekend of 26th/27th August. There was also a display of rolling stock at Southend. In this view at Wickford three eras of travel are represented. In bay platform 1, 302 200 forms the 11.57 to Southminster, in platform 2 312 728 and 312 794 form a service to Southend Victoria. In bay platform 4, 321 325 waits to operate the late evening Southminster service. On the London Fenchurch Street–Southend Central–Shoeburyness line, 1989 also marked the conversion of the last two short stretches of line from 6.25 kV to 25 kV. *Michael McGowan*

◄Network SouthEast took delivery during March 1989 of a new self-propelled snowblowing machine built by Beihack, West Germany. During severe winter weather it will augment Network's fleet of snowploughs and de-icing trains which help keep the Sector's 2,500 miles of track open for business. For the rest of the year it can be readily converted to work as an adjustable mobile inspection platform, a shrub cutting unit and a shunting locomotive. It is seen waiting for the bad weather which never came outside Stewarts Lane depot. *BR*

◄The centenary of the Weymouth Tramway was celebrated on 30th December. This line, disused since the transfer of ferry services to Poole saw a number of special trains. Class 438 (4 TC) unit 8023 leads 8001 and Class 33/1 No. 33117 down the tramway past a load of parked cars. *Mervyn Turvey*

Provincial

The most important event of 1989 was, paradoxically, the non-arrival of the Class 158 'Express' DMUs. The £150 million fleet on order was delayed because of construction and operating problems. BR were reportedly unhappy about build quality of the initial batch too. Other important happenings were the 'Sprinterisation' of a large number of routes in Scotland and the full implementation of the new routing strategy through central Manchester.

THE MONOPOLIES AND MERGERS COMMISSION REPORT

The Monopolies and Mergers Commission published its detailed report into BR's Provincial sector in February. It endorsed the sector's pricing, investment and cost-cutting strategies since inception in 1982, the year sectorisation into five railway businesses took place. The success of the PTEs was noted and possible new ones were suggested.

In July the British Railways Board made an interim response to the report. Recommendations to which the Board had already responded included a rationalisation of fares policy. On the same day new quality targets were given to Provincial by the secretary of state for transport.

On Express and longer rural services 90% of trains would have to arrive within 10 minutes of the right time; 90% of urban or shorter rural trains would have to arrive within 5 minutes. In the former category at least 99.5% of trains should run, in the latter 99%. All trains should be cleaned inside every day, outside at least every other day.

At telephone enquiry bureaux 95% of calls should be answered within 30 seconds. Maximum times of 5 minutes/3 minutes at peak/off-peak times in ticket office queues were envisaged.

Interestingly, no published targets were set for overcrowding limits on Express/longer rural services. For urban/shorter services the limit would be 135%/110% of seating capacity on sliding/slam door stock respectively, with a maximum standing time of 20 minutes.

As with the change on InterCity, Provincial's guards were designated conductors from October to reflect their changing roles – supposedly more ticket-checking, on-train announcements and customer liaison as well as traditional guards' duties.

NETWORK NORTH WEST

April saw the launch of Network NorthWest, a marketing initiative designed to reflect the improved travel opportunities possible from the recast of services in May using a now full service over the Windsor Link in Salford and greater use of Piccadilly station. Although a good idea, the partnership of BR, Greater Manchester PTE and Lancashire County Council did not seem to have the momentum of the 1986 launch of Network SouthEast. The new livery (see page 55) only appeared on a few DMUs, the first being 150 201, and the pace of station refurbishments was relatively slow. The main problems, however were shortage of DMUs resulting in train cancellations or short trains and poor timekeeping, often, but not always, due to the use of single-power car old DMUs on trains timed for Sprinters or Pacers.

Manchester was at the heart of the new network, the Hazel Grove Chord (opened in 1986) and Windsor Link (1988) transforming the system. The three important stations at Deansgate, Oxford Road and Piccadilly had all seen improvements, with £2 million being spent on the latter. Track layouts and signalling had been completed early in 1989 at Piccadilly too.

Manchester Victoria's importance diminished but remained base for local services to Huddersfield and Leeds via Halifax, and Bury, Oldham and Rochdale. Some services were extended to provide through local trains to Bolton and Southport or Liverpool (via St. Helens Junction). Services to Wigan and Barrow-in-Furness were improved.

To alleviate congestion on the Cornbrook Jn.–Manchester Piccadilly line, a route recently used only for freight trains between Skelton Jn.(Altrincham) and Edgeley Jn.(Stockport) was reopened and the Chester–Manchester Oxford Road service was diverted over it, thus providing Stockport with a direct service to Altrincham and Chester. Certain trains were extended to Warrington Central. A new half-hourly service from Liverpool to Manchester Piccadilly via the more southerly Warrington Central and Birchwood route was inaugurated. TransPennine services were included in this diversion, thereby ending the sight of these key services at Victoria and on the St. Helens Junction (Chat Moss) route. East of Piccadilly, Trans Pennine services travelled via Guide Bridge to Stalybridge where the Diggle route to Huddersfield and Leeds was rejoined. A half-hourly 'fast' service was therefore provided between Manchester and Leeds, the hourly Liverpool–Newcastle/Scarborough services complementing the hourly Manchester–Hull service.

Stalybridge, east of Manchester, became an interchange for most North Wales coast trains (from Holyhead, Bangor, Llandudno/Junction, Wrexham (and Chester)) with the Liverpool–Newcastle/Scarborough TransPennine expresses. These North Wales trains continued to travel via Runcorn East, Warrington Bank Quay, Earlestown, Newton-le-Willows, (Chat Moss), Eccles and Manchester Victoria.

EXPRESS

Demand on East Anglia/Nottingham–North West routes continued to grow with overcrowding remaining a problem. Extra services were provided between Nottingham and Blackpool, with the East Anglia–North West service running to Liverpool every hour instead of alternating with Blackpool. Express developments in Scotland are covered in the 'ScotRail' section.

RURAL ROUTES

The re-introduction of two-shift working between Boston and Skegness followed Lincolnshire County Council's agreement to meet half the cost of automating the line's antiquated level crossings. A much more attractive all-day service was therefore offered. The Gainsborough–Barnetby closure proposal is discussed in 'BR Network'.

PASSENGER TRANSPORT EXECUTIVES

The year saw, on the one hand, an often strained relationship between PTA/PTEs and BR. The root cause was poor availability of new DMUs, both 'Pacers' and 'Sprinters' and the resulting strains on life-expired DMUs, locomotives and coaches. The non-arrival of Class 158 'Express' DMUs caused yet more problems in that the cascading of 'Super Sprinters' and 'Sprinters' was prevented. On the other hand, electrification plans progressed on several routes.

During 1989 BR Provincial was also withdrawing three DMU vehicles or three loco-hauled carriages for every new DMU vehicle introduced, the latter consisting almost entirely of Class 156. The long hot summer in particular saw continuing withdrawals and frequent failures, giving rise to poor time keeping, cancellations, reduced train formations and loco-haulage on services such as Liverpool–Preston, Manchester–Wigan/Southport, the 'Oldham loop', Sheffield–Leeds (via the Dearne Valley) and Newcastle–Middlesbrough. Such routes would generally offer Class 31-hauled trains of Mark 1 stock.

West Yorkshire PTA and Greater Manchester PTA both gave BR an ultimatum to improve services. There was talk of financial penalties if things failed to improve. One reason for poor reliability in the WYPTA area was that Provincial's fitters at Neville Hill depot were not paid the 'going rate', and less than InterCity's fitters, and so staff shortages continued all year with a resultant maintenance backlog. South Yorkshire PTA and Humberside County Council also complained about BR service reliability in their areas.

In late September, WYPTE and BR reached agreement on the conversion of the remainder of the 'Pacer' DMU fleet to more reliable Voith transmission. GMPTA, Mersey PTA, Tyne & Wear PTA had already agreed this re-engineering.

On a brighter note, West Midland PTA authorised for submission to the Department of Transport a £33.5 million Cross-City Line electrification from Lichfield Trent Valley through central Birmingham to Redditch; just under half of this amount is for the purchase of new EMUs.

Merseyrail agreed to support the southward extension of electrified services to Ellesmere Port and Chester with a £3.2 million investment. Later in the year it decided to invest £20.35 million on a centralised control system, mainly for the Northern and Wirral lines; this will house operating, passenger information, policing and signalling functions. They also launched a campaign to bring its suburban stations up to the standards of those in the city centre. Schemes at Hunt's Cross (joint 'winner' of 'The Daily Telegraph' worst station awards), Birkenhead Central, Bromborough, Thatto Heath and St. Helens Central progressed. A 'Railside Revival' project was included.

A report by Transmark Worldwide on Bradford rail services, commissioned by Bradford City Council, West Yorkshire PTE and BR was published on 25th April. A gradual programme of electrification and more frequent services linking Skipton, Ilkley, Bradford (Forster Square) and Leeds, with Shipley being an interchange. The study shows no useful future for the Wortley Curve and no case for a cross-city rail link from Bradford (Forster Square) to Bradford (Interchange). The Leeds–Bradford (Interchange) service should be extended to Halifax to form a high-frequency service.

Also in West Yorkshire, the first phase of Neville Hill depot's £5.5 million modernisation was marked by BR and WYPTA. These parties were also responsible for the production of the West Yorkshire Railplan 1, a document analysing past performance and outlining proposals for rail development over the next two years. Overcrowding, poor punctuality and reliability were cited by passengers as areas for improvement. However, against a background of fast-growing business, the forward-looking authority would give priority to new signalling and track to expand capacity – particularly Leeds/Bradford–Keighley/Ilkley. The operating body 'Metro' would also continue to improve stations, try to strengthen train formations (subject to government spending limits) and install close-circuit TV and ticket-issuing machines at stations. The report also covers the possibility of operating passenger services on the Pontefract–Wakefield line and for passenger services to Brighouse and Elland.

Strathclyde PTE unveiled public transport proposals in December, the result of a two-year Strathclyde Transport Development Study. An expanded Glasgow Underground network is rejected. Expansion of the ScotRail suburban network by using certain disused alignments and present freight-only lines is mentioned. Construction of new stations along these lines, particularly in the north Glasgow suburbs and on the Rutherglen–Coatbridge line are suggested. Options are given for improving rail links between Glasgow and its airport.

South Yorkshire PTE opened a new station at Dodworth (see page 8), but its new three-platform Swinton station was not finished by the end of the year. A major development for a rail-bus-tram transport interchange at Meadowhall was announced which would be at the junction of the Sheffield–Barnsley and Sheffield–Rotherham lines and would serve the giant new Meadowhall development.

▲With the virtual cessation of loco-hauled workings on the Bristol–Portsmouth/Weymouth route from the summer timetable, the need for Malago Vale carriage sidings was removed. The weeds are already taking over as 'Slim Jim' Class 33/2 No. 33211 prepares to leave with the e.c.s. for the 16.00 Bristol T.M.–Portsmouth on 15th May, the last day of opening.
Graham Scott-Lowe

◄Although NSE stopped using Class 33/1s on passenger workings from the start of the summer timetable, Provincial continued to use this class for two return trips between Weymouth and Bristol on summer Saturdays. 33108 is seen passing Cole with the 10.30 Weymouth–Bristol with 2 Class 438 (4 TC) units.
A.J. Woof

PROBLEMS WITH NEW DMUs

►1989 started with all Class 155s out of service due to doors opening between stations. This resulted in Class 156 units earmarked for Scotland being sent new to Cardiff Canton, together with some existing Class 150/2s and 156s. Class 150/2 units were working to Penzance by April, as can be seen in this photograph of unit No. 150 282 shortly after arriving with the 04.56 ex-Cardiff on 27th April, the next working being the 10.40 to Plymouth. The overall roof of this station was undergoing refurbishment involving the removal of all the glazing. *G.F. Gillham*

►The 155s started to reappear after modification during April, the first ones to be modified being the Neville Hill allocated ones owned by West Yorkshire PTE. The Cardiff ones started to return during May, their first regular workings being on the Bristol–Weymouth route on which they had not previously appeared. On 27th May, unit No. 155 314 is seen near Yetminster on the 15.06 Bristol–Weymouth. *G.F. Gillham*

▼Towards the end of the year, the first Class 158 eventually appeared, many months late. The late delivery of this class had disastrous results on Provincial's plans. By the end of the year, only the first of the class, unit No. 158 701 had been delivered, albeit in an incomplete form. The unit is seen at Leicester on 11th October after a trial run from Derby. *L.A. Nixon*

PROVINCIAL
LOCO-HAULED TRAINS

◄Due to severe overcrowding on certain sprinter workings on the Cardiff–Portsmouth route on summer Saturdays in 1989 Provincial sector had hired from Inter-City a Class 47 and stock to form an unadvertised relief working. This was the 09.15 Swansea–Southampton, seen here climbing away from Westbury on 5th August behind 47433. The stock worked back as the 15.13 Southampton–Cardiff. Perhaps because these workings received little publicity, they usually ran almost empty.

G.F. Gillham

◄Instead of the customary DMU, Provincial Services Wales produced the exceedingly rare spectacle of a locomotive-hauled passenger train with loaned InterCity stock between Swansea and Crewe via the scenic Central Wales line on Saturday 4th November. Heavy demand for extra DMUs and sprinter services in South Wales on that day emanated from the Wales v All Blacks rugby game. Although DMU failures have produced locomotive assistance in the past it must be many years since a booked loco-hauled service train ran over the Central Wales line. Class 37 No. 37426 'Vale of Rheidol' is seen heading north from Craven Arms with the 09.48 Swansea–Crewe.

Geoff Bannister

▼On Mondays to Fridays during Potteries district holidays, a loco-hauled relief train was run between Blythe Bridge and Blackpool North. The motive power was usually a pair of Class 20s. 20035 and 20110 are seen at Blackpool North on 31st August with the 18.42 to Blythe Bridge.

B.G. Hughes

▲Poor availability of Class 142 pacers at Newton Heath meant that certain trains in the Lancashire area were loco-hauled for much of the year with Class 31 haulage. The 06.46 Preston–Liverpool Lime Street is seen at Springs Branch Jn., Wigan on 10th June with 31147 in old Railfreight livery with a rage of Mark 2A/B/C coaches (including one in Provincial livery with 'Trans-Pennine' branding). *Paul A. Senior*

▶To accommodate peak flows from the East Midlands and Sheffield to Blackpool, a return loco-hauled train was run between Nottingham and Blackpool on Mondays to Fridays, generally hauled by a Class 47. Unfortunately due to the fact that it had an unattractive timing, it generally ran almost empty, with the DMUs running overcrowded. For the last few weeks that the train ran, a Cardiff Class 37/4 was diagrammed with a shorter load. 37408 'Loch Rannoch' is seen climbing away from Sheffield with the 08.15 Nottingham–Blackpool on 25th October. *L.A. Nixon*

▼For a short time during August, shortage of Class 150/1 units due to engine failures resulted in the operation of a number of Derby–Crewe services with either Class 31s or pairs of Class 20s. Some of the coaches used had been cannibalised ready for departmental conversion and had had to be hastily restored for passenger service. As they had Southern Region 750 V heaters, the heating jumpers had been removed so that they could not be coupled up to 1000 V e.t.h. locos. 20065+20228 with no heating capability leave Derby with the 15.11 to Crewe on 5th August. *Peter Fox*

▲Class 114 DMU (53006+54010) arrives at the new station at Hednesford on a gala-day shuttle from Walsall. On 8th April the public were given a foretaste of travel on the newly re-opened passenger service with a flat return fare of £1 from Hednesford to Birmingham. Trains at half-hourly intervals were very heavily loaded. Full timetabled services started on Monday 10th April at hourly intervals between Hednesford and Walsall. *Colin Boocock*

▼1989 saw the Sunday re-opening of the former GWR branch from Blaenau Ffestiniog to a temporary platform in the goods yard at Maentwrog Road. The service, which ran from 23rd July to 10th September was a joint venture between BR, the CEGB and Gwynydd County Council. The CEGB provided a temporary bus service to Trawsfynydd nuclear power station. A Class 108 power twin, bearing the set number 'CH 602', rounds the curve near the former Teigl Halt with the 10.55 ex-Blaenau Ffestiniog on 3rd September. *Andrew Bannister*

▶▼The 10.55 Cleethorpes–Sheffield formed of a Class 101 power car and a Class 108 trailer passes Kirton Lime Works on 23rd October. This stretch of line was proposed for closure to passenger services during 1989 (see pages 9/10) although the section from Barnetby to this location would be retained for freight traffic. *A.J. Woof*

SCOTRAIL

Following the introduction of Sprinters to the south west of Scotland in late 1988, it was the Provincial sector's intention to operate almost all other non-electric internal passenger routes in Scotland with new-generation diesel multiple units by the end of 1989. Unfortunately this aim was not achieved in full, mainly due to factors outside the control of the sub-sector within Scotland.

The first was the mass withdrawal of all Class 155 units in England which resulted in a number of ScotRail-allocated Class 156 units being transferred, or delivered new, to Cardiff as temporary replacements. As a result, the original introduction date of these units to the West Highland and Far North lines needed to be reviewed. Fortunately, sufficient West Highland units had been delivered and tested on time. Services started operating from Edinburgh and Glasgow to Oban, Fort William and Mallaig on Monday 23rd January, as planned, replacing the now ageing Class 37/4s and, more importantly, the early Mark 1 and 2 rolling stock, but the Far North routes i.e. those from Inverness to Aberdeen, Wick/Thurso and Kyle of Localsh etc. were not officially converted to Sprinter operation until 15th May, some four months later than planned, not helped, but not stopped by, the collapse of the Ness Viaduct in Inverness. In fact ScotRail's commitment to these lines by getting the Sprinters in use at all, North of the Moray Firth, must be applauded.

The second obstacle to Provincial's strategy was the non-appearance, due to late delivery, of the Class 158 Express Sprinter units which had been due to enter squadron service on the Glasgow/Edinburgh–Aberdeen/Inverness routes in May. This factor more than any other caused Provincial most problems because the Class 47/7 locomotives and rolling stock on these routes were generally life-expired or had deteriorated to such an extent that replacement was critical; delays and cancellations were frequent later in the year. Adding to this problem was the fact that two of the sixteen Class 47/7s were transferred to Network SouthEast in early 1989 leaving ScotRail short of suitably equipped locomotives and it was not uncommon to see English-based locomotives used on these routes or in some cases Class 156 Sprinters or conventional DMUs on peak-hour Edinburgh–Glasgow services.

On a more positive note, May saw the transfer north of some additional Class 150s to Haymarket. This allowed the Dunblane–Edinburgh and Dunfermline–Edinburgh routes to join the existing east of Scotland Sprinter network. On 7th August new Class 156 Metro Cammell Sprinters in Strathclyde

Transport livery entered service (two months ahead of schedule) on the Glasgow Queen Street–Cumbernauld route followed on 2nd October (as planned) on the Glasgow Central–Kilmarnock/Barrhead/East Kilbride routes. These new units permitted Provincial to withdraw, or transfer out of the region, some of the older units (mainly Class 101s) and the last of the Scottish-allocated Class 120s.

Other notable events in conjunction with Provincial in Scotland were the opening of five new stations in the Strathclyde Transport area at Greenfaulds (Cumbernauld), Stepps, Drumgellach (Airdrie), Airbles (Motherwell) and Milliken Park (Johnstone) while refurbishments or modernisation took place at Elgin, Neilston and Bellshill. As part of the introduction of Class 150 Sprinter units to the Dunfermline route, the south side curve at Thornton Junction was reinstated to passenger traffic allowing a new Fife circular service to run via Dunfermline, Cowdenbeath and Kirkcaldy to Edinburgh. Meanwhile, parliamentary approval was sought on creating a new curve at the south end of Cowlairs carriage depot which will eliminate the need for Glasgow Queen Street–Cumbernauld trains to reverse at Eastfield diesel depot while much more controversial is the proposal to create a new East Kilbride town centre station just under one mile closer to the town than the existing terminus and which would result in the demolition of a number of town houses.

On the technical side the first stages of the SSI installation at the new Yoker signal box were commissioned and the wholly-owned Railfreight sector signal box at Millerhill was opened. ScotRail revealed that its new centralised security system covering more than 140 stations in the Strathclyde area has cut crime by over 50%. The system is based at Glasgow Queen Street and allows an immediate response from British Transport Police, in liaison with civil police authorities.

On the locomotive front, the rundown of ScotRail's Class 20 fleet continued, with at one point, only three examples of the class operating around the middle of the year although this number did increase later when stored locomotives at Ayr were reinstated. The introduction of Sprinters to the West Highland, and for North lines, allowed surplus Class 37/4s to be transferred south of the border, most of them receiving CEMs at BRML Springburn either before or after their transfer.

The 10.14 Glasgow Queen Street–Cumbernauld arrives at Stepps on 15th May, the first day of operation of the station, although the official opening was not until the following day. Cumbernauld services now run to and from Queen Street High Level, with reversal at Cowlairs, calling at Springburn en route. Tom Noble

ALL CHANGE IN THE HIGHLANDS

◄On 23rd January, Class 156 'Super Sprinters' took over the Glasgow–Fort William–Mallaig/Oban services from Class 37/4s (with the exception of the Euston–Fort William sleeper). On 21st January 37408 passes Crianlarich Lower Jn. with the 12.50 Oban–Glasgow Queen Street. *Maxwell H. Fowler*

◄Class 156s did not commence operation on the routes from Inverness to Aberdeen, Kyle of Lochalsh, Wick and Thurso until 15th May, taking over from locomotive-hauled trains of Mark 2 stock. 156 478 is seen arriving at Kyle of Lochalsh with the 07.22 ex-Dingwall on 25th August. *Steve Turner*

▼An Aberdeen–Inverness service is seen at Keith on 31st May with a three-car Class 156 set No. 156 485. The Aberdeen–Inverness services were formerly worked by Class 47/4 locos. *Les Nixon*

FAR NORTH ISOLATION

▲▲Dingwall became the southern terminus for Far North and Kyle line services following the collapse of the Ness Viaduct on 7th February (see page 10). A dedicated bus service was provided between Inverness and Dingwall for connecting purposes with little overall effect on journey times. This photograph taken on 22nd March shows 37419 stabled in the bay behind 37416 on the 12.06 Dingwall–Wick. The tail end of the 10.40 Dingwall–Kyle of Lochalsh can be seen which was hauled by 37415.

L.A. Nixon

▲A temporary maintenance depot was erected at Muir of Ord. In this view (10th August), four Mark 2 Provincial sector coaches can be seen, together with InterCity charter Mark 1 and Pullman stock.

Allan Mott

►Locos and stock were transferred between Invergordon and Inverness by road. 37419 is seen on 24th April on the main A9 road at the Invergordon turn-off.

Tom Noble

▲Strathclyde PTE opened five new stations on 15th May (see also page 51). In this view, Class 107 set No. 107 746 with appropriate headboard arrives at the new Drumgelloch station on 16th May with VIP guests to officially open the station which is a terminus on a one mile extension from Airdrie. The station opened to passengers 24 hours before this official ceremony.   *Maxwell M. Fowler*

▼On the first day of the new timetable (15th May), 150 207 passes Northenden on the newly reopened Stockport–Altrincham line with the 15.36 Blackpool North–Chester.   *Paul Shannon*

PROVINCIAL COLOURS

▲Early in 1989, Class 47/4 No. 47475 received Provincial livery, the only member of the class to be so-treated. It is seen arriving at York with the 16.10 Newcastle–Liverpool Lime Street on 26th March.   *John Augustson*

◄Class 156 units Nos. 156 501–14 were delivered to Corkerhill depot (Glasgow) in Strathclyde PTE livery, unlike other units of this class which are in Provincial livery. 156 511 is seen leaving Newcastle with the 12.52 service to Stranraer Harbour on 2nd October.   *John Augustson*

▼The new Network NorthWest livery has been applied to certain Class 150/2s allocated to Newton Heath depot (Manchester). The only variations on the standard Provincial livery are that the light blue stripe is replaced by a grey stripe in the centre of the vehicle and a red stripe at the ends, and the vehicle carries a red BR logo and the distinctive Network NorthWest logo. Despite the relative ease of modification to this livery, only seven out of Newton Heath's 28 Class 150/2s had been repainted by the end of the year. 150 207 is seen crossing the viaduct between Manchester's Oxford Road and Piccadilly stations on 18th June.   *A.J. Woof*

SPRINTER WORKINGS

▲Class 156s replaced Class 37/4s on the Oban line on 23rd January, three car formations being required to cope with the heavy demand. 156 450 heads west out of Crianlarich with the 12.10 Glasgow Queen Street to Oban on 19th July.　　*Douglas Young*

▼On the 'North & West' route, shortage of units meant that certain Cardiff–Liverpool/Manchester workings were loco-hauled throughout the year. Deputising for a Class 155, Class 37 No. 37425 'Sir Robert McAlpine/Concrete Bob' heads the 11.13 Liverpool–Cardiff south of Church Stretton in typically-attractive scenery. The date is 10th June.　　*Tom Clift*

Railfreight

During 1989 Railfreight was able to announce its best results of the decade, having achieved an operating surplus of £69.4 million in the 1988/89 financial year. This was 50% better than the previous year's figure, and provided good grounds for optimism about the future of the business. Carryings, too, were on the increase: the 1988/89 total of 149.5 million tonnes was the highest in the second half of the decade and for the first time exceeded the annual tonnage immediately before the miners' strike. All the bulk sub-sectors – Coal, Metals, Construction and Petroleum – recorded increases in traffic.

RAILFREIGHT COAL

The continuing upheaval in the coal industry required greater flexibility from Railfreight, as more collieries were closed down and new flows of imported fuel were established. Amongst the rail-served collieries closed in 1989 were Betteshanger, Baddesley, Oakdale, Marine, Merthyr Vale, Trelewis, Cynheidre, Holditch, Barnburgh, Bilston Glen and Monktonhall, leaving only a handful still operational in South Wales and none at all in Kent and Scotland. A new coal import terminal for British Steel was opened at Immingham in April 1989, and further expansion of port facilities in the Immingham area seemed likely to enable power stations such as Cottam and West Burton to be served. And all this was happening not far away from the terminal which, in 1983, used to handle up to 30 trains a day of British coal for export! Other ports from which Railfreight began or resumed carrying imported coal in 1989 were Hull, Liverpool Gladstone Dock and Bidston. Developments in the British coalfield were not all negative, especially where opencast activity was concerned. During 1989 Railfreight acquired new flows of Scottish coal from Ravenstruther and Blindwells to Leith, ultimately destined for Scandinavia. New loading facilities were constructed or brought into use at Wardley, Allerton Bywater and Melkridge, whilst in North East England a Section 8 grant worth £0.75 million was awarded to fund the provision of rail access to a new coal discharge terminal at Bates staithes, on the south side of the River Blyth.

Tonnages of domestic coal conveyed by Railfreight, originally marketed under the name of Speedlink Coal but since renamed Network Coal, continued to decline in 1989. Several depots were closed during the year, whilst others had their service reduced from daily to two or three times a week. One of a small number of new Network Coal services introduced during the year was a direct link from Washwood Heath to Birkenhead, a destination which previously had received its coal by scheduled Speedlink (i.e. Railfreight Distribution) services. New uses continued to be found for surplus HEA coal hopper wagons, including a batch rebuilt as barrier wagons for nuclear flask traffic.

RAILFREIGHT CONSTRUCTION

Railfreight Construction continued to increase its carryings of aggregates in 1989, especially limestone and other crushed rock destined for the construction industry in South East England. Several new receiving depots were opened during the year, and new destinations with only basic rail facilities were found for the Redland self-discharge train which made its debut in 1988. Section 8 grants were awarded to RMC Roadstone and G.G. Papworth in 1989 to provide new rolling stock and discharge facilities for Peak Forest–Ely limestone traffic.

Existing rail-based refuse disposal schemes in London, Manchester and Avon were joined in late 1989 by a new operation in Edinburgh. A loading terminal was constructed at Powderhall, on the former Granton branch, and a discharge terminal was provided next to the Tarmac Econowaste site at Kaimes, near Kirknewton. The project as a whole was expected to cost Edinburgh District Council £2.5 million.

In addition to pursuing its long-term refuse contracts, the Construction sub-sector carried waste on a short-term basis from two London sites to Stewartby, in Bedfordshire, during 1989. The first was a disused factory site at Barking which was to be redeveloped for housing, whilst the second forwarding location was Willesden, where considerable quantities of spoil were to be generated by the widening of London's North Circular Road. British Rail no longer keeps stocks of wagons available for use in instances such as these, so a private wagon leasing company had to be found to provide the rolling stock: in the event the waste from both Barking and Willesden was carried on bogie container wagons operated by Tiphook Rail.

METALS & PETROLEUM

The trend away from individual wagon marshalling towards an increased reliance on block trains continued to make itself felt during 1989. The bulk sub-sectors, notably Metals and Petroleum, found that it was more efficient to provide their own services than continue to use the Speedlink network as they have done for some smaller consignments of freight. In some cases this resulted in new block trains, such as direct services from Lackenby to Blackburn and Wakefield, whilst in other cases different traffic flows would be combined to create a limited wagonload service, such as one from Tees yard conveying Metals traffic from various originating points to Stranraer. In Scotland there were examples of two or more sub-sectors combining their wagonload traffic into a single 'Bulklink' service, such as one which would carry oil, coal and cement to Inverness on behalf of the Petroleum, Coal and Construction sub-sectors respectively.

RAILFREIGHT DISTRIBUTION

The new Railfreight Distribution organisation, formed in October 1988 from the merger of Freightliners and Speedlink Distribution, conducted a major reappraisal of its activities during 1989. Some expansion was achieved on the container-carrying side, headed by a brand new £2.2 million Freightliner terminal for Teesside. This was constructed on ICI land at Wilton and provided better access to principal customers on the south bank of the Tees. It replaced the poorly sited facility at Stockton. Rail services to Harwich container terminal started again in February 1989 after a gap of three years, thanks to the decision to use Felixstowe only for deep-sea containers and transfer European traffic to Harwich. Later in the year Railfreight Distribution increased the capacity of its Harwich operations by 15%, allowing the daily throughput of wagons to rise to 85.

It was Railfreight Distribution's wagonload services which saw the biggest changes in 1989. The Speedlink network as it stood was not viable, especially perhaps after the removal of much oil, cement and steel traffic as mentioned above. A new scheme was drawn up under the heading of Network 90, with services recast in line with the quantities of traffic on offer. The pattern of local trip working came under particular scrutiny, since local trips often tie up a locomotive and crew for a whole shift in order to move just a handful of wagons to or from one customer's sidings. Some little-used terminals would lose their rail connection altogether, whilst others would be served less frequently. Most of the features of Network 90 would not take effect until January 1990, but in some parts of the network alterations were made in autumn 1989. In November 1989 Railfreight Distribution withdrew its shunting operations at Tyne and Millerhill yards, as well as its trunk services over the East Coast Main Line between those two points. Ironically the ECML and Millerhill yard would still be used by some of the 'Bulklink' services mentioned above, carrying traffic transferred from Speedlink!

Railfreight Distribution operates block trains as well as wagonload services, and March 1989 saw the introduction of a new china clay service from Burngullow to the recently commissioned Caledonian Paper plant at Irvine. The trains were scheduled to run twice a week and were hauled throughout by one or two Laira-based Class 37 locomotives. A fleet of 27 90-tonne stainless steel tank wagons was constructed by French builders NAF for this traffic. The Caledonian Paper mill also started taking in raw timber by rail, generally in wagonload consignments from the Western Highlands.

THE NETWORK

A pleasing addition to the Railfreight network during 1989 was the reopening of certain lines on the Trafford Park industrial estate in Manchester. Considerable investment was necessary to enable the system to carry high-capacity wagons, and two Class 08 shunters were acquired from BR to haul trains to and from the exchange sidings. The first two customers to make use of the reopened railway were Norton Metals, who dispatch scrap metal to Cardiff, and Cerestar, who dispatch starch to Kent and Scotland. Both firms had previously taken their wares to Ardwick freight terminal on the other side of the city, a facility which BR no longer wished to retain. The freight network also suffered some losses in 1989, particularly amongst its remaining rural outposts. Apart from colliery closures such as those mentioned above, the year saw the end of freight traffic to/from Caldon Low (stone), Dereham and North Elmham (agricultural products), Carbis Wharf (china clay), Dunstable (oil), York Foss Islands (oil) and Elswick (bitumen).

LOCOMOTIVES

The freight locomotive scene in 1989 was dominated by the arrival of Class 60, the locomotive type on which so many of

In summer 1989 March depot was reopened. Class 37/3 No. 37354 undergoes brake block replacement there on 27th September.
Michael J. Collins

Railfreight's hopes for the future are pinned. The first of the 100 machines on order. No. 60001, was delivered on time from Brush on 30th June, a remarkable achievement considering that only 13½ months had been allowed for design and construction of the type. Before No. 60001 made its first appearance on BR tracks it was named 'Steadfast' by Railfreight Director Colin Driver. It then proceeded to Derby, for extensive testing at the RTC and on the Mickleover test track. Further locomotives soon rolled off the production line and by the end of the year locomotives up to No. 60005 had appeared on BR metals. Trials in revenue-earning service commenced on 11th December, when No. 60005 worked the morning Mountsorrel–Radlett stone train. Names were chosen during the year for all but two of the fleet of Class 60s, following the themes of mountains, reformers and scientists.

New construction was not limited to the Class 60, as during the summer, West Country quarriers Foster Yeoman took delivery of their fifth American-built machine, Class 59 No. 59005. The design clearly impressed rival firm ARC, who after conducting their own haulage trials placed an order for four of their own Class 59s. At the other end of the power spectrum, 1989 saw the end of the Class 03 shunter in revenue-earning service, with just two examples left on the Isle of Wight for departmental work.

Locomotive modifications included the experimental derating of several Class 56 locomotives to 2400hp, in order to assess the feasibility of a new low-powered locomotive type for short-haul merry-go-round work. On the electric side, Railfreight identified ten Class 85 locomotives which it wished to keep as dedicated freight haulers beyond the life of the rest of the class. They had their speed restricted to 75 mph, their ETH isolated, and were renumbered in the 851xx series. Further alterations were made to the Class 86 fleet during the year: the Railfreight 86/5 variant became extinct, whilst a number of Class 86/4 locomotives were restricted to 75 mph and formed a new Railfreight sub-class 86/6.

WAGONS

Amongst the new wagons to enter service in 1989 were large fleets of aggregate-carrying wagons operated by Tiphook Rail Ltd. Both hoppered and flat-bottomed types were produced, and they were put to use on services from Grain, Angerstein Wharf, Merehead and Peak Forest. Foster Yeoman also took delivery of a fleet of a new design of 102-tonne hopper wagon, built by Orenstein & Koppel in Germany. These wagons were delivered by road to Westbury and were formed into permanently-coupled sets, with only the outer wagons of each set having normal couplings. On the debit side, the decision was taken to scrap the entire fleet of Procor aluminium-bodied hopper wagons during 1989 after only five years in revenue-earning service, thanks to excessive maintenance costs. Railfreight Distribution invited tenders during the summer for renewal of its container-carrying wagon fleet. As well as 700 standard flat wagons the order would include 45 vehicles mounted on small-wheel bogies which would be able to carry 9'6" containers within the BR loading gauge. The ranks of vacuum-braked wagons in service on BR continued to diminish during the year. The last flow of roadstone to rely on ageing MSV wagons went over to air-braked operation in the early part of the year, this being the flow from Peak Forest to Leeds. In Scotland, however, 29 MDV scrap-carrying wagons were given a new lease of life when they were transferred to private ownership for continued use in the Glasgow area.

▶ 1989 was the year when the Milk Marketing Board finally disposed of its fleet of milk tankers. Nos. 31123 and 31102 leave Swindon with 36 of the condemned vehicles on 13th July, running as 8Z85 20.40 Swindon–Leicester. A total of 66 tankers had been reconditioned in 1981 for possible use in an emergency, but their remaining lives were to be spent mainly in storage at locations such as Chard Junction and Lostwithiel.
Mike Goodfield

► The first completed Class 60 locomotive, No. 60001 'Steadfast', stands at Toton depot on 27th December. The bodyside carries the Railfreight Construction logo, indicating that this locomotive will find itself hauling block trains of aggregate in due course, most probably from the Leicestershire quarries.
Michael Rhodes

▼ Class 56 No. 56012 was named 'Maltby Colliery' at a ceremony at Maltby on 22nd June, in connection with the opening of a new £23 million preparation plant there. The new Railfreight Coal livery for both locomotive and wagons is displayed to good effect in this photograph taken just after the naming.
Brian Morrison

TRACTION CHANGES

►On 9th August Class 90 No. 90030 hauled a special test train from Willesden to Ipswich and back with 25 Freightliner flats loaded with old rail, in order to assess the capabilities of Class 90s before diagramming them on East Anglian Freightliner services. The test train formation included Test Car 10 and 'dead' Class 47 No. 47234, and the ensemble is pictured at Brantham during its return journey. Similar test runs were made with No. 90030 over the East Coast Main Line between Willesden and Doncaster on 11th and 12th August. *Michael J. Collins*

▲▲The fifth Foster Yeoman Class 59 locomotive, No. 59005, is pictured at Felixstowe Beach on 5th June, having been offloaded the previous day at the nearby docks. It has been coupled up to Class 31 No. 31209 for transfer to the Railway Technical Centre, Derby via Ipswich and March. *Michael J. Collins*

▲Now fully serviceable and bearing the name 'KENNETH J. PAINTER', No. 59005 passes Gravesend with a loaded test train from Grain to Hither Green on 16th September. This was the first occasion that a Class 59 had hauled a train through Gravesend, but for the following two weeks Class 59s were given extended trials over Southern Region metals, working from the Foster Yeoman loading terminal at Grain to receiving depots at Crawley and Shakespeare Cliff. *David Brown*

◄A view inside the Brush Electrical Machines works at Loughborough on 15th August, showing Class 60 locomotives Nos. 60007 (left) and 60004 (right) at different stages of construction. The bodyshells for this class are built by Procor at Horbury and brought down to Loughborough by road. *Colin J. Marsden*

▲The last location where Class 03s were used for shunting Railfreight traffic was Birkenhead Docks. Their use here came to an end in March 1989, after which any shunting in the area was carried out by main line locomotives. Most dockside terminals at Birkenhead had stopped receiving railborne traffic by the end of 1988, and the only flow with a reasonable medium-term future, namely domestic coal to Birkenhead North coal depot, was concentrated on a new thrice-weekly block train from Washwood Heath (Birmingham) from January 1989 onwards. In this photograph, dated 13th February, Class 37 No. 37212 has just arrived at Birkenhead Cavendish Sidings with seven loaded HEAs, running as 6F46 Washwood Heath–Birkenhead. Class 03 No. 03079 waits in the adjacent siding, ready to take the wagons forward to the coal depot.

Paul Shannon

▲Most Freightliner services over the North London line became diagrammed for electric haulage from the May 1989 timetable change. Services were hauled initially by pairs of Class 86/4 locomotives, which worked through to Anglia Region destinations at Tilbury, Harwich Parkeston Quay and Ipswich. On 13th July Nos. 86431 and 86425 approach Caledonian Road station with 4L75, the 07.32 Garston–Felixstowe South service, which will be electrically hauled as far as Ipswich yard. The additional trackwork for the North London line AC electrification comprises an extra single line between Camden Road and Dalston, with a loop at each end.   *Paul Shannon*

▲Newly redesignated Class 85/1 locomotive No. 85101 passes Castlefield Junction, Manchester, with an additional 4Z88 10.35 Trafford Park–Glasgow Freightliner service on 9th December. It is about to pass over what has become one of the worst bottlenecks on BR – the double-track section between Deansgate and Piccadilly. The vantage point is the G-MEX car park, which together with the viaduct visible on the right will eventually become part of the formation of Manchester's new MetroLink system.
Paul Shannon

▶Class 86/4 locomotives Nos. 86432 and 86431 approach Colchester with a Freightliner working from Felixstowe on 6th July.
Ian Cowley

VACUUM-BRAKED SURVIVORS

►Vacuum-braked MSV wagons remained in use during 1989 on coal slurry traffic from Westfield and Killoch to Methil. Class 26 locomotives Nos. 26037 and 26006 pass near Kinglassie with G01 trip, the 15.00 Westfield–Methil, on 15th September. The MSVs are expected to be replaced by a new build of MEA wagons, of which prototype versions were tried out during the year.

Brian Denton

►▼The 1989/90 sugar beet season saw the freight-only Wirksworth branch brought into use again, and still with vacuum-braked HTV wagons. On 30th October Class 20 locomotives Nos. 20078 and 20151 join the main line at Duffield with 17 loaded HTVs from Wirksworth to South Lynn. The hill in the background is known as the 'Chevin', and is said to be the most southerly hill of the Pennine Chain. *Paul Shannon*

▼Killoch colliery on 6th April, with a train-load of coal slurry passing over the weighbridge behind Class 37s Nos. 37675 William Cookworthy and 37674. These Laira-based locomotives had reached Scotland on the previous night's Burngullow–Irvine china clay train, and were being used on local services in Ayrshire before their scheduled return trip to England. Coal traffic from Killoch dwindled to nothing for a time in 1988 but was considerably more healthy by the middle of 1989: as well as slurry to Methil there were new flows of domestic fuel to Haymarket and industrial coal to Northern Ireland via Ayr Harbour.

Paul Shannon

SERVICES WITHDRAWN

▲Class 58 No. 58017 waits for its merry-go-round train to be loaded by mechanical shovel at Baddesley colliery, West Midlands, on 22nd April 1989. The colliery closed shortly afterwards, leaving no further use for the short freight-only branch from Kingsbury.
P.A. Waterman

▼Yet another South Wales colliery to close during 1989 was Merthyr Vale, the last freight user on the Merthyr branch between Abercynon and Black Lion. Class 37 No. 37692 waits at Merthyr Vale as the first of its wagons is loaded on 2nd May. When ready the train will depart as 6B62, the 13.00 Merthyr Vale–Abercwmboi.
Don Gatehouse

►A number of changes were made to the Speedlink Coal Network during 1989, some involving the closure of depots, and others involving alterations to servicing arrangements. The two Lancashire depots at Blackburn and Preston had been served from Healey Mills since the inception of the Speedlink Coal Network in 1987, but with the running down of Healey Mills yard the service was altered in October 1989 to run from Washwood Heath instead. This meant the loss of one of the few regular freight services over the Copy Pit line. On 31st March Class 37 No. 37264 heads east near Portsmouth, on the Copy Pit line, with 6E80, the 10.30 empties from Preston Deepdale to Healey Mills.   *Paul Shannon*

►The last coal train to the Rugby Cement works at Chinnor ran on 20th December 1989, complete with ceremonial headboard. The train was hauled by Railfreight Distribution locomotive No. 47258 and is pictured on the doomed single-track branch from Princes Risborough to Chinnor. The flow of imported coal from Newport Docks to Chinnor was reliant on a fleet of now elderly, increasingly unreliable HTV hopper wagons, and no funding could be found to provide modern replacements.
Brian Morrison

▼Another service which used vacuum-braked wagons until its withdrawal in 1989 was the flow of sulphur from Mostyn to Amlwich. Class 47 No. 47323 crosses Tan-y-Lane viaduct, near Colwyn Bay, with empty HJVs for Mostyn on 16th January. At one time Railfreight had hoped to carry liquid sulphur from Runcorn to Amlwch as a replacement for the Mostyn flow, but this was not to be.   *Larry Goddard*

STEEL SECTOR CHANGES

◄The Metals sub-sector made definite moves away from using the Railfreight Distribution Speedlink network during 1989, with the establishment of a number of dedicated Metals services for both trainload and wagonload consignments. A new service operated up to twice a week from Lackenby to Blackburn, bringing steel coil to Fogarty's Blackburn railhead. This traffic would previously have been conveyed by trunk Speedlink services to Warrington and by the connecting Warrington–Blackburn feeder service. Class 37/5 No. 37419 arrives at Blackburn on 31st March with 6Z50, the 04.50 departure from Lackenby, comprising a mixture of wagons owned by Railfreight, VTG and Tiphook. Priority will be given to unloading this train in the Fogarty transhipment shed, and No. 37519 will set off again with the empties within two or three hours.
Paul Shannon

►After October 1989 traffic to and from the Metal Box factories at Worcester, Wisbech and Westhoughton was abstracted from Speedlink and handed over to the Metals sub-sector's own services. Under the new scheme a Cardiff-based Class 37/7 or 37/9 locomotive works north overnight from Cardiff to Trafford Park with any available Metals traffic and then works a feeder service to Westhoughton and back if there is any traffic for Metal Box. The Class 37 then returns to South Wales in the evening. In this view of the Metal Box sidings at Westhoughton, empty SHA coil wagons to form the return service to Trafford Park are being shunted by 37718. *Paul Shannon*

▼Ex-BR Class 08 shunter No. 08423 trundles along the Trafford Park Estates Internal system with thirteen POA scrap wagons on 20th July. The wagons have been loaded at the now rail-served premises of Norton Metals and are destined for Allied Steel & Wire, Cardiff. No. 08423 will remain in charge of the train as far as the BR exchange sidings at Trafford Park, where a Metals sub-sector locomotive will take over for the trunk haul to Cardiff Tidal sidings. *Paul Shannon*

NEW FREIGHT FLOWS

▶A new destination for the Redland self-discharge aggregates train was Chelmsford. Class 56 No. 56063 Bardon Hill approaches Badgeney crossing, March, with the empties from Chelmsford on Saturday 18th August. *Michael J. Collins*

◀A short-term contract to move imported coal from Bidston Dock to Rugeley commenced on 20th October, with trains using a new access curve at Bidston in order to avoid interfering with New Brighton line passenger services. Class 20 locomotives Nos. 20106 and 20113 approach Canning Street North, Birkenhead, with a Bidston–Rugeley MGR train on 3rd November. *R.W. Cragg*

▼Class 37/5 locomotives Nos. 37670 and 37669 pass Bodmin Parkway with the 11.48 Burngullow–Irvine clay slurry train on Sunday 16th July. These Laira-based locomotives will remain in charge of the train all the way to the Caledonian Paper factory at Irvine. *John S. Whiteley*

◀The opening of Cleveland Freightliner terminal on 16th June, with Class 47 No. 47363 Wilton Endeavour ready to depart with the first outward service to Leeds.

Michael J. Collins

▼During 1989 a new daily Freightliner service was introduced between Leeds and Immingham, where containers were loaded and unloaded by mobile crane. Class 47 No. 47285 approaches Stainforth & Hatfield with the outward working, 11.19 Leeds–Immingham, on 5th September.

Les Nixon

▼▼Freightliner services returned to the Harwich branch in February 1989 after a gap of just over three years. Services were originally planned to commence in early January, but introduction was delayed by an industrial dispute so that the first trains did not run until the end of February. Class 31 No. 31408 is pictured near Wrabness on 4th March with 4F85, the 08.53 Ipswich–Parkeston (Harwich) service.

Michael J. Collins

TEMPORARY CONTRACTS

▶Railfreight gained a useful contract to remove industrial waste from Barking to Stewartby during 1988, and this traffic continued to operate until summer 1989. For operational reasons the trains ran via Ripple Lane yard. InterCity-liveried Class 47 No. 47430 has just run round its loaded train in Ripple Lane West sidings and will head for Stewartby by way of the Midland Main Line and a second reversal at Bedford.
Paul Shannon

▶▼The second short-term waste contract to operate during 1989 involved the removal of spoil from Willesden to Stewartby. A service of 22 trains a week was scheduled to commence in September 1989 and last for approximately ten months. As with the Barking flow, the waste was carried in sheeted containers loaded on to Tiphook bogie flat wagons, but the normal motive power for the Willesden trains was a pair of Construction sub-sector Class 31s, in contrast to the single Class 47 used from Barking. On 31st October Class 31 locomotives Nos. 31209 and 31301 approach Stewartby station, shortly after leaving the London Brick landfill sidings, with 6A16, the 12.15 empties to Willesden. *Paul Shannon*

▼To the same siding at Barking which was used for outgoing waste traffic, Railfreight operated regular block trains of limestone from Merehead quarry. These trains were indentifiable by the inclusion of a bogie brake van in their formation, needed because of the awkward reversal at Barking. The unique Class 47/9 locomotive No. 47901, carrying new Railfreight Construction livery, passes West Ealing on 22nd August with the loaded Merehead–Barking working. *David Brown*

THE SPEEDLINK SCENE

◀A Speedlink trip working to convey timber to the Kronospan factory at Chirk was inaugurated in January 1989. The firm had successfully applied for a Section 8 grant to install a new siding at its premises, and the traffic was to be conveyed in a specific fleet of OTA wagons, painted in Kronospan livery. Class 31 No. 31248 approaches Frodsham with 6J47, the 13.10 Warrington Arpley–Chirk service, on 10th August. Timber was conveyed to Chirk in 1989 from East Anglia, the Scottish Highlands and Kent. *Paul Shannon*

▼Trunk Speedlink services over the West Coast Main Line were rationalised in October 1989 as a prelude to the more widespread changes to the Speedlink network in January 1990. On 23rd August 1989, Class 85 No. 85038 approaches Castlethorpe with one of the few daytime WCML Speedlink trains, 6S73 10.18 Dover–Mossend. The load includes steel rods from Sheerness, a traffic flow which would soon be transferred to the Metals sub-sector's own services. The itinerary of 6S73 was cut short to Warrington in October, and from January 1990 the train was expected to run no further than Willesden, though still with connecting services for the North. No. 65038 just lived long enough to see the end of the decade – it was withdrawn on 2nd January 1990. *Paul Shannon*

▲Railfreight Distribution withdrew its Speedlink trains from the East Coast Main Line north of Newcastle in November, at the same time as it stopped using Tyne and Millerhill yards as attaching and detaching points. Railfreight Distribution's own traffic would in future have to travel via Carlisle and Mossend, whilst certain bulk commodities formerly carried by Speedlink but belonging to other sub-sectors, such as cement, would still travel over the East Coast Main Line but in redesignated 'Bulklink' trains. The old order of Speedlink traffic north of Newcastle is illustrated by 6S63, the 17.50 Tees Yard–Aberdeen service, which is seen passing Alnmouth behind Class 37 No. 37042 on 29th June.

Stephen Miller

▶During July and early August the TGWU strike immobilised a number of ports, and imports of Volkswagen cars were switched from Immingham to Scrabster, near Thurso. The cars were loaded on to railway wagons at a temporary terminal adjacent to Inverness carriage depot and taken to Bathgate and Immingham for distribution. Here No. 37428 hauls an Inverness–Immingham car train near Dalnaspidal on 26th July.

Michael J. Collins

▶In the declining years of BR's vacuum-braked wagonload network it was not unusual to find supposedly revenue-earning trains carrying nothing but departmental traffic. In 1989 the reverse situation could be found in Devon, where Speedlink traffic was often conveyed by the 14.15 Tavistock Junction–Exeter Riverside engineers' service. This train is pictured near Ivybridge on 30th June, with Class 50 No. 50021 Rodney hauling a mixture of vans and covered hopper wagons carrying china clay, OCA open wagons carrying bricks, and empty LPG and bitumen tanks. *Don Gatehouse*

▲Many more Railfreight locomotives received the latest sub-sector livery styles during 1989, including the small fleet of slow-speed fitted Class 26s allocated to Eastfield for merry-go-round work. A pristine No. 26004 pulls away from Blindwells opencast disposal point on 20th March with the 10.35 working to Cockenzie power station.
Michael J. Collins

▼Despite a high-level directive to limit the number of different locomotive liveries on BR and to outlaw 'one-off' schemes perpetrated by individual depots, Class 50 No. 50019 'Ramillies' was outshopped from Laira during May in now non-standard plain blue livery with a white roof. It is allocated to the Western Region civil engineer's pool and should in theory carry departmental grey livery. It is seen entering Hinksey yard, Oxford, with a train of spent ballast from the Banbury line on 23rd July.
Martin Loader

▲ Sub-sector liveries have started to find their way on to a number of railway-owned wagon types. On HAA hopper wagons the red band has been superseded by a yellow one. A train consisting entirely of reliveried HAAs is pictured heading south at Moore, near Warrington, on 19th July. Traction is provided by Nos. 20135 and 20080, and the train is 6D25 Fidlers Ferry–Point of Ayr empties. *Paul Shannon*

▶ Nondescript grey livery was applied to departmental locomotives of Classes 31, 33, 37, 47 and 73 during 1989. Class 47 No. 47352 passes Cossington with 6E98 Mountsorrel–Peterborough ballast train on 5th September. *Paul A. Biggs*

PREPARING FOR 1992

In January 1989 two new sets of sorting sidings were opened at Ebbw Vale. The site of the old yards, which were known as Waunllwyd, was needed for the planned 1992 Garden Festival at Ebbw Vale. Class 37/7 No. 37710 departs from the new Ebbw Vale south yard on 8th July with ten empty BBA wagons from Ravenscraig. *Michael Rhodes*

COLLIERY HAPPENINGS

◄A delightful scene which passed into history in 1989 was the electrified colliery railway at Westoe, on the south bank of the River Tyne. Coal traffic over the system ceased in 1988, but shale traffic continued until the commissioning of a conveyor belt in August 1989. The line was originally owned by the Harton Coal Company and ran from South Shields to Westoe, Marsden and Whitburn Colliery, the line from South Shields to Westoe being electrified at 550 V dc in 1908. On 26th May English Electric 400 hp Bo–Bo No. 12 returns to Hilda exchange sidings after working a loaded shale train to the terminal visible in the background. *Michael Rhodes*

▼A ticket from the passenger service which used to operate on the route.

▼ A rail link to Allerton Bywater colliery was restored during 1989, in order to handle a new flow of 'sweetener' coal from Allerton Bywater to Gascoigne Wood. Standing beside the former Ledston station platform at Allerton Bywater is Class 56 No. 56107, just after reversing up the branch from Castleford with a trainload of empty HAAs. *Michael Rhodes*

►Class 56 loco No. 56093 is seen at Euston station on 29th November awaiting departure with three HAA wagons after having been named 'The Institution of Mining Engineers' in commemoration of the Institution's centenary.   *Brian Morrison*

▼The centenary was an excuse for a series of railtours down colliery branches, some of which had possibly never seen a passenger train before! One such tour ran on 23rd April formed of two 3-car suburban units plus a Class 114 2-car. It is seen at Silverhill Colliery (middle photo) and at Warsop Colliery (bottom photo).   *Les Nixon*

RAILFREIGHT 89

A major Railfreight exhibition was held in the former maintenance shed at Cricklewood in April 1989. On show were the latest developments in wagon design, handling methods and service. There was also a separate purpose-built exhibition hall where over sixty stands were available for industry. A major part in the exhibition was played by Railfreight Distribution, keen to accrue new business in readiness for European deregulation and the opening of the Channel Tunnel. As well as contributing to the wagon displays, Railfreight Distribution provided a Channel Tunnel exhibition coach, showing the sub-sector's plans for a network of international freight services, and demonstrations of various road-rail transfer systems, including a full display of swapbody equipment. Swapbodies are already used on mainland Europe and their use is expected to spread to Britain once the problem of our restricted loading gauge has been alleviated by the construction of Lowliner low platform height wagons.

◀▲ Standard Railfreight 51-tonne heavy duty open wagon No. RLS4607 stands inside the main exhibition hall. This design is widely used for carrying scrap metal, hence the additional bracing.   *Colin J Marsden*

◀ Tiphook Piggyback wagon No. TIPH 96500 stands on display outside the exhibition hall.   *Colin J Marsden*

▶ Six-wheelers are not dead! This is one of a fleet of fifty three-axle car-carrying wagons, built in France in 1981 but used within Britain for the delivery of Renault cars. Note the variable height of the upper floor roof.
Colin J Marsden

◀ A gleaming new 90-tonne bogie tank wagon built for the recently inaugurated flow of clay slurry from Burngullow to Irvine, with its stainless steel finish not yet tainted by the slurry spillages! Although intended for operation within Great Britain, this design is equipped for train ferry operation and carries international numbers, a trend which is likely to spread during the 1990s.
Colin J Marsden

Parcels

The Parcels sector had a relatively quiet year in 1989. The sector's loss of £12.4 million for the 1988/89 financial year was not unexpected and reflects the level of change which the sector has undergone since the demise of the newspaper traffic in July 1988. The sector's prospects for the next few years seemed good, with carryings of Post Office mail assured until the expiry date of the present contract in 1994. This provided a useful breathing space during which the sector could begin to formulate a policy for replacement of its ageing fleets of locomotives, vans and multiple units.

At the end of 1989 the sector's traction resources comprised 16 Class 31/4 locomotives based at Crewe, 56 Class 47/4 locomotives shared between Crewe, Bristol and Old Oak Common and 17 AC electric locomotives of Classes 85, 86 and 90 for the West Coast Main Line. The Class 127 multiple unit fleet was withdrawn in May 1989, and the year also saw the end of the few Class 105 sets which had survived in parcels traffic, so by the end of the year the diesel unit fleet was limited to Classes 114 and 128, comprising 18 and 5 vehicles respectively. There was little change to the sector's complement of hauled stock, except that Post Office red livery started to appear on BGs and GUVs as well as Travelling Post Office vehicles.

► The last Class 127 DMU cars were withdrawn from service in May 1989, having been converted for parcels duties in 1985. Nos. 55975 and 55976 are hauled north past Horfield by Class 47 No. 47580 'County of Essex' on 13th March.   *Martin Loader*

▼ Southern Region Class 419 Motor Luggage Vans Nos. 9004 and 9001, both carrying Royal Mail red livery, pass Coulsdon with a Redhill–London Bridge mail train on Saturday 11th March. These were the only two of their type to receive Royal Mail livery, as a change of policy led to Network South-East colours being applied instead.
David Brown

▼ With many parcels services now loading to only three or four vehicles, it is not surprising that the sector is looking to increase its use of multiple units on all but the longest distance workings. Class 47 No. 47471 has plenty of power to spare as it passes Helsby with three empty vans from Holyhead to Red Bank on 15th April. This working was diverted to Preston following the closure of Red Bank carriage sidings.
J.C. Hillmer

◄▲▲ Blue-liveried Class 73/0 No. 73005 heads 3B01, the 15.59 Waterloo–Bournemouth van train through Winklebury, Basingstoke, on 29th September. This had previously been a regular Class 33 turn but the use of Class 33s on parcels workings had all but ceased by the autumn.
Peter Tandy

◄▲ Following the withdrawal in March Class 105 parcels cars were stored in the sidings at the south end of Cambridge station. This view shows Class 105 car No. E 53373 parked in its temporary home whilst Class 317 EMU No. 317 367 departs with the 16.40 to King's Cross, a duty which once would have been familiar to E 53373!
David Percival

◄ Cambridge depot has assumed the role of principal servicing depot for parcels stock. Inside the shed on 7th January are Post Office Sorting Van No. 80303 and Class 128 single unit No. M55993. *Michael J. Collins*

► For much of 1989 the Wednesday–only Carlisle–Preston parcels train produced a Class 26 locomotive, although substitutions by other classes were not uncommon. On 31st May No. 26031 climbs past Thrimby on the northern approach to Shap with this train. *Michael J. Collins*

A Glimpse of Ireland

▲ 2–6–4T No. 4 worked the RPSI's first rail-tour specially for UK enthusiasts in June 1989. The 'Sea Breeze' ran from Dublin to Rosslare and back, and was a sell out. After servicing at the pierhead, No. 4 brings the e.c.s. into the new station at Rosslare Harbour before the return journey.
David Percival

◀ NIR Metrovick No. 106 pilots English Electric No. 103 on the 'Irish MV' railtour at Crumlin on 7th October. *E. Dunkling*

▼ The first NIR Mark 3 push-pull Dublin outer suburban stock entered service in March 1989. First of the DTSO driving trailers, No. 6101, brings up the rear of the 09.35 to Maynooth, leaving Dublin Connolly on 24th June. *David Percival*

Accidents

REPERCUSSIONS OF CLAPHAM

In November BR accepted the full findings of the judicial inquiry (under Sir Anthony Hidden) into the Clapham train crash of 12th December 1988. Most of the Report's 93 recommendations applied to the railway and action was being taken to put them into effect BR said.

The inquiry endorsed BR investigators' findings (used in the internal inquiry set up after the accident) that the prime cause of the collision was faulty workmanship: a loose wire in Clapham A relay box causing a 'rogue' electrical circuit. As a result, the signal failed to detect the presence of the Basingstoke–Waterloo train and to show the 'danger' aspect to protect it.

Following the internal inquiry (under Maurice Holmes, director, safety) it was deemed essential that working practices, communication of grievances, supervision, management, testing and quality control needed to be improved. Recruitment, pay structure and training needed transforming. The pressures caused by under-staffing and excessive hours of work prior to the Clapham crash were criticised.

Distinguishing the immediate causes of the accident at Clapham with those at Purley and Bellgrove, BR admitted that the root causes were the same – human error. 'The culture must be developed further that seeks to minimise the incidence of erratic behaviour and to ensure, through design and override systems, that such behaviour is countered by failsafe reponses.'

Adopting all of the Hidden Report recommendations would cost a lot of money, estimates varying as to how much. Unfortunately, cost-benefit analysis, which would take into account safety considerations (along with environmental and social benefits) is not used for railway investments, strict financial appraisal being the norm, unlike road investment cases.

4th MARCH, PURLEY, SOUTH LONDON

Only twelve weeks after the Clapham crash, six people died when the 8-car 11.47 Portsmouth Harbour/12.17 Littlehampton–London Victoria (formed of Class 421 EMUs 1280 + 1295) collided with the rear of the 4-car 12.50 Horsham–Victoria (Class 423 No. 3441) just north of Purley station. The Littlehampton train had been travelling at about 55 mph, the front six carriages becoming derailed in the severe impact and careering down the embankment into people's back gardens.

The crash occurred at 13.39 and emergency services were again quick on the scene. It took two days to clear the line and, with the help of up to three cranes, six days to remove all the carriages.

An internal inquiry found that the Littlehampton train had gone through a signal at red at about 80 mph at which point the emergency brakes were already applied. The Horsham train had been crossing from the up slow to the up fast line at about 25 mph. On collision this train stayed upright. Human error, rather than faulty signalling (as at Clapham), was blamed.

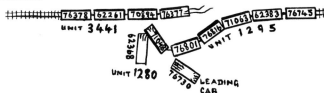

▼The worst rail accident of 1989 at Purley is clearly shown in the aerial photographs here and overleaf.The impact was such that only the front three carriages of the Horsham–Victoria train and the last carriage of the Littlehampton–Victoria train stayed on the tracks.   *202 Squadron, RAF Manston*

▲▲Coach No. 76816 of Class 421/2 (4Cig) No. 1295 is at the centre of this view taken the day after the accident.
Brian Morrison

▲The relatively intact state of the Horsham–Victoria train still standing on the main line can be seen in these aerial views.
202 Squadron, RAF Manston

▶Car No. 76816, minus bogies, is hoisted over the rooftops to a road transporter.
Press Association

6th MARCH, BELLGROVE, GLASGOW

The 12.20 Milngavie–Springburn, operated by 303 071 collided head-on with the 12.39 Springburn–Milngavie (303 005). The accident occurred on the down line of the double track Springburn branch just beyond the main line junction (about 300 metres east of Bellgrove station on the Airdrie–Helensburgh line). Two people were killed, including the driver of the Milngavie-bound train. The crash is pictured, by mistake, in 'Today's Railways Review of the Year' Volume 2 where the caption refers to the Hyndland accident of 1988. Sorry!

An internal inquiry indicated that the surviving driver of the Springburn-bound train had been at fault. The junction at Bellgrove had recently been simplified. It took eight hours to prise the leading vehicle of 303 071, No. 75837 from the Milngavie train's 75605. Train services resumed two days later and a public inquiry was launched in April. Failure to observe a stop signal on leaving Bellgrove station was blamed. The BR rulebook, though altered after the Paisley accident of 1979, was unclear in certain respects over signalling procedure, the Sheriff stated. (The Paisley accident was also caused by a driver passing a signal at danger. The BR rulebook was altered –

wrongly, in the editor's opinion – so that the guard should not give the authority to proceed unless the signal was clear. This could lead to a false sense of security for the driver). He also criticised the siting of a single-lead junction near to the station, the absence of a secondary safety device to prevent a train passing a red signal, and the lack of a preceeding warning signal. Train timetabling across the single lead was also criticised. (However, in the UK, the timetable is not used as the means of preventing collisions, as it is in certain other countries – ed).

This accident, plus the Purley crash, increased the pressure for BR to develop and install a nationwide system of Automatic Train Protection (ATP). By the end of the year, BR was planning to install it on the Chiltern lines from Marylebone and Paddington–Bristol (and Heathrow). The key feature of ATP is that should the driver fail to respond correctly to signals and speed restrictions after a warning is given, the brakes are applied automatically so that the train stops before the danger signal is reached, or the speed is reduced in time for the speed restriction. Such famous accidents as Morpeth (1984) and Paddington (1983) might also have been avoided had ATP been installed.

EXPRESS TRAIN DERAILED BY VANDALS

▲After two decades of service, 50025 'Invincible' was destroyed by vandals after its train, the 21.15 Oxford–Paddington, was derailed at speed at West Ealing on 6th August. Miraculously, no-one was killed. Derailment by placing objects on lines and stone-throwing attacks on trains in certain areas (often known as 'bomb alleys') is a grave problem for BR. Here, the locomotive is righted the following morning.
Brian Morrison

◀One of the sadder sights of the year, 50025 stands in the adjacent supermarket's car park. The loco was condemned a few days later due to the cost of repairs in relation to its age. *Chris McKee*

▼Mark 2A FK No. 13442 is ready for hoisting from the crash scene on 7th August. *Chris McKee*

▼On 3rd September, Class 442 'Wessex Electric' unit No. 2407 ran away from Bournemouth depot, demolishing buffers and coming to rest in Wharfedale Road. No-one was hurt. Like the accident at Cricklewood on 28th October 1988, this provided a good picture story for some of the national papers! *By kind permission of the Bournemouth Evening Echo*

ACCIDENTS MENTIONED IN 'DIARY' SECTION

▲ On 17th April the rear of the Class 37-hauled 6A18 04.55 Robeston–Theale Murco oil train, on its usual route via Bath, Avon valley and the Berks and Hants route, became derailed on the Westbury East Chord at Hawkeridge Junction. The derailed wagons were PR 82648 and PR 84117, there being slight leakage of oil from the former. Firemen survey the damaged track and foam-covered bogies of 82648.

Steve McMullin

◄A van driver had a lucky escape from his Ford Transit van, when it was hit on the unmaned lights only level crossing, at Appledore, on the Romney Marsh, by the 07.31 Ashford to Hastings service, on 31st July. The train was slowing down for Appledore station, which is adjacent to the level crossing. No passengers on the train were injured, but the van driver was detained in hospital. The Network SouthEast-liveried Class 205/1 DEMU No. 205 101, had only superficial damage. This incident, yet again, highlights the fact that unmanned, no-barrier level crossings in rural areas, are abused.

Ian G. Feather

BR Stock Changes 1989

LOCOMOTIVES

New

90019	WN	05/01/89
90020	WN	31/01/89
90021	WN	31/01/89
90022	WN	14/02/89
90023	WN	24/02/89
90024	WN	19/03/89
90025	WN	17/03/89
90026	WN	20/03/89
90027	WN	03/04/89
90028	WN	29/03/89
90029	WN	18/04/89
90030	WN	29/05/89
90031	WN	14/09/89
90032	WN	17/09/89
90033	WN	21/09/89
90034	WN	27/09/89
90035	WN	29/09/89
91010	BN	07/04/89

In addition locomotives 60001 to 60005 inclusive had been delivered to BR between 30/06/89 and the end of the year, but none had been released for traffic as at 31/12/89.

Reinstated

08527	SF	06/06/89
20031	TO	10/11/89
31124	SF	30/01/89
33110	EH	28/09/89
33115	EH	27/05/89
37113	IS	21/08/89
45128	TI	20/02/89
47097	TI	17/01/89
47189	CD	06/01/89
47298	TI	24/12/89

Withdrawn

* Subsequently reinstated.

7	VR	17/04/89
8	VR	17/04/89
9	VR	17/04/89
10	VR	17/04/89
03073	BD	23/05/89
03162	BD	23/05/89
03170	BD	23/05/89
08202	CF	23/05/89
08463	DY	16/03/89
08527	SF	05/05/89*
08650	EH	11/09/89
08669	LO	23/05/89
08763	HA	05/10/89
08769	LE	23/05/89
08785	CF	13/03/89
08846	AN	13/10/89
20005	TO	27/07/89
20008	TE	20/02/89
20009	TE	19/07/89
20031	IM	04/10/89*
20044	TO	11/09/89
20054	TO	11/09/89
20083	TO	20/03/89
20097	TO	11/09/89
20100	TO	05/05/89
20126	IM	18/09/89
20134	TO	19/07/89
20147	TO	18/05/89
20158	TO	18/05/89
20171	TO	08/12/89
20178	IM	18/12/89
20179	TO	28/02/89
20192	TO	11/09/89
20193	TO	19/07/89
20202	TO	08/12/89
20204	ED	10/05/89
20205	IM	18/12/89
20217	TO	21/07/89
20218	TO	04/10/89
20219	TO	20/03/89
20225	TO	20/03/89
26031	ED	04/10/89
26034	ED	08/09/89
31118	TE	20/02/89
31124	SF	10/01/89*

31127	TE	21/06/89
31131	TE	20/03/89
31138	CD	02/02/89
31141	CD	25/01/89
31152	IM	01/06/89
31173	SF	14/04/89
31189	SF	26/05/89
31225	IM	07/03/89
31226	SF	03/01/89
31259	TI	02/03/89
31278	TE	29/03/89
31281	TE	15/05/89
31283	TE	03/11/89
31284	TI	30/08/89
31311	SF	07/02/89
31320	TE	15/05/89
31322	IM	28/07/89
31323	SF	08/06/89
31443	CD	03/07/89
33011	SL	23/03/89
33013	SL	14/03/89
33015	EH	28/07/89
33016	SL	04/10/89
33022	SL	24/12/89
33031	SL	06/02/89
33035	SL	20/10/89
33039	SL	18/05/89
33055	SL	24/12/89
33055	SL	24/12/89
33107	EH	16/05/89
33110	EH	11/09/89*
33115	EH	10/05/89*
33119	EH	26/10/89
37062	TI	13/03/89
37113	ED	20/03/89*
37260	IS	21/08/89
45106	TI	20/02/89
45128	TI	20/04/89
47008	TI	17/10/89
47012	TI	15/12/89
47012	TI	15/12/89
47097	TI	03/01/89*
47101	CD	13/03/89
47110	TI	02/05/89
47124	TI	05/06/89
47143	TI	01/12/89
47189	CD	16/03/89*
47198	CF	20/04/89
47203	TI	27/03/89
47298	IM	01/12/89*
47411	IM	30/06/89
47428	CD	25/01/89
47469	IS	19/03/89
47542	BR	03/04/89
50012	LA	16/01/89
50025	OC	14/08/89
50039	OC	04/06/89
81005	GW	20/02/89
81007	GW	14/11/89
81011	GW	05/04/89
81013	GW	01/11/89
81019	GW	03/01/89
83009	WN	19/03/89
83012	WN	20/03/89
85002	CE	17/05/89
85014	CE	16/10/89
85019	CE	01/12/89
85022	CE	20/02/89

Renumbered

37002 to 37351		03/05/89
37033 to 37719		20/03/89
37050 to 37717		24/01/89
37084 to 37718		08/02/89
37094 to 37716		15/01/89
37165 to 37374		10/02/89
37303 to 37271		26/01/89
37304 to 37272		19/01/89
37306 to 37273		17/02/89
37308 to 37274		01/02/89
37310 to 37152		14/09/89
37311 to 37156		05/09/89
37312 to 37137		23/02/89
37313 to 37145		14/09/89
37320 to 37026		06/09/89
37321 to 37037		21/04/89
37323 to 37088		18/09/89
37324 to 37099		13/09/89
37325 to 37108		18/09/89
37326 to 37111		23/06/89

37352 to 37008		06/07/89
37353 to 37032		05/06/89
37356 to 37068		05/06/89
37374 to 37165		17/01/89
37374 to 37165		09/07/89
47551 to 47801		11/09/89
47552 to 47802		13/07/89
47553 to 47803		21/03/89
47563 to 47831		10/05/89
47560 to 47832		14/06/89
47571 to 47822		31/03/89
47577 to 47847		/12/89
47589 to 47827		22/05/89
47590 to 47825		02/05/89
47591 to 47804		29/07/89
47602 to 47824		20/04/89
47607 to 47821		29/03/89
47608 to 47833		23/06/89
47609 to 47834		27/07/89
47610 to 47823		15/04/89
47611 to 47837		13/10/89
47612 to 47838		03/11/89
47613 to 47840		23/11/89
47618 to 47836		31/08/89
47619 to 47829		09/06/89
47620 to 47835		02/08/89
47621 to 47839		10/11/89
47622 to 47841		15/12/89
47629 to 47828		01/06/89
47632 to 47848		/12/89
47637 to 47826		10/05/89
47638 to 47845		/11/89
47647 to 47846		/11/89
47649 to 47830		29/06/89
47650 to 47805		03/08/89
47651 to 47806		19/07/89
47652 to 47807		10/07/89
47653 to 47808		21/07/89
47654 to 47809		06/07/89
47655 to 47810		21/02/89
47656 to 47811		04/08/89
47657 to 47812		31/07/89
47658 to 47813		23/07/89
47659 to 47814		16/06/89
47660 to 47815		31/08/89
47661 to 47816		21/02/89
47662 to 47817		20/07/89
47663 to 47818		21/02/89
47664 to 47819		24/06/89
47665 to 47820		11/09/89
50149 to 50049		22/02/89
85004 to 85111		07/11/89
85006 to 85101		09/06/89
85009 to 85102		18/06/89
85010 to 85103		02/07/89
85012 to 85104		09/06/89
85016 to 85105		06/07/89
85021 to 85106		14/07/89
85024 to 85107		15/06/89
85032 to 85108		12/06/89
85035 to 85109		29/06/89
85036 to 85110		31/10/89
86233 to 86506		26/01/89
86241 to 86508		02/02/89
86402 to 86602		09/11/89
86407 to 86607		07/08/89
86408 to 86608		17/09/89
86409 to 86609		30/06/89
86413 to 86613		/12/89
86420 to 86620		18/05/89
86421 to 86621		27/07/89
86427 to 86627		07/09/89
86432 to 86632		31/08/89
86433 to 86633		11/09/89
86435 to 86635		04/09/89
86436 to 86636		08/08/89
86501 to 86258		27/11/89
86502 to 86222		20/10/89
86503 to 86205		03/11/89
86504 to 86217		01/11/89
86505 to 86246		26/09/89
86506 to 86233		07/08/89
86507 to 86239		24/07/89
86508 to 86241		23/06/89
97204 to 31970		19/08/89
97472 to 47472		15/05/89
97480 to 47971		02/08/89
97545 to 47972		20/07/89
97561 to 47973		15/07/89
97800 to 08600		by 27/08/89

In addition 73101 and 73105 were renumbered 73801 & 73805 for a short period, but as this was done by the SR without BRB sanction they reverted to their former numbers almost immediately.

Locos Transferred to Departmental Status and Renumbered

33018 to ADB 968030

Locos. Withdrawn from Departmental Service:

ADB 968028 ED 15/09/89

Withdrawn Locos. taken into Departmental Service:

45111
45125
45126
45148

COACHING STOCK

New

10300	BN	16/06/89
10301	BN	16/06/89
10302	BN	31/07/89
10303	BN	02/09/89
10304	BN	25/09/89
10305	BN	25/09/89
10306	BN	30/11/89
10307	BN	13/12/89
11200	BN	16/06/89
11201	BN	18/05/89
11202	BN	18/05/89
11203	BN	14/07/89
11204	BN	21/08/89
11205	BN	27/07/89
11206	BN	17/08/89
11207	BN	17/08/89
11208	BN	31/10/89
11209	BN	30/10/89
11210	BN	30/11/89
11211	BN	30/11/89
11212	BN	13/12/89
11213	BN	13/12/89
12200	BN	31/05/89
12201	BN	14/09/89
12202	BN	25/07/89
12203	BN	24/08/89
12204	BN	31/10/89
12205	BN	30/11/89
12206	BN	13/12/89
12300	BN	31/05/89
12301	BN	14/07/89
12302	BN	18/08/89
12303	BN	31/10/89
12304	BN	30/11/89
12305	BN	13/12/89
12400	BN	31/05/89
12401	BN	21/08/89
12402	BN	17/08/89
12403	BN	24/08/89
12404	BN	30/08/89
12405	BN	26/10/89
12406	BN	26/10/89
12407	BN	26/10/89
12408	BN	30/11/89
12409	BN	30/11/89
12410	BN	30/11/89
12411	BN	21/12/89
12412	BN	13/12/89
12413	BN	13/12/89

Reinstated

* Subsequently withdrawn.

1859	PH	20/05/89*
4366	HT	12/08/89

4634	FW	04/11/89
4785	HT	12/08/89
6505	LA	25/03/89
9007	FW	04/11/89
17021	FW	04/11/89
17055	CF	09/09/89
18576	LL	17/06/89
18712	LL	17/06/89
18716	LL	17/06/89
18734	LL	17/06/89
18756	MA	17/06/89
18806	MA	17/06/89
18957	LL	17/06/89
25008	FW	04/11/89
26125	FW	04/11/89
35459	MA	17/06/89
35470	LA	20/05/89
93646	EN	25/03/89

Withdrawn

* Subsequently reinstated.

1815	BN	30/03/89
1859	PH	13/12/89
1861	BN	11/08/89
1868	NC	30/03/89
1965	OM	17/07/89
3135	BN	11/08/89
3918	CL	02/01/89
3919	DY	25/08/89
3924	DY	23/10/89
4066	DY	23/10/89
4366	HT	31/05/89*
4392	DY	23/10/89
4422	PH	06/09/89
4425	PH	06/09/89
4484	HT	31/05/89
4785	HT	31/05/89*
4786	HT	09/03/89
4787	HT	09/03/89
4789	HT	09/03/89
4790	HT	09/03/89
4796	HT	09/03/89
4802	HT	09/03/89
4804	HT	17/07/89
4805	HT	09/03/89
4816	PC	21/09/89
4821	HT	31/05/89
4822	HT	31/05/89
4823	HT	09/03/89
4824	HT	31/05/89
4826	HT	31/05/89
4828	HT	09/03/89
4829	HT	31/05/89
4832	PH	13/12/89
4844	PH	06/09/89
4847	EN	03/02/89
4871	PH	06/09/89
4921	OM	02/01/89
4941	OM	02/01/89
4957	OM	02/01/89
5034	OM	02/01/89
5070	CL	21/06/89
5072	CL	09/03/89
5076	CL	09/03/89
5088	CL	09/03/89
5099	CL	09/03/89
5114	CL	21/06/89
5125	NL	19/07/89
5143	IS	02/09/89
5165	OM	22/08/89
5201	IS	22/09/89
5205	OM	22/08/89
5245	CF	30/03/89
5252	LL	13/10/89
5302	LA	17/02/89
6402	DY	10/04/89
6410	OY	06/03/89
6413	DY	08/12/89
6504	LA	11/08/89
7074	LA	03/11/89
7154	CF	09/03/89
7162	NL	09/03/89
7196	NL	09/03/89
7199	NL	09/03/89
7209	CF	11/08/89
7214	EN	15/09/89
7233	HT	09/03/89
7238	HT	09/03/89
9227	PH	06/09/89
13438	OM	15/11/89

17003 IS 09/05/89
17021 IS 02/01/89*
17022 IS 09/05/89
17024 IS 02/01/89
17030 OY 13/10/89
17035 CF 09/03/89
17038 HT 09/03/89
17041 OY 23/10/89
17048 HT 09/03/89
17055 PC 09/05/89*
18287 CF 09/03/89
18293 NL 09/03/89
18303 IS 10/05/89
18414 HT 09/03/89
18568 HT 09/03/89
18576 CF 07/06/89*
18610 LA 09/03/89
18624 NL 09/03/89
18626 NL 09/03/89
18716 CF 09/03/89*
18726 CF 09/03/89
18733 CF 03/11/89
18744 NL 09/03/89
18758 CL 09/03/89
18759 HT 09/03/89
18760 NL 09/03/89
18776 OM 02/01/89
18778 OM 02/01/89
18795 OM 02/01/89
18817 CL 09/03/89
18820 CF 09/03/89
18822 CL 09/03/89
18823 HT 09/03/89
18825 LL 30/03/89
18826 NL 09/03/89
18844 HT 09/03/89
18848 NL 09/03/89
18853 OM 02/01/89
18856 OM 02/01/89
18868 CL 09/03/89
18871 OM 02/01/89
18872 IS 09/05/89
18881 CL 09/03/89
18888 NL 09/03/89
18892 CL 09/03/89
18894 CL 09/03/89
18926 CF 21/06/89
18951 CF 09/03/89
18956 CF 09/02/89
18957 CF 09/03/89*
18983 CL 09/03/89
18994 OM 02/01/89
18998 CL 09/03/89
19015 CF 09/03/89
19017 HT 09/03/89
19018 NL 09/03/89
19489 DY 08/12/89
19497 WB 04/08/89
19500 DY 08/12/89
19537 OM 15/09/89
21238 OM 02/01/89
21240 SA 03/11/89
34663 HT 09/03/89
34674 HT 09/03/89
34940 EH 09/03/89
34950 EH 09/03/89
34952 EH 09/03/89
35012 EH 09/03/89
35053 CF 09/03/89
35116 PH 17/05/89
35120 LA 09/03/89
35184 LL 02/01/89
35195 LA 09/03/89
35204 CF 09/03/89
35210 OM 17/07/89
35300 CL 04/08/89
35305 CL 12/04/89
35320 DY 09/03/89
35321 CF 09/03/89
35330 CL 09/03/89
35332 CL 04/08/89
35336 CF 11/08/89
35342 CL 09/03/89
35451 CL 17/02/89
35460 HT 09/03/89
35463 DY 11/08/89
35467 OY 12/04/89
35470 LA 09/03/89*
35472 CL 09/03/89
35478 OY 21/06/89
35480 CF 09/03/89
35481 OY 21/06/89

Renumbered

3170 to 6215
3171 to 6222
3173 to 6221
3175 to 6220
3176 to 6212
3177 to 6209
3179 to 6216
3180 to 6203
3183 to 6206
3184 to 6217
3185 to 6230
3189 to 6231
3190 to 6235
3191 to 6202
3193 to 6205
3194 to 6223
3195 to 6224
3196 to 6210
3197 to 6227
3198 to 6200
3199 to 6232
3200 to 6225
3201 to 6228
3204 to 6207
3205 to 6208
3206 to 6233
3207 to 6234
3208 to 6213
3209 to 6218
3210 to 6201
3211 to 6214
3212 to 6229
3213 to 6219
3215 to 6211
3216 to 6204
6450 to 3403

DMUs
New

52469 CF 11/01/89
52470 CF 16/01/89
52471 CF 17/01/89
52472 CF 22/01/89
52473 CF 23/01/89
52474 CF 30/01/89
52475 NL 02/02/89
52476 NL 03/02/89
52477 IS 20/02/89
52478 HA 02/03/89
52479 NL 18/02/89
52480 NL 21/02/89
52481 NL 21/02/89
52482 NL 02/03/89
52483 NL 14/03/89
52484 NL 22/03/89
52485 IS 31/03/89
52486 NC 04/03/89
52487 NL 09/03/89
52488 NL 07/04/89
52489 NL 13/04/89
52490 NL 15/04/89
52491 NL 20/04/89
52492 IS 29/04/89
52493 IS 03/05/89
52494 IS 04/05/89
52495 IS 07/05/89
52496 IS 07/05/89
52497 NL 13/05/89
52498 NL 15/05/89
52499 NL 23/05/89
52500 HA 28/05/89
52501 CK 08/06/89
52502 CK 15/06/89
52503 CK 22/06/89
52504 CK 26/06/89
52505 CK 25/07/89
52506 CK 24/07/89
52507 CK 08/08/89
52508 CK 09/08/89
52509 CK 15/08/89
52510 CK 16/08/89
52511 CK 21/08/89
52512 CK 15/09/89
52513 CK 02/10/89
52514 CK 02/10/89
52701 HA 04/10/89
57469 CF 11/01/89
57470 CF 16/01/89
57471 CF 17/01/89
57472 CF 22/01/89
57473 CF 23/01/89
57474 CF 30/01/89
57475 NL 02/02/89
57476 NL 03/02/89
57477 IS 20/02/89
57478 HA 02/03/89
57479 NL 18/02/89
57480 NL 21/02/89
57481 NL 21/02/89
57482 NL 02/03/89
57483 NL 14/03/89
57484 NL 22/03/89
57485 IS 31/03/89
57486 NC 04/03/89
57487 NL 09/03/89
57488 NL 07/04/89
57489 NL 13/04/89
57490 NL 15/04/89
57491 NL 20/04/89
57492 IS 29/04/89
57493 IS 03/05/89
57494 IS 04/05/89
57495 IS 07/05/89
57496 IS 07/05/89
57497 NL 13/05/89
57498 NL 15/05/89
57499 NL 23/05/89
57500 HA 28/05/89
57501 CK 08/06/89
57502 CK 15/06/89
57503 CK 22/06/89
57504 CK 26/06/89
57505 CK 25/07/89
57506 CK 24/07/89
57507 CK 08/08/89
57508 CK 09/08/89
57509 CK 15/08/89
57510 CK 16/08/89
57511 CK 21/08/89
57512 CK 15/09/89
57513 CK 02/10/89
57514 CK 02/10/89
57701 HA 04/10/89

52467, 52468, 57467 & 57468 were new 12/88 but not shown in volume 2.

Reinstated

* Subsequently withdrawn.

51441 CA 04/05/89
51445 CA 04/05/89
51513 CF 08/09/89
51526 NL not wdn 11/88
51532 NH 08/09/89*
52061 LE 08/09/89
53843 CF 08/09/89*
59383 LE 08/09/89

Withdrawn

* Subsequently reinstated.

51057 CH 05/05/89
51095 CH 05/05/89
51183 CF 12/12/89
51197 CH 04/09/89
51203 HT 21/09/89
51206 CH 04/09/89
51216 HT 08/12/89
51217 HT 21/09/89
51227 NH 08/09/89
51243 NL 08/12/89
51305 LA 11/08/89
51307 CF 11/08/89
51310 CF 28/07/89
51320 LA 11/08/89
51325 CF 28/07/89
51430 CA 19/07/89
51439 CA 19/07/89
51441 CA 30/03/89*
51441 CA 19/07/89
51445 NL 09/03/89*
51446 NL 23/10/89
51449 CF 21/09/89
51454 NL 08/12/89
51456 NL 23/10/89
51458 NL 23/10/89
51465 NL 29/06/89
51467 HT 21/09/89
51510 NL 23/10/89
51513 CF 11/08/89*
51515 HT 21/09/89
51516 HT 21/09/89
51517 NL 23/10/89
51519 NL 08/12/89
51520 NL 23/10/89
51521 HT 08/12/89
51522 NL 23/10/89
51523 CF 04/09/89
51526 NL 23/10/89
51527 HT 20/01/89
51529 CF 11/08/89
51532 CF 21/09/89
51538 NL 23/10/89
51795 CF 21/09/89
51798 CF 11/08/89
51801 NL 29/06/89
51809 NL 29/06/89
51812 NL 21/09/89
51827 NL 08/12/89
51828 NL 14/12/89
51835 NL 29/06/89
52061 LE 11/08/89*
52067 NL 21/09/89
52081 NL 04/08/89
52084 NL 09/03/89
52209 NH 24/04/89
52212 NL 24/04/89
53008 TS 08/12/89
53026 TS 20/03/89
53037 TS 20/03/89
53038 CA 09/03/89
53039 TS 08/12/89
53080 CF 21/09/89
53089 CF 28/07/89
53122 CF 21/09/89
53131 CF 11/08/89
53141 NL 08/12/89
53150 NC 23/10/89
53159 NL 08/12/89
53162 NL 23/10/89
53182 HT 21/09/89
53186 HA 08/12/89
53187 HA 08/12/89
53188 HT 08/12/89
53195 CH 04/10/89
53218 CA 17/05/89
53219 CF 04/09/89
53221 CA 19/07/89
53222 CH 20/03/89
53229 NL 29/06/89
53230 CA 17/05/89
53233 CA 19/07/89
53235 NL 23/10/89
53237 NL 14/12/89
53240 CF 21/09/89
53251 NH 09/03/89
53255 CA 19/07/89
53257 HT 21/09/89
53263 CH 04/10/89
53264 CH 04/09/89
53290 ED 22/11/89
53303 CF 26/10/89
53306 CH 04/10/89
53307 CH 05/05/89
53309 CH 05/05/89
53317 CF 21/09/89
53318 CH 05/05/89
53319 LE 24/10/89
53323 CH 05/05/89
53324 CF 21/09/89
53325 CF 21/09/89
53334 NL 08/12/89
53335 NL 29/06/89
53336 CH 05/05/89
53337 CH 05/05/89
53338 CH 20/03/89
53355 NH 13/06/89
53361 CA 09/03/89
53364 CA 30/03/89
53365 CA 09/03/89
53367 CA 30/03/89
53368 CA 09/03/89
53373 CA 09/03/89
53421 NH 04/10/89
53425 CH 24/10/89
53427 CP 09/03/89
53443 NH 08/09/89
53460 CP 09/03/89
53464 NH 08/09/89
53465 CH 04/09/89
53468 CH 21/09/89
53472 CH 07/06/89
53474 CP 09/03/89
53476 CH 04/10/89
53478 CH 07/06/89
53487 NH 08/09/89
53492 CH 04/09/89
53496 CP 09/03/89
53499 CH 04/10/89
53500 NH 17/05/89
53501 CP 09/03/89
53504 CH 04/10/89
53507 CH 04/10/89
53511 NH 08/09/89
53518 NH 17/05/89
53520 CH 04/10/89
53522 CH 04/09/89
53530 CH 07/06/89
53532 NH 08/09/89
53536 CH 08/12/89
53541 CH 24/10/89
53556 NH 17/05/89
53601 NL 21/09/89
53606 NL 23/10/89
53607 NL 23/10/89
53613 BR 27/04/89
53658 HA 23/10/89
53682 HA 13/09/89
53686 HA 23/10/89
53699 HA 23/10/89
53700 HA 13/09/89
53732 HA 23/10/89
53733 HA 23/10/89
53812 NH 17/05/89
53843 CF 11/08/89*
53843 CF 21/09/89
53848 CF 21/09/89
53855 CF 12/12/89
53857 NH 09/03/89
53858 CF 21/09/89
53866 NH 09/03/89
53869 NH 09/03/89
53887 CF 21/09/89
53908 CF 12/12/89
53911 CF 21/09/89
53922 NH 09/03/89
54013 TS 20/03/89
54019 TS 20/03/89
54024 TS 08/12/89
54042 CA 17/04/89
54054 CP 17/05/89
54071 NH 17/05/89
54080 NL 08/12/89
54091 NL 21/09/89
54179 OO 02/11/89
54184 OO 02/11/89
54196 NL 21/09/89
54213 BY 23/11/89
54335 NL 08/12/89
54348 NL 08/12/89
54350 CP 17/05/89
54355 NL 08/12/89
54375 NH 27/04/89
54381 CP 17/05/89
54391 HT 21/09/89
54398 CP 09/03/89
54401 CP 17/05/89
55966 LO 15/05/89
55967 LO 15/05/89
55968 LO 15/05/89
55969 LO 15/05/89
55970 LO 15/05/89
55971 LO 15/05/89
55972 LO 15/05/89
55973 LO 15/05/89
55975 LO 15/05/89
55976 LO 15/05/89
55977 LO 15/05/89
55978 LO 15/05/89
55979 LO 15/05/89
55980 LO 15/05/89
55981 LO 15/05/89
55982 LO 15/05/89
55983 LO 15/05/89
55984 LO 15/05/89
55985 LO 15/05/89
55986 LO 15/05/89
55987 LO 15/05/89
59050 LE 24/10/89
59073 HA 08/12/89
59082 CH 24/10/89
59085 NC 23/10/89
59096 NL 29/06/89
59113 HA 08/12/89
59137 CH 24/10/89
59144 NL 23/10/89
59148 CH 24/10/89
59149 CH 05/05/89
59152 CH 05/05/89
59153 HA 24/10/89
59155 CH 24/10/89
59168 NL 08/12/89
59183 CH 24/10/89
59195 ED 08/12/89
59207 CH 24/10/89
59305 HA 08/12/89
59330 CP 09/03/89
59383 LE 11/08/89*
59417 RG 09/03/89
59482 LA 11/08/89
59553 HA 08/12/89
59562 NL 29/06/89
59565 NL 29/06/89
59666 TS 17/05/89
59690 NL 08/12/89
59697 LE 08/12/89
59709 CF 28/07/89
59710 LE 13/09/89
59739 BY 23/11/89
59748 CP 17/05/89
59793 ED 08/12/89

59798	ED	08/12/89
59810	NL	21/09/89
59812	CP	17/05/89
60113	SU	by 30/10/89
60144	SU	by 30/10/89
60618	SU	by 30/10/89
60663	SU	by 30/10/89
60813	SU	by 30/10/89
78709	NL	23/10/89
78711	NL	21/09/89
78712	NL	23/10/89
78713	NL	23/10/89
78714	NL	21/09/89
78717	NL	23/10/89
78718	NL	23/10/89
78719	NL	23/10/89
78722	NL	09/03/89
78959	NL	23/10/89
78960	NL	23/10/89
78961	NL	21/09/89
78962	NL	23/10/89
78964	NL	21/09/89
78967	NL	29/06/89
78968	NL	23/10/89
78969	NL	23/10/89
78971	NL	23/10/89

Note: 59478 was withdrawn 12/88 but not shown in the last edition.

Renumbered

53015 to 55929
53018 to 55928
54009 to 54903
54015 to 54904
60014 to 60152
60015 to 60153
60100 to 60154
60101 to 60145

* Official Period Ending date. In reality these cars were not physically renumbered until much later.

Transferred to Departmental Status and Renumbered

53197 to TDB 977652 /11
53290 to TDB 977651 /11

Withdrawn from Departmental Service:

TDB 975227 LMR 17/02/89
RDB 975386 RTC 31/07/89
TDB 977177 ScR 20/07/89

ADB 977048 was withdrawn 11/88 but not shown in the last edition.

EMUs

New Units

2423	BM	13/01/89
2424	BM	25/02/89
321 312	IL	12/01/89
321 313	IL	05/01/89
321 314	IL	09/01/89
321 315	IL	13/01/89
321 316	IL	17/01/89
321 317	IL	20/02/89
321 318	IL	23/01/89
321 319	IL	03/02/89
321 320	IL	31/01/89
321 321	IL	06/02/89
321 322	IL	07/02/89
321 323	IL	10/02/89
321 324	IL	21/02/89
321 325	IL	23/02/89
321 326	IL	27/02/89
321 327	IL	28/02/89
321 328	IL	02/03/89
321 329	IL	03/03/89
321 330	IL	06/03/89
321 331	IL	13/03/89
321 332	IL	16/03/89
321 333	IL	21/03/89
321 334	IL	29/03/89
321 335	IL	06/04/89
321 336	IL	07/04/89
321 337	IL	11/04/89
321 338	IL	14/04/89
321 339	IL	21/04/89
321 340	BY	03/05/89
321 341	BY	05/05/89
321 342	BY	04/05/89
321 343	BY	08/05/89
321 344	BY	14/06/89
321 345	BY	19/05/89
321 346	BY	31/05/89
321 401	BY	06/07/89
321 402	BY	06/07/89
321 403	BY	07/06/89
321 404	BY	07/06/89
321 405	BY	16/07/89
321 406	BY	14/07/89
321 407	BY	20/07/89
321 408	BY	24/07/89
321 409	BY	02/08/89
321 410	BY	04/08/89
321 411	BY	08/08/89
321 412	BY	10/08/89
321 413	BY	30/08/89
321 414	BY	30/08/89
321 415	BY	25/08/89
321 416	BY	31/08/89
321 417	BY	01/09/89
321 418	BY	06/09/89
321 419	BY	08/09/89
321 420	BY	12/09/89
321 421	BY	15/09/89
321 422	BY	20/09/89
321 423	BY	25/09/89
321 424	BY	/10/89
321 425	BY	03/10/89
321 426	BY	09/10/89
321 427	BY	13/10/89
321 428	BY	17/10/89
321 429	BY	23/10/89
321 430	BY	/11/89
321 431	BY	/11/89
321 432	BY	/11/89
321 433	BY	/11/89
321 434	BY	/11/89
321 435	BY	/12/89
321 436	BY	/12/89
321 437	BY	04/12/89
321 438	BY	07/12/89
321 439	BY	11/12/89
321 440	BY	13/12/89
321 441	BY	15/12/89
321 442	BY	18/12/89
321 443	BY	20/12/89
483 001	RY	13/07/89
483 002	RY	25/09/89
483 003	RY	02/10/89
483 004	RY	02/10/89

The following units were new in 1988 but not shown in the last edition:

November: 321 301, 321 302.
December: 321 306, 321 308, 321 309, 321 310, 321 311, 2422.

Vehicles Reinstated

70824	BM	/01/89
70827	BM	/06/89
70845	BM	/01/89
70859	BM	/06/89
76323	BM	02/10/89
77106	SL	/09/89
77111	SL	/09/89

Vehicles Withdrawn

47	RY	/07/89
55	WC	21/09/89
71	WC	10/11/89
79	WC	21/09/89
14575	SU	01/12/89
61092	IL	02/01/89
61094	IL	21/09/89
61096	IL	19/04/89
61097	IL	21/09/89
61100	IL	17/04/89
61102	IL	21/09/89
61103	IL	21/09/89
61104	IL	21/09/89
61105	IL	21/09/89
61106	IL	21/09/89
61107	EM	21/09/89
61108	EM	21/09/89
61115	IL	21/09/89
61117	IL	21/09/89
61123	IL	21/09/89
61124	IL	21/09/89
61127	IL	21/09/89
61128	IL	21/09/89
61129	IL	21/09/89
61130	IL	21/09/89
61194	EM	21/09/89
61198	IL	21/09/89
61198	IL	21/09/89
61198	IL	21/09/89
61204	EM	02/01/89
61205	IL	21/09/89
61206	IL	21/09/89
61207	EM	21/09/89
61211	EM	21/09/89
61212	EM	21/09/89
61213	IL	21/09/89
61215	EM	21/09/89
61218	EM	21/09/89
61463	IL	11/04/89
61485	GW	15/11/89
61506	GW	19/05/89
61511	GW	27/07/89
61533	SG	17/04/89
61812	LG	26/10/89
61817	LG	26/10/89
61818	GW	15/11/89
61820	GW	09/03/89
61826	LG	26/10/89
61829	LG	26/10/89
61833	LG	26/10/89
61840	GW	09/03/89
61843	LG	26/10/89
61844	GW	15/11/89
61847	GW	02/11/89
61854	LG	26/10/89
61857	GW	15/11/89
61862	GW	15/11/89
62124	BM	11/04/89
62146	BM	11/04/89
62163	GW	15/11/89
62165	GW	09/03/89
62166	GW	09/03/89
62168	GW	15/11/89
62172	GW	09/03/89
62368	BI	11/04/89
69022	BM	09/05/89
69023	BM	09/03/89
69024	BM	08/11/89
69025	BM	08/11/89
69321	BM	11/04/89
69325	BM	09/03/89
70067	IL	21/09/89
70090	IL	21/09/89
70092	IL	21/09/89
70094	IL	21/09/89
70096	IL	21/09/89
70100	IL	21/09/89
70102	IL	21/09/89
70104	IL	21/09/89
70105	IL	21/09/89
70106	IL	21/09/89
70107	EM	21/09/89
70112	IL	21/09/89
70113	EM	21/09/89
70115	IL	21/09/89
70124	IL	21/09/89
70127	IL	21/09/89
70128	IL	21/09/89
70129	IL	21/09/89
70132	EM	21/09/89
70194	EM	21/09/89
70195	EM	21/09/89
70201	IL	21/09/89
70205	IL	21/09/89
70206	IL	21/09/89
70207	EM	21/09/89
70211	EM	21/09/89
70212	EM	21/09/89
70227	EM	21/09/89
70784	BM	11/04/89
70803	BM	11/04/89
70818	BM	07/11/89
70820	BM	07/11/89
70831	BM	07/11/89
70837	BM	07/11/89
70842	BM	07/11/89
70846	BM	07/11/89
70850	BM	07/11/89
70854	BM	07/11/89
70857	BM	07/11/89
70863	BM	07/11/89
70884	BM	11/04/89
71000	WD	14/12/89
71048	BI	11/04/89
71156	BM	07/11/89
71164	BM	07/11/89
75204	IL	19/04/89
75206	IL	19/04/89
75208	IL	19/04/89
75210	IL	21/09/89
75214	IL	11/04/89
75230	IL	21/09/89
75231	IL	21/09/89
75238	IL	21/09/89
75239	IL	02/01/89
75241	IL	21/09/89
75242	IL	21/09/89
75243	IL	21/09/89
75246	EM	21/09/89
75251	EM	21/09/89
75252	EM	02/01/89
75254	IL	21/09/89
75255	IL	21/09/89
75262	IL	21/09/89
75263	IL	21/09/89
75264	EM	21/09/89
75268	EM	21/09/89
75278	IL	19/04/89
75284	EM	21/09/89
75290	IL	21/09/89
75291	IL	21/09/89
75293	IL	21/09/89
75294	IL	21/09/89
75295	IL	21/09/89
75296	EM	21/09/89
75300	EM	21/09/89
75302	EM	21/09/89
75304	IL	21/09/89
75305	IL	21/09/89
75307	EM	21/09/89
75313	IL	21/09/89
75314	IL	17/04/89
75315	IL	21/09/89
75318	IL	21/09/89
75320	EM	21/09/89
75321	EM	21/09/89
75327	EM	19/04/89
75333	IL	19/04/89
75337	EM	18/12/89
75338	IL	21/09/89
75339	EM	21/09/89
75342	IL	21/09/89
75343	EM	21/09/89
75345	IL	21/09/89
75351	EM	21/09/89
75360	IL	21/09/89
75496	IL	11/04/89
75548	IL	11/04/89
75570	GW	15/11/89
75591	GW	19/05/89
75596	GW	15/11/89
75598	GW	15/11/89
75605	GW	15/11/89
75615	GW	09/03/89
75631	GW	09/03/89
75633	GW	15/11/89
75746	LG	26/10/89
75751	LG	26/10/89
75754	GW	09/03/89
75758	GW	15/11/89
75760	LG	26/10/89
75763	LG	26/10/89
75767	LG	26/10/89
75774	GW	09/03/89
75777	LG	26/10/89
75778	GW	15/11/89
75781	GW	02/11/89
75788	LG	26/10/89
75791	GW	15/11/89
75796	GW	15/11/89
75802	LG	26/10/89
75807	LG	26/10/89
75814	GW	15/11/89
75816	LG	26/10/89
75819	LG	26/10/89
75823	LG	26/10/89
75830	GW	27/04/89
75833	LG	26/10/89
75834	GW	15/11/89
75837	GW	02/11/89
75844	LG	26/10/89
75847	GW	15/11/89
75852	GW	15/11/89
76237	BM	11/04/89
76281	BM	07/11/89
76282	BM	07/11/89
76285	BM	07/11/89
76286	BM	07/11/89
76300	BM	02/01/89
76307	BM	07/11/89
76308	BM	07/11/89
76319	BM	07/11/89
76320	BM	07/11/89
76323	BM	20/09/89
76329	BM	07/11/89
76330	BM	07/11/89
76357	BM	11/04/89
76403	GW	15/11/89
76405	GW	27/04/89
76406	GW	27/04/89
76408	GW	15/11/89
76412	GW	27/04/89
76422	GW	15/11/89
76424	GW	27/04/89
76425	GW	27/04/89
76427	GW	15/11/89
76431	GW	15/11/89
76730	BI	11/04/89
76801	BI	11/04/89
76816	BI	03/11/89
76945	BM	07/11/89
76946	BM	07/11/89

NPCCS

New

82102	WB	06/02/89
82103	WB	06/02/89
82104	WB	06/02/89
82105	WB	15/02/89
82106	WB	20/02/89
82107	WB	20/03/89
82108	WB	30/03/89
82109	WB	18/04/89
82110	OY	25/04/89
82111	OY	22/05/89
82112	OY	22/05/89
82113	OY	13/06/89
82114	OY	13/06/89
82115	OY	13/06/89
82116	OY	04/07/89
82117	WB	18/08/89
82118	WB	04/07/89
82119	OY	11/07/89
82120	OY	31/07/89
82121	OY	31/07/89
82122	OY	31/07/89
82123	WB	05/10/89
82124	OY	18/08/89
82125	WB	16/08/89
82126	WB	20/09/89
82127	WB	05/10/89
82128	WB	20/09/89
82129	WB	05/10/89
82130	WB	05/10/89
82131	WB	05/10/89
82200	BN	27/07/89
82201	BN	24/08/89
82202	BN	14/09/89
82203	BN	12/10/89
82204	BN	31/10/89
82205	BN	30/11/89
82206	BN	13/12/89

Reinstated

93646	EN	25/03/89

Withdrawn

80537	CA	11/08/89
80743	HT	10/08/89
80965	IS	07/06/89
84084	CA	10/11/89
84090	DY	04/01/89
84093	CA	04/10/89
84111	BJ	09/05/89
84141	BN	19/04/89
84152	CA	15/08/89
84328	BJ	04/10/89
84330	CA	15/08/89
84433	EH	19/04/89
84449	BJ	11/08/89
84462	BJ	24/10/89
92191	EN	11/08/89
93148	CA	24/10/89
93242	CA	21/09/89
93472	CA	21/12/89
93778	BJ	24/10/89
93941	BJ	04/10/89
94057	CA	09/05/89
94075	CA	17/07/89
96250	WB	30/03/89
96251	WB	30/03/89
96252	WB	30/03/89
96253	WB	30/03/89
96254	WB	30/03/89
96255	WB	30/03/89
96256	WB	30/03/89
96257	WB	30/03/89
96258	WB	30/03/89
96259	WB	30/03/89
96260	WB	30/03/89
96261	WB	30/03/89
96262	WB	30/03/89
96263	WB	30/03/89
96264	WB	30/03/89
96265	WB	30/03/89
99624	SA	20/06/89

Renumbered

93385 to 96160
93646 to 96163
93647 to 96162
93756 to 96167
93782 to 96178
93784 to 96165
93834 to 96166
93843 to 96180
93875 to 96181
93880 to 96164
93910 to 96179
93937 to 96169
93944 to 96182
93978 to 96168
93980 to 96177

BR Namings and Denamings

LOCOMOTIVES NAMED DURING 1989

No.	Name	Place	Date
08647	Crimpsall	BRML Doncaster	11/05
08691	ESCAFELD	Tinsley TMD	/12
09026	William Pearson	Redbridge	04/03
31201	Fina Energy	Immingham TMD	/03
33025	Sultan	Eastleigh TMD	/01
33207	Earl Mountbatten of Burma	Eastleigh TMD	08/08
37113	Radio Highland	BRML Doncaster	21/08
37702	Taff Merthyr	Cardiff Canton TMD	20/11
43023	County of Cornwall	Truro	30/11
43032	The Royal Regiment of Wales	Cardiff Central	05/12
43106	Songs of Praise	York	13/06
43108	BBC Television Railwatch (Temporary Name)	London King's Cross	13/02
43109	Yorkshire Evening Press	York	15/05
43114	The National Garden Festival Gateshead 1990	London King's Cross	10/08
43115	Yorkshire Cricket Academy	Leeds	07/06
43169	The National Trust	London Paddington	14/07
47010	Xancidae	Crewe TMD (D)	/05
47210	Blue Circle Cement	Eastfield TMD	23/12
47527	Kettering	Kettering	05/05
47528	The Queen's Own Mercian Yeomanry	Worcester Shrub Hill	10/11
47586	Northamptonshire	Wellingborough	20/09
47803	Woman's Guild	Eastfield TMD	/06
47831	Bolton Wanderer	Bolton	09/06
56012	Maltby Colliery	Maltby Colliery	22/06
56030	Eggborough Power Station	Eggborough PS	02/09
56062	Mountsorrel	Mountsorrel	21/03
56080	Selby Coalfield	Gascoigne Wood Colliery	30/10
56091	Castle Donington Power Station	Castle Donington PS	18/06
56093	The Institution of Mining Engineers	London Euston	29/11
56099	Fiddlers Ferry Power Station	Fidlers Ferry PS	15/07
58019	Shirebrook Colliery	Shirebrook Colliery	01/10
60001	Steadfast	Brush Works	/06
60002	Capability Brown	Brush Works	/08
60003	Christopher Wren	Brush Works	/11
60004	Lochnagar	Brush Works	/08
60005	Skiddaw	Brush Works	/10
60006	Great Gable	Brush Works	/11
60007	Robert Adam	Brush Works	/11
60011	Cader Idris	Brush Works	/12
86401	Northampton Town	Northampton	13/05
89001	Avocet	London King's Cross	16/01
90001	BBC Midlands Today	Birmingham International	28/09
90009	Royal Show	London Euston	21/05
90010	275 Railway Squadron (Volunteers)	London Euston	15/11
90015	BBC North West	Carlisle	25/10
91001	Swallow	London King's Cross	20/09
91004	The Red Arrows	London King's Cross	07/11
97561	Midland Counties Railway 1839–1989	Derby	23/05

LOCOMOTIVE NAMES REMOVED DURING 1989

No.	Name	Date
31309	Cricklewood	/12
33027	Earl Mountbatten of Burma	/08
33114	Sultan	/01
37188	Jimmy Shand	/05
37260	Radio Highland	/08
37412	Loch Lomond	14/05
43017	HTV WEST	/05
43019	City of Swansea/Dinas Abertawe	/06
43038	National Railway Museum The First Ten Years 1975–1985	/11
43047	Rotherham Enterprise	/06
43051	The Duke and Duchess of York	/01
43057	Bounds Green	/10
43064	City of York	/10
43077	County of Nottingham	/05
43085	City of Bradford	/11
43088	XIII Commonwealth Games Scotland 1986	/02
43093	York Festival '88	
43113	City of Newcastle Upon Tyne	05/03
43116	City of Kingston upon Hull	/08
43122	South Yorkshire Metropolitan County	/08
43124	B.B.C. Points West	11/02
43151	Blue Peter II	/11
43152	St Peters School York AD 627	/05
43153	University of Durham	/07
43196	The Newspaper Society FOUNDED 1836	/02
47010	Xancidae	28/10
47119	Arcidae	/10
47611	Thames	/10
47612	TITAN	/10
47613	NORTH STAR	/11
47623	VULCAN	/07
47628	SIR DANIEL GOOCH	/12
47705	Lothian	/05
47714	Grampian Region	/02
47826	Springburn	/11
47831	Woman's Guild	/05
47836	Fair Rosamund	/09
47839	Royal County of Berkshire	/12
47841	The Institution of Mechanical Engineers	/12
56035	Taff Merthyr	/07
56124	Blue Circle Cement	/10
56132	Fina Energy	/03

On, arguably, the most important day for InterCity since the introduction of HSTs between Bristol and London in October 1976, the InterCity 225 concept is launched with the naming of the first Class 91 locomotive 'Swallow', before a press run to Leeds and back. At King's Cross on 21st September are James Prior, chairman of GEC (speaking), Sir Robert Reid, BR chairman (right) and Dr. John Prideaux, director InterCity.   *Peter Fox*

MULTIPLE UNIT CARS NAMED DURING 1989

No.	Name	Place	Date
62937	BEAULIEU	Brockenhurst	30/06
62938	COUNTY OF HAMPSHIRE	Eastleigh	07/04
62955	BBC SOUTH TODAY	Southampton Central	05/09
71776	Partnership for Progress	Selhurst TMD	06/10
71891	Southend-on-Sea	Southend Victoria	11/10

LOCOMOTIVE MISCELLANY

▲Six Class 20 locomotives have been sold to Hunslet-Barclay for use on weedkilling trains and reclassified 20/9. The trains are operated either by Chipman's or Schering's. The Schering train is a new train made up of converted Mark 1 coaches and makes a fine sight in this view taken at Lockwood Viaduct on 22nd June. The locomotives in use are 20902 and 20903. The train originated at Healey Mills and should have run the previous day, but was cancelled because of a strike. *David Rodgers*

▲British Rail Research-allocated Class 47/4 No. 97561 was painted maroon for the occasion of the 150th anniversary of the Midland Counties Railway. It was also named 'Midland Counties Railway 1839–1989'. The loco is seen passing Bordesley Junction on an excursion from Derby to Bristol on 30th May. *Chris Morrison*

◄Two Class 47/7s were transferred from the Scottish Region to Old Oak Common depot for Network SouthEast services, their push-pull equipment not being used. 47714 is on InterCity duty as it hauls a motley collection of Mark 1 stock past Slough forming the 09.06 Swansea–Paddington on 22nd May. *Brian Denton*

Preservation Scene

1989 is probably a year many in the preservation movement would rather forget. Declining living standards prompted by rises in interest rates meant that the public had less money to spend on leisure activities. The support for main line steam hauled excursions in particular saw a catastrophic drop due to a continuation of high fares, unattractive itineraries and, from some cities, difficulty of access. Perhaps predictably the preserved lines offering travel at the lower end of the fare scale suffered less; indeed a number reported a significant rise in the number of tickets sold. A notable example was the West Somerset Railway whose receipts increased by a phenomenal 25% although it is certain that the presence of 'EVENING STAR' on the line for the summer season had some beneficial effect. Other lines, notably the Kent and East Sussex were financially embarrassed as a result of the government's Education Reform Act which resulted in a dramatic fall in the number of school visits. In contrast with previous years there have been fewer new share flotations to raise capital but those carrying over from 1988 reached their targets. The Peak Rail issue had reached £200,000 by April, the WSR issue raised £352,000 while the same sum was realised for the SVR Boiler Shop appeal. The latter was formally opened by ScotRail chairman and owner of A4 No. 60009, John Cameron on 14th July. A sum of £306,500 changed hands in March when the Brecon Mountain Railway at last became the new owners of the Vale of Rheidol narrow gauge line. The Strathspey Railway, under the banner of the Highland Locomotive Company, announced a rights issue of 4,000 ordinary shares at £5 each while the Cholsey and Wallingford launched an appeal for £60,000 over three years to finance capital work.

More modest financial locomotive appeals were for £20,000 by the Scottish Railway Preservation Society for the restoration of 'MAUDE' and for £15,000 by the Humberside loco preservation group for the completion of the restoration of No. 777 'SIR LAMIEL', and £60,000 for the repair to main line order of 'KING GEORGE V'. Still on financial matters, in the autumn there was a long overdue attempt to coax more passengers on to steamhauled excursions by introducing graduated fare structures on the North Wales and Cumbrian Mountain Expresses.

◀Now there are *two* fully restored Kings! At long last the efforts of the volunteers of the Buckinghamshire Railway Society were rewarded when No. 6024 'KING EDWARD I' was returned to steam and rededicated by the Duke of Gloucester at a special ceremony on 25th April. The King was on show alongside Castles Nos. 5080 'DEFIANT' and 7029 'CLUN CASTLE' at Tyseley's 'Castles and King' weekend of 15th October. Meanwhile the third of the surviving King trio, No. 6023 'KING EDWARD II', was on the move from Bristol Temple Meads to Didcot.   *Stephen Hansford*

▼Over the years many preserved steam locomotives have crossed Mytholmes Viaduct on the KWVR but a notable addition to the list was V2 2–6–2 No. 4771 'GREEN ARROW' on 13th May. The engine was stabled overnight at Haworth after working a southbound Cumbrian Mountain Express earlier in the day; its first trip over the line for almost ten years.   *D.C. Rodgers*

There is little doubt that the reintroduction of regular steam services to the North Wales holiday resorts and Holyhead was the most eagerly-awaited event of the year. Initial fears of financial disaster, prompted by poor loading statistics, were quickly dispelled during the school holiday period. On the other side of the country however the fortunes of steam-hauled trains to Scarborough reached an absolute nadir. Most were cancelled through lack of support and at the time of writing it seems unlikely that Scarborough will feature regularly in the 1990 steam programme.

STEAM LOCOMOTIVES

The year brought the usual crop of new steam locomotives out on to the main line. 'TAW VALLEY', 'BURTON AGNES HALL', 'GREEN ARROW' and 'BAHAMAS' have all performed well but the limelight was certainly stolen by the surprise appearance of 'THE GREAT MARQUESS' in early July when it was hurriedly moved north to Scotland for two weeks' activity on the Mallaig line. A move which provided the rare spectacle of no fewer than three steam locomotives, Nos. 3442, 5407 and 44871 at Fort William. LMS enthusiasts were however disappointed by the news that the long-awaited return to traffic of 'DUCHESS OF HAMILTON' would not now take place until 1990.

There was also the usual batch of steam newcomers to the preserved lines, some after very lengthy overhaul periods. These included: Terrier No. 11 (in Isle of Wight Central Railway livery) on the Isle of Wight Railway; pannier tanks No. 5764 on the SVR and No. 5786 to Bulmers Railway Centre, Hereford; BR Class 4MT 2–6–0 No. 76079 on the ELR; GWR 2–6–2T No. 4561 on the WSR; Turkish Stanier 8F No. 45160 on the Swanage Railway; Class N7 0–6–2T No. 69621 at the East Anglian Railway Museum and last, but certainly not least, King No. 6024 'KING EDWARD I' at the Buckinghamshire Railway Centre.

Out of main line service was A4 'SIR NIGEL GRESLEY' which suffered a cracked boiler end plate while working an excursion in the spring.

The visit of Class 5 No. 44932 to various Middlesex locations of the Southern Region in the late autumn was a pleasant surprise for many. It would appear that steam and third rail electrification are not mutually exclusive after all!

A new BR requirement was for newly-renovated steam locomotives to undergo a loaded test run, generally between Derby and Sheffield, before they could be passed for main-line running. The first such test run was on 19th May with 'Jubilee' Class 4–6–0 No. 45596 'BAHAMAS'.

New developments in the engineering side of the business included the manufacture of a brand new lead driving axle for 'UNION OF SOUTH AFRICA' by Ring Rolled Products Ltd. of Rotherham. It even transpired that discounts were now being sought for bulk order of quite major parts. No fewer than 21 connecting rods were ordered from John Hesketh & Son for fitment to former BR Standard locomotives.

The Barry saga, at long last, came to an end during the year when GW 2–8–0 No. 3845 left for Brighton. GWR 2–6–2T No. 5553 remains, and will be displayed at Barry as a permanent reminder of the tremendous contribution Dai Woodham has made to the railway preservation movement.

The year also saw a growing trend to change the identity of locomotives. Apart from the well-known identity problems of the GCR Class N2 tank and A4 'BITTERN', S&D No. 53808 switched to sister engine No. 53807 for a period to commemorate 25 years since the last 7F ran on the Somerset and Dorset.

For two weeks in mid July the Glens of the West Highland extension echoed once again to the Gresley three cylinder beat. Class K4 2–6–0 No. 3442 'THE GREAT MARQUESS' takes its six coach BR train up the bank to Glenfinnan on 24th July.   *A.J. Woof*

▲ 'TAW VALLEY' was the latest Bulleid Pacific to obtain a main line ticket in 1989 when it was soon drafted into the small pool of locomotives earmarked to work the new BR sponsored North Wales Coast expresses. Passenger receipts during the early weeks of operation were disappointing when there was even talk of some cancellations but in the event loadings were excellent during the school holiday period – in spite of the best summer for many a year. On the return leg on 19th July No. 34027 was caught by the camera passing Abergele at speed. *L.A. Nixon*

◄ Back home! 'FLYING SCOTSMAN' is hoisted on to dry land at Tilbury on 14th December after its six week voyage home from Sydney, Australia. Urgent repairs will be undertaken at Southall during the winter months and it is hoped to have her back on the main line by early summer 1990; possibly in lined BR brunswick green.

C.J. Marsden

▶ The Swanage Railway's Turkish Class 8F 2–8–0 No. 45160 arrived in Britain at Immingham (of all places!) on 11th June and was moved by road later in the month to Dorset. The engine must have passed within a mile or two of Swanage as it sailed up the English Channel. The locomotive was found to be in good mechanical order and was soon in steam making its inaugural movements on the line during the Steam Gala weekend on 16th September.

Mervyn Turvey

Table of Steam Locomotive Movements:

3217 Didcot to Bluebell Railway
3440 Didcot to Utrecht (NS 150) and back
3822 Nene Valley to Didcot
3862 Barry to Northampton Steam Railway
4141 SVR to Swindon
5199 Wolverhampton to Llangollen
5080 Tyseley to GCR to Tyseley
5952 Gloucestershire and Warwickshire to Llangollen
6023 Bristol to Didcot
6106 KWVR to GCR to Didcot
7027 Tyseley to Buckfastleigh
7752 Tyseley to Swanage
7760 Tyseley to Llangollen
7821 Gwili to Llangollen
9466 Dean Forest to Swindon
9642 BP Chemicals, Baglan Bay to Swansea Vale Railway
9681 Dean Forest to Swindon

  926 USA to Sail and Steam Brightlingsea to Pickering
32640 KESR No. 10 to Tyseley
34027 SVR to Crewe to Southall
35005 Steamtown to GCR
35011 Barry to Preston Park

5231 GCR to Nene Valley
5305 Hull to Fort William
5593 Tyseley to GCR
5596 Dinting to Steamtown
6115 Dinting to Tyseley
44871 Steamtown to Fort William to Steamtown
46443 SVR to Swanage
46464 Strathspey to Brechin

 1306 GCR to Hull Dairycoates
 3442 SVR to Fort William to SVR
 4472 Sydney to Southall
60009 Markinch to SVR
60019 NRM to Tyne and Wear Stephenson Museum

65894 NYMR to Tyne & Wear Stephenson Museum
69023 NYMR to Didcot then North Norfolk Railway

92220 NRM to West Somerset Railway

DIESEL

It has been a quieter year on the modern traction front. In contrast to 1988 when Class 45s and surviving Class 25 and 40s were ready targets for preservation bids there was no major BR class to become extinct. Nevertheless a few ex-BR locomotives were transferred to preservation sites from industrial locations.

Table of Diesel Locomotive Movements

(Movement of Locomotives for open days/diesel weekends not listed)

D99 to Peak Rail, Matlock
D2059 Colchester to IOWR
D3476 Fowey to South Yorkshire Railway Museum
D7671 Derby to Midland Railway Centre
D8233 ELR to Mangapps Farm Railway
07001 RMC Roadstone, Peak Dale to South Yorkshire Railway.
12074 Swalwell Disposal Point to South Yorkshire Railway
12088 Swalwell Disposal Point to South Yorkshire Railway
24061 Vic Berry's for preservation
27000 to Utrecht (NS 150) and onto Ilford
40012 to Midland Railway Centre

MAIN LINE COACHING STOCK

The prestige coaching formations continued to catch the public eye. The VSOE set extensively roamed the BR network but it was unusually noted on the Mid Hants Railway hauled by a BR Class 47 No. 47833 in connection with the making of the film 'Bullseye'. It was also announced that 1989 would be the last year when the early 1960s preserved coaching stock comprising 2 x SK, 2 x SLF and BSK would be used in the Royal Scotsman formation.

PRESERVED LINE PROGRESS

During the year there was the usual frenzied activity in some quarters constructing new lines. Work progressed on the extension on the IOWR to Smallbrook, to East Grinstead on the Bluebell, to Northiam on the Kent and East Sussex, to the Deeside loop on the Llangollen Railway, to Birkhill and Manuel on the Forth Valley line, to Conwil on the Gwili Railway, and Holywell Halt to Draughton on the Yorkshire Dales Railway. The first train ran the full eight mile length of the East Lancashire Railway from Bury to Rawtenstall on 5th November. A brand new line was the laying of the first section of Peak Rail's track, from Darley Dale almost to Matlock. In East Anglia the first track was laid at County School station on the Wensum Valley Railway on the old Norwich–Wells branch. A totally new standard gauge preservation centre to open its doors was John Jolly's Mangapps Farm Railway at Burnham-on-Crouch. A notable development in the south east was the commencement of track relaying in the old steam shed at Tunbridge Wells by the Tunbridge Wells and Eridge Preservation Society.

The Department of Transport awarded Light Railway Orders to the operators of two former GW branches; the Cholsey and Wallingford and the Bodmin and Wenford lines. The latter also became one of the few preserved lines to carry freight traffic when in early December the first revenue earning freight, comprising two VGAs hauled by a Class 08, travelled the branch to Bodmin Parkway.

A surprising development early in the year was the announcement that the landlord of the Dinting Railway Centre, Jack Warburton, had decided to evict the preservation group; formal notice was given that all locomotives and exhibits were to be moved forthwith. Former Dinting based engines which have already made the move include 'BAHAMAS' and 'SCOTS GUARDSMAN'.

Significant structures on the move in the year included Frome North signal box to Didcot to complement the earlier acquisition from Radstock North. Further north the redundant box at Bamford was relocated at Darley Dale, Matlock. Deep in the south Brading box was moved for eventual use at Smallbrook. The pre-war W.H. Smith bookstall at Manchester Victoria station was donated to the SVR and moved to Kidderminster. Another significant Peak Rail acquisition was a bridge from Hull which was moved to Derbyshire where, in the long term, it is to be used to span the A6 at Rowsley. By far and away the most impressive achievement in this field though was the erection of a brand new, but home made, coaler at Grosmont depot on the NYMR. Even BR, courtesy of local councils, made a token gesture to the continued well-being of main line steam when they formally opened the new triangle at Valley, Holyhead on 20th June.

On the station front Irwell was opened on the ELR Rawtenstall extension. Freshfield Halt on the Bluebell was closed and demolished but another halt was built at Ketches Farm close to Sheffield Park. Ingrow West on the KWVR was formally opened on 22nd July. The old station at Monifieth, formerly on the Dundee–Arbroath line, finally found a permanent home at Birkhill on the Bo'ness Railway. Yet another interesting development was the BR approval, at least in principle, of the Strathspey Railway's proposal that they might be allowed to use the rarely-used platform 4 of Aviemore station.

The Bo'ness line in Scotland extended its sphere of activity when its long awaited extension to Birkhill was formally opened on the 25th March. The new station, seen here with Caledonian Railway 0-4-4T No. 419 waiting to depart with a train for Bo'ness, was formerly at the 1988 Glasgow Garden Festival and before that was the BR station at Monifieth. At the close of the year work on the further extension to the main line at Manuel was well advanced. By this time ScotRail had already installed a connection with the main line via a ground frame electrically operated from Polmont panel.

L.A. Nixon

▲ Peak Rail has made steady progress towards its first objective of restoring a public passenger service to the Matlock–Darley Dale section of the old Midland main line to Buxton. Starting from Darley Dale level crossing the rails at the time of writing were within 3/4 mile of linking up with BR at Matlock. The redundant signal box from Bamford in the Hope Valley has been bought and, as seen here, installed at the southern end of the up platform where it will eventually be used to control movements over the crossing. It is hoped that an LRO will be granted in 1990 with passenger services operating by early summer.   *L.A. Nixon*

►▲ There will no doubt be those who are none too happy with the new SVR boiler shop which has just been built to the north of Bridgnorth station. It certainly appears to dominate the scene and is hardly compatible with the steam age era but it is a vital asset to the steam preservation movement. The shop was pictured nearing completion on 13th May.   *Stephen Widdowson*

► One of the interesting preservation movements during the year was the transfer of the 1930s-style W.H. Smith bookstall from Manchester Victoria station to Kidderminster. It was donated to the SVR on 27th September where it has been restored to its original dark green livery complete with roller blinds. With so much emphasis today on the preservation of locomotives and rolling stock it is a pleasure to find that some of the peripheral items of railwayana are being saved for posterity.
Stephen Widdowson

▲ A new standard gauge preservation scheme for 1989 is at Mangapps Farm near Burnham on Crouch where there is a collection of rolling stock and railway ephemera together with a mock up Great Eastern style station. It was opened on August Bank Holiday Monday to coincide with the nearby centenary celebrations at Southend. Arguably the star attraction is the former BR Class 15 BTH type 1 seen on the left of this picture. On the right is Bagnall built 0–6–0ST 'DEMEIZA' ex-NCB Cadley Hill colliery. At the time of writing the running line extends to 600 yards.

M.J. Collins

◀On 15th May, the Llangollen Railway ran a freight train privately-hired for photographic purposes. It is seen just beyond Dee Bridge hauled by GWR 0-6-0PT No. 7760.

Doug Birmingham

On a sadder note there were a number of tragic deaths which included Richard Levick who was killed in a workshop accident at Butterley on 17th August; former boiler inspector Jack Street who died (24th April) on the footplate of 'PRINCESS ELIZABETH' and Lord Lindlay (31st July) owner of 'THE GREAT MARQUESS'. Particular reference however must be made to the passing of two of the most respected railway photographers of the 50s and 60s; Ivo Peters who died on 7th June and W.J.V. (Bill) Anderson whose death occurred on the 23rd September. Both will be long remembered and new generations will know of them through their everlasting classic railway photographs of the Somerset & Dorset and Scotland.

Preservation personalities in the news were Les Barwick who was awarded a BEM for 20 years of continuous work on the permanent way of the North York Moors Railway. Twenty years was also the time span of Dr Peter Beet's association with Steamtown. In 1989 he announced that he was to sever his links with the centre and transfer his locomotives (Ivatt No. 46441, SNCF 231K Pacific and DB 01.10 Pacific) probably to the Crewe Heritage Centre. Indeed the whole future of Steamtown began to look a little insecure; other assets up for grabs included their former Old Oak Common steam crane, for sale at £20,000. Meanwhile Peak Rail managed to acquire Toton's redundant 36-ton steam crane ADRC 95223 which was moved to Matlock in the autumn.

MUSEUMS

The National Railway Museum, perhaps unintentionally, hit the enthusiast headlines in 1989. First there came the bombshell that 'DUCHESS OF HAMILTON' would be un-

likely to be restored to running order until 1990 and even then it would be restricted to a nominal four or five runs per year. It was announced that the Leeman Road building, formerly York steam shed, would have to be closed for urgent roof repairs. While the old exhibition hall was repaired it was disclosed that there would be a new alternative display entitled 'The Great Railway Show' on the other side of Leeman Road in the Sir Peter Allen building. In the autumn work started on the construction of a new pedestrian tunnel to link the two sites and plans were well-advanced for the temporary transfer, early in the New Year, of some of the major exhibits to Swindon. Controversy with a capital C however centred on the museum's decision to eliminate one of the two turntables from the old exhibition hall. The enthusiast movement was almost universal in its condemnation of the proposal; some of the more polite phrases voiced included 'official vandalism' and 'total irresponsibility'.

Other museum news included the transfer of A4 No. 60019, masquerading as No. 2509, from the NYMR to the Tyne and Wear Stephenson Museum. The NRM also decided it was time to change the exhibit at Darlington station; NER 0–6–0 No. 1275 had been there since the Rainhill celebrations of 1975 and its place was taken by NER 2–4–0 No. 910. At the Birmingham Railway Museum permission was granted by BR for passenger services to use the new Tyseley (Warwick Road) station. Meanwhile, Bressingham finally became the legal owners of Terrier 0–6–0 No.672 'MARTELLO', Class B4 0–4–0T No. 102 'GRANVILLE', 6233 'DUCHESS OF SUTHERLAND' and Scot No. 46100 'ROYAL SCOT'.

▶ In 1989 the County of Cornwall got its first operational standard gauge preserved railway when the Bodmin and Wenford Railway was awarded its Light Railway Order on 31st August. 'ALFRED', the diminutive Bagnall 0–4–0ST from the Port of Par, is hardly appropriate power for this steeply graded line although it was giving short brake van rides at Bodmin General station when this picture was taken on 31st July. The line has already achieved a unique status in that it carries freight traffic to the main line at Bodmin Parkway. The first revenue earning freight, comprising two 18-tonne VGA freight wagons loaded with light fittings from the factory of the FitzGerald Lighting Co., ran on 2nd December hauled by Class 08 No. 08444.

Stephen Widdowson

▶ Languishing in the shadow of nearby Didcot, the Cholsey and Wallingford Railway is finding the establishment of its line on the UK railway preservation map an uphill task. However the award of a Light Railway Order will mean that 1989 will go down as a significant date in their short history. The small band of volunteers have plenty of hard work ahead of them judging by this view of Wallingford terminus on 20th November. At the time of writing the railway is still looking for its first operational steam engine although some progress is being made on GW 2–8–0T No. 4247. The frames are presently receiving attention at Butterley. The future success of the line is seen by many to rely upon a positive BR decision to allow them to run into the long redundant bay platform at the main line station at Cholsey.   *L.A. Nixon*

1989 was also a unique year in that a British preserved steam locomotive broke several records, albeit on the other side of the world. 'FLYING SCOTSMAN' became the first steam engine to cross Australia unassisted, broke an Australian speed record at 88 mph while working a 360-ton train and set a new record of 422 miles for a non-stop run from Parkes to Broken Hill. The A3 returned to the UK in December when it was moved to Southall for the winter months.

The Dorset preserved line centred at Swanage moved from strength to strength with a £200,000 loan promised by the County Council to help them reach their Corfe Castle and Worgret Junction objectives. The line held their first steam gala weekend in September when the undoubted star attraction was their latest addition to stock in the shape of former Turkish Railways 8F No. 45160. Another steam engine imported from abroad was former South African Railway's Class 11 2–8–2 which is a new resident at the Buckinghamshire Railway Centre. Meanwhile in South Wales the Swansea Vale Railway acquired a secure base when it occupied a disused foundry near to the site of Upper Bank locomotive shed, Swansea. It was formally opened on 21st April when the new depot was home for 0–6–0PT No. 9642 and Austerity 0–6–0ST No. 3829 of 1955.

Plans to promote even more preserved lines were made public during the year. There was a serious bid to secure the threatened four-mile-long BR Princes Risborough–Chinnor branch and rumours persisted that both the Warcop and the former Hawes branches off the Settle & Carlisle line were being actively investigated as potential preservation projects. Interest in the latter was no doubt prompted by the welcome announcement from the Secretary of State for Transport on 11th April that this main-line route was not to close.

Diesel days continued to gain in popularity with even the NRM getting in on the act when Class 40 No. D200 and Class 03 No. 03090 made short runs up and down the yard on 1st May. Yet another Society to hold a successful diesel event was the Great Western at Didcot.

During the year there was the inevitable crop of major and minor centenary and sesquicentenary celebrations. Centenary events were held on the Chesham Metropolitan branch; at Southend to commemorate the opening of the lines to Shenfield and Southminster; on the West Highland when a special steam-hauled train was run from Fort William to Crianlarich to commemorate the cutting of the first sod in 1889. The 150-year event was the Midland Counties 150 jamborees centred on Derby and Nottingham although, not to be outdone, the south commemorated the formation of the London and South Western Railway.

A celebration of the 25th anniversary of the commissioning of a power station would seem to be one of the last events of the year you would expect to see reported in these columns. However, Padiham B power station celebrated the event in fine style over the weekend of 7th/8th October when no fewer than eight steam engines including 'Jinty' No. 7298 and 'BAHAMAS' were brought in to entertain the many visitors.

A novel development of 1989 which augurs well for the future of preserved main line steam operation in Scotland was the decision by ScotRail to hire Class 5 No.5305 for a period of four weeks for crew training in steam locomotive firing and driving techniques.

Finally reference must be made to the achievement of the KESR who obtained an ARPS awards in recognition of the line's contribution in bringing railway preservation into the public eye through the BBC TV series 'Challenge Anneka'.

ANNIVERSARY EVENTS

▲ The centenary of the Chesham Metropolitan branch was celebrated over the first two weekends of July. In addition to LT electric locomotive No. 12 'SARAH SIDDON', steam was represented in the shape of GW pannier tanks Nos. 9466 and 7715 (formerly London Transport No. L99) and Metropolitan 0–4–4T No. 1, all on contract hire from the Buckinghamshire Railway Centre. The steam locomotives were in operation on the Chesham to Wembley Park, Watford and Harrow on the Hill sections. In this delightful scene No. 1 leaves Watford for Chesham on 9th July.
Ian Cowley

▲ The main line outings of the Dinting restored double-chimneyed Jubilee 'BAHAMAS' gladdened the hearts of many enthusiasts during 1989. As forerunner to its memorable trips over the Settle & Carlisle No. 45596 worked from Derby–Didcot on 27th May. With not a leak of steam in sight it is pictured here pounding away from Derby en route to Burton and Birmingham.　　*L.A. Nixon*

▼ The Midland Counties 150 'Lincolnshire Poacher' excursions from Derby to Lincoln were poorly patronised – in contrast with the MC 150 Derby–Nottingham steam hauled shuttle services. Standard Class 4MT 2–6–4T No. 80080 waits at Derby for joining passengers from St Pancras with the morning departure for Lincoln on 3rd June.　　*A.O. Wynn*

▲ A surprising development of the year was the BR decision to introduce the railway equivalent of the MOT test for steam locomotives destined for main line use. Engines were required to deal with substantial trains of around ten bogies on a circular route from Derby via Chesterfield, Beighton and Sheffield. LNER Class K4 2–6–0 No. 3442 'THE GREAT MARQUESS' passed the test with flying colours on 30th June and is seen here easing its train into platform 6 at Sheffield for a water stop.   *L.A. Nixon*

▼ Another old faithful which returned to service after an absence of almost six years was Severn Valley pannier tank No. 5764. Portraying the perfect Great Western branch line scene it takes the evening autumn air with a Kidderminster–Arley local near Victoria Bridge on 24th September.   *L.A. Nixon*

BLACK 5s IN THE NEWS

▲Class 5 No. 5407 was a regular performer on the North Wales Coast Express during 1989. The loco makes a fine sight as it skirts the Irish Sea near Penmaenmawr on 8th August. Llandudno and Penmaenbach Point can be seen in the distance.
Doug Birmingham

► The 23rd October marked the centenary of the digging of the first sod on the route between Fort William and Crianlarich on the West Highland Railway. British Rail ran a four coach special to commemorate the occasion when Class 5 No. 5305 provided the motive power. The train is pictured arriving at Crianlarich. *Mervyn Turvey*

► Preserved steam is rarely allowed to wander on to Southern Region metals but in early December the 140th anniversary of the arrival of the railway at Windsor and Eton Riverside station was celebrated. In attendance was Butterley based Class 5 No. 44932 but here it is pictured at Richmond as part of a Richmond Victorial evening on 8th December. The locomotive also found its way to the end of the Shepperton branch early one morning! *Kevin Lane*

STEAM MISCELLANY

◄ Castle No. 5080 'DEFIANT' was one of the many steam locomotives on the move during the year when, during the summer, it became one of the star attractions at the Great Central Railway at Loughborough. It was in service during their 'Thomas the Tank Engine' weekend of 16th September when it and several other locos were adorned by funny faces. Purist enthusiasts may find this practice singularly unattractive but these events, aimed at the family market, pay handsome financial dividends. The Great Western Society event at Didcot attracted no fewer than 20,000 visitors over one weekend with up to three mile traffic jams in the nearby town. *L.A. Nixon*

► It is a long time since Ivatt Class 2 Mogul No. 46464 has been in the news. It has languished at Aviemore for many years following serious damage as a result of an attempt to raise steam with no water in the boiler. In 1989 it was on the move, hopefully to a more active future. The engine was pictured at Aviemore looking remarkably spick and span on 3rd June just prior to its move by road to Brechin. *L.A. Nixon*

◄ The end of an era. The 212th and very last steam locomotive to leave Dai Woodham's Barry scrapyard was the hulk of former Great Western 2–8–0 No. 3845, pictured here among the weeds on 21st June. When the engine left for Brighton on 9th November it concluded the Barry saga; just 21 years had elapsed since the first locomotive, KWVR Class 4F No. 43924, escaped in 1968. Your editor wonders how long it will be before TODAY'S RAILWAY REVIEW OF THE YEAR is reporting the first steaming of No. 3845. *Graham Scott-Lowe*

▲ A preservation moment to savour! Newly arrived from a sojourn on the Gwili Railway Manor No. 7828 'ODNEY MANOR' poses alongside sister locomotive No. 7822 'FOX-COTE MANOR' at Llangollen during their Great Western weekend on 18th June. Other recent GW transfers to Llangollen have included Hall No. 5952 'COGAN HALL' and Manor No. 7821 'DITCHEAT MANOR' from the Gloucester and Warwickshire Railway along with dismembered Class 5100 2–6–2T No. 5199 from Wolverhampton. The Hall has received a cosmetic repaint and is currently a static display at Llangollen.

A.O. Wynn

►No apologies are given for publishing yet another shot of Jubilee Class 4–6–0 No. 45596 'BAHAMAS', the return of a member of this class to the Settle & Carlisle line being too important to miss. 'BAHAMAS' is seen on 17th August 1989 crossing Ais Gill Viaduct on the Southbound 'Cumbrian Mountain Express'.

Doug Birmingham

DIESELS IN THE NEWS

▲ The second KWVR diesel weekend extravaganza featured green liveried locomotives which included East Lancs. Hymek No. D7076 and Class 24 No. D5054 along with Deltic No. D9016, Class 14 No. D9531 and Crewe Heritage Centre Class 47 No. D1842. In this scene the Hymek and Class 24 storm through Oakworth with a non-stop service on Saturday 11th November.   L.A. Nixon

▲ It doesn't seem all that long since Peaks were in everyday BR service but now preserved examples are in demand at Open Days and modern traction weekends on preserved lines. Matlock based Class 45 No. D100 'SHERWOOD FORESTER' made its first revenue earning visit to the Severn Valley for their October diesel weekend. Here it waits its next turn of duty at Bridgnorth while Western No. D1013 'WESTERN RANGER' departs with a train for Kidderminster. *P. Crumpton*

▲ The collection of ex-BR and industrial shunters continued to grow at the Meadowhall site of the South Yorkshire Railway. One of the more interesting arrivals in 1989 was Class 07 No. 07001 (D2985) from RMC Roadstone Peak Dale where it had been in service since 1978. *Brian Cuttell*

◄ En route to the Open Day at Coalville on 11th June are Class 25 No. D7671, Deltic No. 55015 'TULYAR', Class 40 No. 40012 'AUREOL' hauled by Class 4MTT No. 80080 and Jubilee No. 45596 'BAHAMAS'. The cavalcade was pictured passing Clay Mills near Burton on Trent on 10th June. *A.O. Wynn*

► 'SHERWOOD FORESTER' was obviously a focal point of interest at the Gloucester Rail Open Day on 17th September judging by the crowds surrounding it in the small shed. The weekend celebrations also included a rail tour with Class 20 haulage to Swindon and a shuttle service to nearby Sharpness Docks, the latter operated 'top and tail' style with a Class 37 and a pair of Class 20s. *Martin Loader*

▲ Intending passengers at St Pancras on Sunday 21st May might have wondered if they had mistakenly arrived at nearby King's Cross, for there to greet them at the end of platform 5 was Deltic No. D9000 'ROYAL SCOTS GREY'. It was the prime exhibit of the InterCity Diesel Day. The Deltic's next port of call was to Didcot, for the Great Western Society Diesel Day on 17th June. Note the society/preservation group stalls and the former London Transport Route Master bus.   *P. Crumpton*

► Apparition at Grosmont! 'Warship' No. D821 'GREYHOUND', alias on one side and one end DB V200 021 'WINDHUND', steals the limelight from GW 0–6–2T No. 6619 on 24th June.
Hugh Ballantyne

◄ On loan from BR Toton Class 20 No. 20001 crosses Butterley Reservoir in passenger use on the Midland Railway Centre's diesel spectacular weekend on 24th June. Other visitors in action included the National Railway Museum's Deltic No. 55002 'KINGS OWN YORKSHIRE LIGHT INFANTRY'.   *Brian Cuttell*

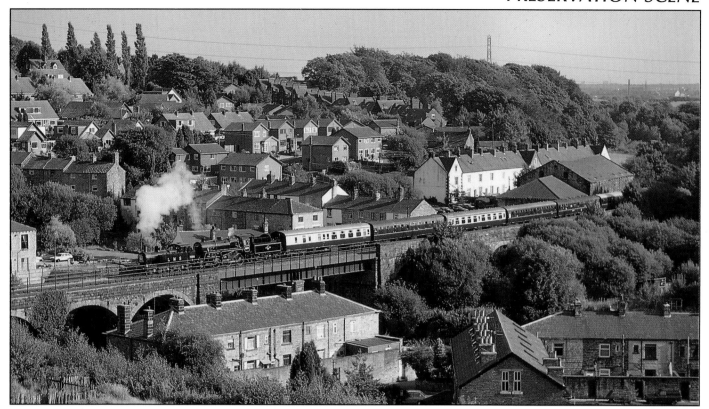

▲ In 1989 Derek Foster's BR standard Class 4 No. 76079 became the second locomotive of its class to be returned to working order. It was returned to revenue earning service on August Bank Holiday weekend when it was paired with his other engine, 'Jinty' 0–6–0 No. 7298. The pair are seen crossing Summerseat Viaduct, arguably the most attractive location on the East Lancashire Railway, on 28th August. *Les Nixon*

◄ One of the more welcome returns to working order in 1989 was that of former Great Eastern Railway Class N7 0–6–2T No. 69621. In a race against the clock the locomotive was declared fit, with only hours to spare, to travel to Southend to take part in the centenary celebrations of the opening of the Shenfield to Southminster and Southend lines. During the August Bank Holiday weekend it operated a shuttle passenger service under the wires to Klondyke Sidings, Prittlewell. Here it is seen at work on home territory at Chappel and Wakes Colne on 14th October. *David Percival*

►On a beautiful still autumn morning the cotton wool exhaust of 'BAHAMAS' hangs in the air as it accelerates away from Westhoughton with the 08.55 Manchester Victoria–Southport excursion on 17th September. Enthusiasts were disappointed to learn that 1989 may well prove to be the last year for these annual steam trips. *D.C. Rodgers*

MAINLINE STEAM EVENTS IN COLOUR

▲ Eclipsed perhaps by 'THE GREAT MARQUESS', 'BAHAMAS' and 'TAW VALLEY' the return to BR main line service of modified Hall No. 6998 'BURTON AGNES HALL' almost went unnoticed. On 10th June it was hard at work on the Welsh Marches Express, recorded here just south of Shrewsbury on the climb to Church Stretton. *Chris Morrison*

▼Perhaps the most unexpected return to main line duty during the year was the long awaited reappearance of three cylinder Gresley Class K4, 2–6–0 'THE GREAT MARQUESS'. Prompted by the serious illness of the owner, Lord Lindlay, the engine was hurriedly brought to main line standards and whisked up to Scotland for a period of two weeks' intense activity on its old stamping ground, the Fort William to Mallaig line. No. 3442 worked up to Scotland via the North and West route and the Settle & Carlisle retracing its steps south on the weekend of 5th/6th August. By this date the death of Lord Lindlay had occurred and hence the locomotive was adorned by a wreath and black draping for the return journey passing Long Meg sidings on 5th August. *Les Nixon*

London Underground

THE SYSTEM

1989 saw the announcement of a major extension to the system, that of the Jubilee Line from Green Park to Stratford, made by the transport secretary, Cecil Parkinson on 16th November. His permission for a parlimentary Bill followed the publication of the East London Rail Study, set up in January.

The 9.5 mile line will give a valuable direct link between Docklands and the City at an estimated cost of some £1 billion, a fair proportion of which, will come from the private sector.

On leaving Green Park the new line will travel to Westminster, where an enlarged station will be necessary, Waterloo, a new station in Blackfriars Road, Southwark, a reconstructed London Bridge, and through another new station in Jamaica Road, Bermondsey. More new stations will be built at Canada Water (to interchange with the East London Line) and Canary Wharf, this time to interchange with the Docklands Light Railway, and Brunswick. The line will come to the surface at Canning Town and follow the existing British Rail line to Stratford, via West Ham. Twenty five new trains are required for the new service with a depot proposed at Stratford Market, although major work will continue to be carried out at Neasden.

The decision to proceed followed months of tense negotiations between the government and developers, particularly Olympia and York, builders of the £3 billion Canary Wharf complex. The capable Michael Portillo had already been put in charge of overseeing transport developments in Docklands and was personally involved in talks with developers anxious to see what is the biggest property development in Europe adequately served by public transport. The government wanted to promote joint public/private infrastructure projects. There was an urgency in the discussions, one reason for the relatively quick decision: 38% of City/Docklands financial sector staff drew their salaries from a foreign-owned bank or institution, for example; if overcrowding got any worse or travel not made easier, these firms could easily move to, say, Paris or Brussels.

John Prescott, Labour's transport spokesman, said the decision was "all about upholding City investment in Docklands and will do nothing to help the majority of passengers left sweating on dirty, crowded tubes."

The East London Line is also to be extended. The proposal is for a northern extension from Shoreditch, currently served only at peak hours and on Sunday mornings, to Dalston via the Broadgate development and along the trackbed of the former North London Line out of Broad Street with stations serving the Hoxton and Haggerston areas. To the south, a short section of line will run just south of Surrey Quays to join the British Rail line, underground trains sharing their tracks to East Dulwich via Queens Road, Peckham and Peckham Rye. If the Bill is deposited in the 1990 parliamentary session, trains could be running by 1993.

There was disappointment at the end of the year that finance was not available for either of the 'Crossrail' LUL/BR projects (Paddington–Liverpool Street/King's Cross–Victoria) advocated in the Central London Rail Study published in January. The report also recommended a £1.5 billion expansion in capacity on existing lines, a more immediate possibility; upgraded signalling is the best short-term measure.

Rather less dramatic is the experimental one year reinstatement of off-peak and weekend trains on the Epping to Ongar section of the Central Line from 30th October. Two trains an hour now run to/from North Weald, now the only intermediate station on the line, with one continuing to Ongar. Proposed leisure developments along the line and at Epping and Ongar stations will hopefully secure these improved services.

An announcement was made in June, of a study into a complete modernisation of the Northern Line (or the Misery Line, as dubbed by its regulars). The line is the second busiest on the system and passenger loadings are increasing steadily – up by nearly 50% since 1981 – requiring a massive investment of some £500 million to replace rolling stock and signalling. In order to increase capacity and reliability, the study is looking into a computer-based automatic train control system called Transmission Based Signalling (TBS). Three TBS systems are under scrutiny including the British Westrace System being developed by Westinghouse. New trains could be running by 1994.

A new name appeared on the underground map from the 24th October when Surrey Docks was officially renamed Surrey Quays, by the Duchess of Kent. The change, which accompanied a renovation of the station, was a joint venture between LUL and the Surrey Quays Shopping Centre, situated across the road. It was also seen to reflect the changing nature of the area, the docks themselves having closed back in 1970, although some local residents were said to be unhappy with the severing of links with the past.

The renaming was the second in the stations history; opened by the East London Railway in 1869 as Deptford Road, it became Surrey Docks in 1911.

The East London Line is to see many improvements in the future, to include platform refurbishments, resignalling, together with the repainting of all trains, the beginning of which were described in last years review. One such 4-car trains of A stock leaves the station on 21st December.

Kevin Lane

ROLLING STOCK

In August came the news that BREL and BRUSH/ABB had been awarded the contract to supply 85 trains for the Central Line, to cost more than £300 million. This follows the various trials with the three sets of Prototype Stock on the Jubilee Line. A couple of weeks before the announcement, on 14th August, a train of the Prototype Stock (but not the BREL cars), were involved in a derailment at Neasden, due to a bracket falling from under one of the carriages. The contract has also been awarded for the resignalling of the Central Line, to Westinghouse, worth £50 million.

Three trains of refurbished stock were unveiled at Acton on 9th September; a complete 8-car train of Victoria Line 1967 stock and two cars each of Metropolitan Line A stock and C stock, the latter used on the Circle, Hammersmith & City and District (Wimbledon branch) Lines. All trains are fitted with fire resistant panelling and floors and include a number of new safety features such as new style passenger alarms, better designed stanchion poles (with the apparent disappearance of swinging grab handles) and improved public address systems.

Furthermore, the Victoria Line stock also features the ability to display digitised speech messages in English, French and German.

There are also improvements to the heating systems and some seating has been rearranged to create more space. The C stock refurbishment also included the addition of end windows to give a less cramped atmosphere and to modify the train braking to give a smoother ride.

Externally, the trains are finished in a white, blue and red livery such a visual improvement on the previous unpainted standard treatment.

The work and design has been undertaken by a variety of firms, including BREL, Vic Berry and the Transport Design Consortium.

STATIONS

The implications of the King's Cross fire continued. Following the publication of Fennell Report (1988), LUL responded in February with a £300 million 3-year safety programme. The recommendations, including installation of sprinkler systems and heat detectors, replacement of all wooden panelling on

◀ Safer and brighter underground trains are to be the order of the day as the industry enters the 1990s. This illustration shows the interior of 1967 stock Driving Motor Car 3010, one of the prototype refurbished vehicles unveiled at Acton on 9th September. Note the rather stylish curved bulkheads.
Brian Morrison

▶ On 14th August, a Jubilee Line train composed of Metro Cammell (red and green) prototype stock, became derailed at Neasden. This was apparently due to a bracket from the underside of one of the cars coming loose and falling onto the track. This resulted in the withdrawal of the trains, although as the evaluation was by then complete, and the decision that the BREL trains had been chosen was to be announced at the end of the month, meant that they were due to be taken out of service anyway, together with the BREL train also. It seems likely that the stock will see further use in the service stock in some capacity or another.

By late November, some of the withdrawn stock could be seen outside Neasden depot, including two of the blue BREL cars photographed (with difficulty!) from a passing Jubilee Line train on the 24th. *Kevin Lane*

▶ An added attraction of a transport event held at Covent Garden on 11th March was the use of four cars of the Prototype Tube Stock (two blue and two green) on the normally peak-hours only Piccadilly Line Aldwych branch. *John B. Gosling*

◀ It is planned that the refurbishment scheme will take up to three years to complete and further cars were repainted late in the year, including this 3-car train of 1972 Mark 1 stock (3522, 3422 and 4522) leading an ordinary 4-car unit into East Finchley on 21st December working a Mill Hill East to Morden via Bank service on the Northern Line. *Kevin Lane*

escalators, clearer management structures and reporting lines, better staff training, etc., were accepted by LUL and work is now well underway. The final cost will be much higher.

Meanwhile the £19.5 million station modernisation of Piccadilly Circus was completed in June. The booking hall, designed by Holden and opened in 1928 is a grade II listed building and has been decorated in its's original style.

On the Northern Line, the £40 million rebuilding of Angel station got underway in November, while back in March Northern Line trains once again began stopping at King's Cross for the first time since the fire in November 1987.

GENERAL MATTERS

Industrial action has been an unfortunate regular occurrence during the first half of the year, with one day strikes on both the buses and the Underground. It was eventually called off on 9th August but some unofficial action rumbled on with a threat from LUL to sack rebel drivers.

On 30th October the London Regional Passengers' Committee published its annual report. Overcrowding, unacceptably high levels of cancellations and the appalling service on the escalators (only 78% working on average) were highlighted.

On 20th December Cecil Parkinson set new targets to be achieved by the Underground by 31st March 1992 at the latest. Objectives were set for improvements in peak capacity and in other areas such as lifts and escalators.

Finally, LUL's staff newspaper, perhaps in response to severe public and political criticism of the state of the Underground, urged drivers to 'see themselves as the host of the train and make ... passengers feel welcome.' More specifically drivers were told to 'adopt Terry Wogan-style charm.'

◀ January saw the first ticket-control gates installed, all Zone 1 stations to be so-fitted at a cost of £19 million. LUL reported an increase in revenue. After complaints from passengers, the gates were modified in various ways, including automatic-opening when the station fire alarm is operated. Barriers, ticket-machines, improved safety and security measures have combined to change the appearance of many stations. A line of ticket-control gates are seen at Tower Gateway on 6th December.

David Carter

▶ The underground event of the year, as far as many were concerned, were the shuttle trains run between Chesham and Watford, on the Metropolitan Line, over the weekends of 1st/2nd and 8th/9th July, in celebration of the centenary of the Chesham branch. As a bonus, it was also possible to travel on the train to and from Wembley Park at the start and finish of services on each day.

The intended motive power was former Metropolitan Railway E-Class 0–4–4T No. 1, based at Quainton Road together with the old faithful, 'SARAH SIDDONS'. However, No. 1 was out of action for the first weekend, resulting in the substitution by ex-GW pannier tank 9466. No. 12 'SARAH SIDDONS', is seen leaving Chesham on 1st July. The stock is a rather unauthentic BR Class 423 unit   *J. Brian Carter*

Light Rail Transit

1989 proved to be a very important year in the development of Light Rail projects in the United Kingdom. Greater Manchester received financial backing from the government and will lead the rush to implement this form of transport in this country. As in last year's Review it is intended to deal with projects individually.

TYNE & WEAR METRO

The Bill presented to Parliament for the Airport extension in November 1984, duly received Royal Assent on 16th November. Fortunately Northumberland County Council, who feared a serious impact on the 'Green Belt' dropped its opposition earlier in the year. A private developer has subsequently submitted a planning application for a hotel and housing project at Woolsington and this will include a station on the airport extension. When the line is built, Newcastle International Airport will become one of the four regional airports to have its own *direct* rail link.

The Tyne & Wear PTA agreed to commission a £125,000 study on the possible extension of the Metro to Sunderland and/or Washington on the 11th April. The study is looking at three distinct corridors:-
1. Gateshead to Washington
2. Washington to Sunderland
3. From a point on the existing South Shields route to Sunderland.

The full range of Light Rail options will be investigated, and although through running onto and from the existing Metro will be essential, street running will be considered.

It is understood that the Metro now carries nearly 50 million passengers a year, equal to 15% of the total number of passenger journeys made in its operating area.

Smoking was banned on all Metro stations and premises from 1st May as a result of the King's Cross fire.

Revenue protection inspectors have proved to be very effective during the year, and it was announced at the end of the year by the home secretary that a Metro police force had been approved.

DOCKLANDS LIGHT RAILWAY

In 1989 the DLR carried higher passenger loads than were predicted in 1984 and which it was built to carry, therefore with the extension in the pipeline the success of the railway is far greater than ever expected.

The Bill presented in 1986 for the Beckton extension finally received Royal Assent on 21st July. The line will be financed principally by the London Docklands Development Corporation through sale of land for development. Consent for the £240 million extension was agreed by the government on 1st August as an integral part of its strategy to regenerate the old Royal Docks and Learmouth areas. Opening in 1992 it will extend the DLR from Poplar to Beckton passing close to the new London City airport.

Contractors, Edmund Nuttall Ltd. continued boring the tunnel on the City extension throughout the year. Changes to the initial railway in preparation for the City extension require considerable possession time by the contractors GEC Mowlem. In consequence, the railway is closed most weekends and after 21.30 hours in the week. A bus service is substituted during these periods.

The ten cars ordered from GEC in 1988 and being built under licence by BREL at York commenced delivery in December. Various revisions in specifications are built into these vehicles due to lessons learned from the King's Cross fire. 21 new trains were ordered in January from BN Constructions of Belgium with Hawker Siddeley Rail Projects as a major subcontractor.

London Regional Transport and the LDDC began feasibility studies during the year for a 3.8 km extension under the Thames to Greenwich and Lewisham which would give direct access to the Docklands area from the south.

GREATER MANCHESTER PTE

October 24th will go down in history as the date when Britain's next generation of tramways (Light Rail) got the green light from the government; Mr Portillo approved a Section 56 grant towards the net capital cost of Phase 1 of 'Metrolink'.

Having received Department of Transport approval work started in early March on site investigations in central Manchester, checking electricity, gas, water, sewers and telecommunications in preparation for laying the on-street tracks, and if necessary moving equipment.

On 27th September, it was announced that the GMA Consortium (Greater Manchester Associates) had won the £110 million first phase contract to design, build, operate and maintain the sections from Bury to Victoria and Altrincham to

Behind Poplar station is the huge Canary Wharf development under construction, seen here on a misty 6th December. Eleven days later the final contract for the £116 million Poplar–Beckton extension of the DLR was awarded, the key to the rejuvenation of the Royal Docks.   *David Carter*

Piccadilly connected via a new section of street tramway alignment. GMA is made up of GEC Alsthom, John Mowlem & Co., Amec and Greater Manchester Buses Ltd.

It was also announced during the year that the light rail vehicles, which will be approximately 28 metres long and 2.65 metres wide, will be built by Firema of Italy, with electrical equipment provided by GEC Alsthom. At the end of the year the bill presented to parliament in 1988 had reached the first reading in the House of Commons. A further bill was presented in November 1989.

A major study was commissioned by the PTE in 1988 to examine all possible Light Rail extensions, to review their feasibility and costs, and to evaluate each extension in terms of operating costs, estimated passenger traffic, and revenues. The initial findings were presented to the PTA in July 1989.

SOUTH YORKSHIRE PTE

After Manchester received the Section 56 grant from the government it was widely predicted that South Yorkshire would receive similar backing, only to be told by Mr Portillo in November that there would be no money made available in 1990/91, although a grant would be given for further evaluation work. This decision will have disastrous consequences on the plans to have 'Supertram' in operation for the World Student Games, to be held in Sheffield in 1991. Both Mr Portillo and the transport secretary Cecil Parkinson had earlier spoken of their full support for the 'Supertram' proposals.

The second 'Supertram' Bill deposited in November 1988, received Royal Assent on 21st December 1989 after the most unbelievable situation arose in the House of Commons. Labour MP's attempting to block a bill to extend port facilities at Immingham infuriated Conservative members who retaliated and blocked various other bills including South Yorkshire's 'Supertram' bill. This whole farce seriously undermines

the suitability of the Private Bill procedure, and questions must be asked when a totally unopposed Bill is delayed for political reasons.

A further bill was presented in November, covering alignment alterations in the Manor area and at Meadowhall.

During the year a limited company was set up by the PTE, under the name 'South Yorkshire Supertram Ltd.' to implement the project and ensure the contract remains on compliance in its design and construction, together with the eventual efficient and profitable operation of the service.

WEST MIDLANDS PTE

The 1989-deposited bill covering the 21 km Line 1 route from Birmingham Snow Hill via Birmingham Jewellery Quarter, Handsworth, West Bromwich, Wednesbury and Bilston to Wolverhampton received Royal Assent on 15th November 1989. The route is mostly on disused ex-GWR formation, but enters Wolverhampton town centre on a 1.8 km on-street alignment to terminate in a pedestrian precinct next to a new supermarket development. The line will also serve the giant 'Sandwell 2000' development at Wednesbury and will serve an estimated population of 150,000.

In November 1989 the PTE (which gained the name 'Centro' during the year!) deposited the second Metro Bill, covering two further lines. These are:

● Line 2. Fiveways (Birmingham), underground through the city centre serving the International Convention Centre, the Town Hall, New Street, Corporation Street, to Aston University then proceeding to serve Castle Bromwich, Chelmsley Wood, National Exhibition Centre and Birmingham International Airport. This section is 26 km in length and would cost approximately £240 million (a significant part being due to the tunnel section 5 km in length).

● Line 3: Wolverhampton town centre via Wednesbury, Willenhall, Walsall, Darlaston to Wednesbury crossing Line 1 at Sandwell to Dudley town centre. This would also be 26 km costing £139 million.

Unfortunately, opposition has already been mounting and a

▼An artist's impression of one of the cars for the Manchester Metrolink scheme. These vehicles are being built by Firema of Italy for GEC-Alsthom. *GEC-Alsthom*

▲ *An artist's impression of a street section of the 'Midland Metro'.*
The car is clearly of Grenoble design. *WMPTE*

few residents' groups are attempting to block their progress.
It should be noted though, that there is all-party political support. A total of 35 cars will be required for Line 2/3 costing
over £30 million.

ADVANCED TRANSPORT FOR AVON LTD.

The first Bill, seeking powers to build and operate a line from
Portishead to a point a quarter of a mile from Bristol city
centre, received Royal Assent on 11th May 1989. Five objections were withdrawn before relevant committee stages.

Two further Bills were lodged in November, covering Bristol
city centre, where a street-running section is included and for
routes to Bradley Stoke (in the north) and to Yate (east of
Bristol). However objections have been lodged from a number
of sources, most ominously from Bristol City Council. The
whole future of the project is possibly now in doubt.

So far, funding of the scheme has been totally from private
sources, however, it is now appreciated that Section 56 grant
will be required from the government if the scheme is to proceed much further. This is in contradiction of earlier proposals
which the government held as the way ahead for public transport infrastructure funding and has possibly influenced the government's policy of private-sector funding for other schemes.

Two development companies, Parkdale PLC and Dutch-
based VOM International had made substantial investments
in the project in the early part of 1989.

LONDON REGIONAL TRANSPORT

In July a contract was awarded for a second stage study on the
potential of Light Rail in Croydon. An initial survey in 1988
identified the basis of an LRT system with the core based on
three legs from East Croydon to West Croydon, New Ad-
dington and Addiscombe on new alignment. The remaining

sections of route would be on existing BR alignment from
Addiscombe to Elmers End and West Croydon to Wimbledon.
The second stage could expand the system to Caterham, Sut-
ton, Tattenham Corner and Beckenham Junction.

LONDON ASSESSMENT STUDIES

In December four Transport Assessment Studies were published, covering South, West and East London together with
a South Circular study. Each of these were completed by different consultants, and a number of Light Rail suggestions
have been identified.

LOTHIAN REGIONAL COUNCIL

On 19th July 1989, Lothian Regional Council, announced a
£184 million, 17.5 km 'tram-style' railway for Edinburgh, including a two-mile £62 million underground section. Running
from Liberton and Gilmerton in the south through the city to
Muirhouse and Davidsons Main in the north.

WEST YORKSHIRE PTE

1989 saw a very confused picture. The WYPTE wishes to see
Supertram LRT. Leeds City Council are interested in an automatic scheme, possibly BRIWAY and the local major bus
company Yorkshire Rider are investigating Guided Bus
technology. Leeds Council were confident that a Bill would
be presented to parliament in November 1989, but due to public pressure against elevated structures this did not take place.

CLEVELAND COUNTY COUNCIL AND TEESSIDE DE-
VELOPMENT CORPORATION

In 1989, a scheme was identified which could link main centres
in Middlesbrough and Stockton with developing areas of Tees-
dale, Preston Farm, Teesside Park and Middlehaven and also
conversion of the BR line to Darlington and Teesside Airport.
On-street sections are proposed for Middlesbrough and
Stockton.

NOTTINGHAM CITY COUNCIL, NOTTINGHAMSHIRE CC, NOTTINGHAM DEVELOPMENT ENTERPRISE

Plans have been announced for an LRT line from Midland Station to Hucknall and Bubbington. Detailed feasibility studies are in progress to identify alignments in the city centre.

SOUTH HAMPSHIRE

A line from Fareham through Gosport to Portsmouth, with a tunnel under Portsmouth Harbour, is being studied.

CARDIFF BAY DEVELOPMENT CORPORATION

A Light Rail line from the Cardiff Central to the Docks has been proposed.

STRATHCLYDE PTE

A consultant's report on Public Transport for the 21st century was released in December 1989 in which Light Rail features very strongly.

OTHER SCHEMES

Numerous other cities throughout the United Kingdom are showing interest in Light Rail, including:-
Dundee, Preston, Hull, Liverpool, Chester, Stoke, Cambridge, Swindon, Reading, Exeter, Plymouth and Belfast. However, all these are at very early stages and are not covered in this article.

DEPARTMENT OF TRANSPORT GUIDELINES

New guidelines relating to public transport Section 56 grants, were announced by the government in November 1989, which substantially change the emphasis in the investment appraisal criteria. The new rules indicate:
  ● that approval of new rail infrastructure grant depends on the scheme being profitable.
  ● that it has to be seen to be the most cost-effective way of meeting the defined social need.
  ● that evidence that efforts to secure private sector contributions have been maximised.
  ● that the cost should be less than the discounted sum of the revenues to be earned from the passengers.
  ● benefits to non-users. Therefore unlike road schemes, financing future public transport investment cannot be justified on the basis of benefits to the users. Instead it will be justified solely on the grounds of external benefits and users will have to pay through fares for their own benefits.
The grant will in future be calculated as a maximum of 50% of the non-user benefit rather than 50% of the cost of the scheme.
  Talk about moving the goalposts!

LIGHT RAIL 89, BRISTOL

Over 130 exhibitors from a number of countries participated in a major exhibition at Bristol between 14th and 16th November, demonstrating the vast interest in Light Rail technology in the United Kingdom. The exhibition was held to accompany a conference on Light Rail which was held in an adjacent building. Copies of Platform 5's first publication on LRT 'Light Rail Review 1', were provided for all delegates.

DEVELOPMENTS ON MAINLAND EUROPE

In France it was announced that approval had been given to commence construction of Light Rail systems in Paris and Rouen whilst Strasbourg declared its intension of developing Light Rail in preference to the VAL system. Nantes commenced an extension to Beaujoire in April.
  The French government have decided to meet 30% of the costs of new Metro and Light Rail lines.
  Extensions opened in the following West German cities:- Bochum, Braunschweig, Karlsruhe, Krefeld and Mainz, with subways opening in Hannover and Köln. Work commenced on a further subway section in Frankfurt.
  Approval was given during the year for extensions in the Dutch cities of Den Haag, Rotterdam and Utrecht. Rotterdam also saw the extension to Pilgrimsstraat in June, whilst Amsterdam started work on the Amstelveen extension. Mention must be made here that the city of Den Haag celebrated 125 years of tramway operation during May and June, and congratulations on this momentous feat are in order.
  Further extensions in Gent (Belgium) Milan and Wien (Vienna), together with the continuing construction in Lausanne complete our look overseas.
  As can be seen from this short chapter, the future of Light Rail looks very rosy. Shortly we in Great Britain will be able to sample the first of the new generation tramways and delight at the opportunity of gliding through city streets in modern, quiet, pollution-free 'Supertrams'.

▼ Although risking advertising coach travel, this view shows the Bank extension of the DLR under construction on 18th September. Tower Gateway station and BR's Fenchurch Street station are nearby on the left. From here the route to Bank in the heart of the City descends in tunnel, the gradient being severe in places.
Allan Mott

European Scene

In January, proposals for a European high-speed rail network were presented to the European Commissioner for Public Works and Transport. The twelve members of the EEC, plus Switzerland and Austria, will build or upgrade key lines, probably with EC funding, to provide a 19,000-mile network, two-thirds of it for trains running at over 240 km/h. The cost will be $100 billion over 25 years. The hope is that trains will do for post-1992 Europe what deregulated airlines have done for America: help tie a huge market together. Paris–Milano could be 5 hours 20 minutes, München–Roma 5 hours 40 minutes. In certain countries re-gauging to standard gauge will be carried out.

France, geographical centre of the EEC, has a head-start, its first TGVs operating between Paris and Lyon in September 1981. The French have shown what can be done because, TGV apart, passenger rail traffic has grown at only 1.6% per year over the past decade. Air traffic has risen by 6% a year. On the Paris–Lyon route air traffic has dropped by 90% since 1981.

Even though political changes in Europe may mean an eastwards shift of the European economy, Paris is likely to become the centre of the high-speed network taking shape. Unless things change dramatically, BR will remain the least-electrified and least-subsidised in the network. The inadequacies of the existing Network SouthEast Folkestone–London line will dilute the benefits of joining the network that the Channel Tunnel provides.

AUSTRIA

Passenger traffic continued to rise during 1989. To cater for this and to attract even more customers the summer timetable saw ÖBB introducing some 250 new trains. Many lines saw improved services, including some branch lines. In Wien there were improvements to the S-bahn services and July saw the introduction of an S-bahn service between Wien Sud and Wien West. The buoyant traffic has stretched ÖBB resources and this resulted in few locos being withdrawn during the year. Indeed overhauls of Class 1018 started again as a decision was made to keep older locos in traffic much longer than originally planned.

ÖBB placed orders for more electric locos of Class 1044 and 1063 and for three Pendolino units which will probably work between Graz and Linz.

More branch lines are reported to be threatened with closure but there was good news too: one line closed by ÖBB, Oberschützen to Rechnitz has been re-opened as a private concern. Freight traffic will be conveyed but tourist trains will also be run.

The changes in eastern Europe affected Austria by Christmas as Czechoslovakia and Austria did away with the need for visas. There was an upsurge in demand for travel with cross border traffic being very heavy and many extra trains had to be provided, some of which will become permanent. Demand for travel from Bratislava to Wien was so great that trains of 15-20 coaches were put on and had to have a locomotive at each end.

On the private lines Stern & Hafferl received some new dual-voltage EMUs for its Lambach–Haag line whilst the Zillertalbahn opened a brand new depot at Jenbach which many a main-line railway would be proud to have, as the facilities provided are excellent.

BELGIUM

1989 saw the demise of the old postal EMUs and their replacement by some 'new' units. These units were originally introduced in 1935 and rebuilt for postal use in 1967. The wheel has turned again so that some 1954-built units have been converted to replace the earlier units. However, due to a new postal contract the eight old units were replaced by 15 new ones.

Another class that was laid up in 1989 was the Class 59 Cockerill Bo–Bo dating from 1955. The last examples were operating from Antwerpen Dam shed and spent some time going in and out of store. Many are stored for possible use on construction trains for the new TGV lines in Belgium, and one member of the class has been painted in original livery and regained its former number as museum stock.

During the summer period excursion trains were run on the cross-border line between De Panne and Dunkerque in a joint operation with SNCF. This line closed to passenger traffic many years ago. Freight services between St. Ghislain and Valenciennes (France) were withdrawn with effect from 28th May and the cross-border line closed.

CZECHOSLOVAKIA ČSD

During 1989 the ČSD celebrated its 150th anniversary. The celebrations were centred on Brno where there were several weekend cavalcades. However, there was a full back-up programme with steam excursions from Brno to Blansko, Slakov, and Breclav. The latter place also shared in the event holding

The SNCB ran steam railtours for the NS 150 celebrations on four weekends during 1989. Here compound atlantic No. 12.004 stands at the head of the 'Pierement Express' at Antwerpen Centraal on 22nd July awaiting departure for Utrecht. The stock was comprised of type 'K1' semi-open firsts built 1933–4 with a 'birdcage' design open brake first of similar vintage.   *Peter Fox*

a large exhibition at the depot and station with many steam, diesel and electric types present plus other rolling stock. The Breclav exhibition was better than the one held in the Brno trade fair grounds.

Later in the year the country experienced great political events which affected the railways and are documented under 'Germany'.

DENMARK   DSB

The prototype IC-3 DMU was exhibited at the 1988 Hamburg exhibition but teething troubles prevented production units from entering traffic until very late in 1989. Most problems were reported to be software-related.

Meanwhile DSB continued to withdraw old diesel shunting locos and some main line locos of Class MX were sold off to private lines. A new shunting loco was ordered from Cockerill and will become Class MJ.

FRANCE   SNCF

Three landmarks were reached for the TGV. On 29th March, TGV Paris Sud-Est services crossed the point of carrying 100 million passengers. The fleet has covered a distance equivalent to 619 times the distance from the earth to the moon!

On 24th September, SNCF officially started 'TGV Atlantique' operations over its second purpose-built high-speed line between Paris Montparnasse and cities in western France. On leaving the Paris terminus – being completely redeveloped – the line uses the 'Gallardon' right of way (for a line that was never built). The Parisien suburbs are hardly seen, being either

hidden from sight by covered sections and walls, or a blur – at Massy units accelerate to 220 km/h, a little further to the maximum speed of 300 km/h. At Courtelain the line diverges, the southern fork to Vêndome and Tours (and then by existing line to Bordeaux) due to open in 1990. The western fork continues to Le Mans where upgraded conventional tracks run to western cities like Nantes and St. Nazaire on one line or to north western cities like Rennes (and Brest) on another. Journey time reductions were dramatic with one hour, for example, being cut from the previous best Paris–Nantes line.

Alsthom's order is for 95 trains, each with two power cars and ten trailers. The trains are dual-voltage (25kV and 1500 V dc) and use in-cab signalling. Trains are serviced at Châtillon depot in Paris.

On 5th December, a short-formation TGV set No. 325 set a new world speed record of 482.4 km/h which rounds off at 300 mph. The record, snatched from West Germany, was made on the un-opened stretch of line north east of Tours.

On the motive power front, TGV production affected the delivery of the Sybic locos. Other new construction centred on more shunting tractors of Class Y 8000, with those from 8401 featuring remote radio control. Otherwise, SNCF was refurbishing DMUs for use on regional services which saw many new liveries being introduced for these subsidised TER services. The year also saw the appearance of the rebuilt CC 1100 and towards the close of the year the first master/slave diesel rebuilt from BB 63500/63000 was just about ready to enter traffic.

Electrification was completed between Nevers and St. Germain des Fossés in time for the summer timetable.

◀Former test loco BB 10004 has now reappeared as BB 15055, its original identity. It is seen here at Strasbourg Depot on 10th September. *E. Dunkling*

◀▼A new route for SNCF Class 72000 locos in 1989 was the service from Paris Nord to Laon. Here CC 72036 waits to leave with the 13.00 express on 27th May. *E. Dunkling*

▼A TGV Atlantique unit about to depart for Rennes stands at temporary buffer stops at Paris Montparnasse on 17th December. The terminus is undergoing a hugh modernisation programme. *David Carter*

TGV-ATLANTIQUE ENTERS SERVICE

►The rear power car (No. 24 007) of the 11.25 Paris–Nantes stands at its destination on 16th December. This service, TGV 8823, runs to a 2 hour 11 minute timing, including stops at Le Mans and Angers.

Darren Galpin

►▼ Shortly before starting service with the winter timetable, TGV A units were working test trains between Paris and Tours. Unit No. 328 is at Tours on 13th September.

E. Dunkling

▲ The bar area and shop of the catering car is shown, this vehicle being marshalled between first and second class. Catering from here and the provision of pre-prepared food in just first class has been awarded to Servair, part of Air France. Standards are high.

David Carter

► After extensive customer surveys, the SNCF decided to adopt a mixture of seating arrangements. First class accommodation, for instance, features 'Club' and open seating. A video/conference room is also offered. First class Club is shown here with the four-seat 'compartments' behind the smoked glass partitions. The passenger environment is superb, as is the train's ride both on high-speed line and conventional track.

David Carter

EAST & WEST GERMANY

These are grouped together as befits the occasion. The story started in Hungary during the summer when Hungary opened its borders which resulted in many East Germans escaping to the West via that country. The scene then moved to Praha later in the year with hundreds of East Germans staging a sit-in at the West German embassy there. Agreement was eventually made to move the refugees to West Germany via East Germany with the latter country giving its word to allow the people to go through.

The result was that the DB had to send several empty trains to Praha to pick up East German citizens and take them to West Germany. The agreed route was via Dresden and the lines in Saxony to the West German border station of Hof. Media coverage meant the word got round and many people in East Germany tried to join the refugee trains. Rail traffic in the Dresden area was reported halted for several hours as there were hundreds of people on the tracks and lineside. Train load after train load ran to Hof where connecting specials were put on to other locations. Will the full story ever be told?

The refugees probably included some East German railwaymen who were probably welcomed with open arms by the DB which has developed an acute staff shortage, particularly of drivers and other operating staff. This started to have a knock-on effect on DB passenger services with delays becoming a daily event. The worst effect was to the freight traffic where trains were held up for hours or indeed days waiting movement. Late in 1989, suburban trains in many areas were carrying advertisements for drivers and shunters etc.

The Class 120.1 locos were still giving problems and consequently some freight diagrams were covered by other classes. However the 120s extended their sphere of operation during the year when they started working IC trains on the Hamburg–Köln–Stuttgart route.

The DB salesmen were still busy selling off old stock and virtually all the Class 221 diesel hydraulics will see further use – in Albania and Greece! Turkey continued to acquire refurbished Class 798/998 railbuses.

▶The München S-Bahn is suffering from overcrowding and during the year a set of NS double-deck stock was tested. 120 151/3 are at the ends of the set at Belzendorf on 18th June. The tests proved successful, and Talbot was given an order.

Philip Wormald

▼The NS's new 6400 Class diesel eletrics went into revenue-earning service at the start of the summer timetable. 6403 'Gijs' heads a long train of hoppers out of Amersfoort Yard. *David Brown*

NETHERLANDS

1989 was Anniversary year for the NS and details of the events which took place are detailed in the separate feature. The expansion of passenger traffic continued with 21 of the new 3-car ICM units being delivered (4074–94) together with some ICR hauled stock. The Benelux push-pull trains were strengthened by the addition of an extra second class coach in each set. The only withdrawals of passenger stock were due to collision damage (units 322, 714 and 938). The removal of a number of 'Hondekop' (dog-head) units from service for extended periods in order to remove blue asbestos insulation led to a severe shortage of stock. This was counteracted by the hire of a number of sets of M2 stock from the SNCB/NMBS (Belgian Railways), which were used on Roosendaal–Zwolle services. Unfortunately, these coaches with their sparten 2 + 3 seating did not meet with the approval of the regular passengers! 1100 Class locomotives are now the normal power on these services. A further 118 double-decker coaches and 38 Class 1700 locomotives were also ordered to help meet traffic increases.

The new 6400 Class diesel locomotives eventually went into service at the beginning of the summer timetable, 26 of them having been accepted by the end of the year. A number of 2200 and 2400 Class locos were withdrawn, together with the last three 500 Class English Electric shunters and No. 2530, the sole member of its class. The 3000 Class postal railcars gained a new livery variant, and the IC3s the generic name 'Koploper', the result of a competition. The literal English translation is "head runner".

For owners of personal computers, the NS timetable became available on floppy disc, an innovation which deserves to be copied by other administrations.

ITALY

The Italian Railways continued to take delivery of the Pendolino EMUs and gradually introduced them into service on specific trains radiating from Roma. More E656 electric locos were delivered allowing the last of the old Class E428 to head for the scrapyard. The aftermath of the political scandal of 1988 left the branch lines intact for the time being but more rumblings are being heard that sweeping changes are in store not only for the branch lines but also on FS organisation and staffing.

Meanwhile, 1989 saw electrification extended along the scenic Fortezza–San Candido line and in Sardinia the first 25 kV catenary was energised. The year also saw FS celebrating its 150th anniversary but this was a very low-key affair centering on yet another 'opening' of Pietrarsa Museum.

LUXEMBOURG

The main news of 1989 was the extension of electrification to Diekirch but, as CFL still has to take delivery of its new EMUs, some SNCF Z 6300s were hired working from their base at Thionville.

NORWAY

Oslo Vest station finally closed with the summer timetable with all services now concentrated on the Sentral station.

PORTUGAL

CP was busy drawing modernisation plans but some of these are dependent on what will happen in Spain. Meanwhile some new DMU cars have been purchased to make up some of the Porto area units to three-car sets. A surprise was the purchase of two redundant RENFE Alco diesel locos of RENFE Class 313. More are expected.

SPAIN

Second thoughts here on the re-gauging of all its principal lines to standard gauge. The cost is reported to be extremely high! During 1989 tracklaying started on the new line to Seville with the first standard gauge tracks going in at Parla. This was soon followed by delivery of the first RENFE standard gauge diesel loco which is a rebuilt 319.2. Another high-speed line is now on the drawing board and this would link Irun with Bilboa with a branch going south towards Victoria allowing this city to be connected easily with Bilboa.

Most of the TER DMUs are now out of service and some Class 592 DMUs have been rebuilt with first class and buffet/bar to replace them.

At Seville the new Santa Justa carriage sidings were brought into use with the winter timetable allowing the old depot

at San Jeromino to be redeveloped as part of the world fair site.

SWEDEN

A quiet year with development of the high-speed EMUs of Class X2 continuing. During the year the first units were nearing completion and one set at least started trial running.

Otherwise SJ continued to rebuild electric shunting locos to radio control and announced a programme to fit some diesel shunters with the same equipment.

SWITZERLAND

SBB took delivery of many new locomotives and stock for the Zürich S-bahn. The new S-bahn locos brought computer-type numbers to SBB locos as did the narrow gauge Brünig locos of Class 101. The old De4/4 EMUs were phased out of use on the Seetal-bahn.

On the private lines the main event was the centenary of the Rhaetische Bahn which was celebrated throughout the summer with various events and special tours.

▲In Spain, Class 269 No. 269 604 has been rebuilt with a streamlined front end as an experimental high speed loco. It is seen at Madrid Fuencarral Depot on 4th April.
E. Dunkling

▼Garratt 282F 0421 built by Babcock and Wilcox in 1960 has been rebuilt and used on excursion trains during 1989 around Barcelona. It is seen here at Barcelona San Andres Condal Depot on 19th February.
E. Dunkling

▲SJ Class RC2 No. 1031 is seen here at Malmo Depot on 27th August in the new Swedish Railways livery.
E. Dunkling

NS 150

1989 was the year in which the Netherlands celebrated the 150th anniversary of the building of their first railway and, as in Germany and Austria, adavantage was taken of this to publicise the railway system. Although the location of Holland's first railway was from Amsterdam to Haarlen, the celebrations were centred on Utrecht, the headquarters of the NS.

Unlike Germany and Austria, there was no spectacular train parade, presumably because of the lack of available Dutch trains to appear in such a parade. Indeed, the NS have only one remaining main-line steam locomotive, Werkspoor 4–6–0 No. 3737, built 1911. Nevertheless, a small steam parade was held on every day (except Mondays) throughout the whole celebration period (22nd June to 6th August). In addition to 3737, the parade included various industrial locomotives plus visiting locomotives.

A large exhibition was held in the Jaarbeurs exhibition hall, adjacent to Utrecht station entitled 'Treinen door de Tijd' (Trains through Time). Each hall had a different theme. These were:

●The Second Dimension. (Railway Art including photography, film and video, graphic design, banknotes, postage stamps, literature, cartoons and children's drawings).
●Present, Past and Future in Perspective. (An exhibition comprising of five main themes – time, space, money, work and travel).
●Railway Connections. Of the indoor exhibitions, this was the most interesting. Various train builders and railway companies were represented, as well as companies and societies providing for railway and model railway enthusiasts. The main Dutch society, the NVBS was well-represented.

Between the exhibition hall and the station area was 'Wonderland', with attractions including a children's playground. The largest feature of this area was a circular track with a full-size replica of one of the first locomotives to run in the Netherlands, the broad gauge 'DE AREND' (The Eagle). There was also a pedal-powered bike-train for children to ride round on – a must for cycle-mad Holland!

The main attraction was, however the train show, held on the sidings behind Utrecht CS. This consisted of various items of NS rolling stock both ancient and modern together with various visiting exhibits from foreign railways. BR was represented (for a short time) by GWR 4–4–0 No. 3440 'CITY OF TRURO' and a Class 156 DMU, but the main British exhibit was the EM2 society's Co–Co No. 27000 'ELECTRA' a veteran of both the Sheffield–Manchester via Woodhead route and the NS, on which it ran as No. 1502.

Other visiting locos included the joint holder of the world speed record for an electric locomotive, SNCF No. CC 7107 and various visiting steam locomotives (see below).

A programme of steam specials was run from Utrecht over various routes, the intention being that theses should be hauled by 3737. A set of withdrawn 'plan E' coaches were overhauled for these trains. Unfortunately, No. 3737 was not up to the job, and after the first few runs was replaced by whatever visiting loco happened to be available, with the addition of 52 8139, acquired by the Stoom Stichting Nederland (Netherlands' Steam Foundation).

The Belgian Railways (SNCB/NMBS) also got in on the act, running specials on four weekends with either the Canadian-built 2–8–0 No. 29.013 or the streamlined atlantic No. 12.004. The specials were steam-hauled on the outward journey from Antwerpen to Utrecht on Saturdays, returning electric-hauled to Roosendaal and diesel-hauled from there to Antwerpen. On Sundays, the procedure was reversed. Unfortunately 29.013 failed on arrival at Utrecht on the first trip on 8th July, its place being taken from Utrecht to Roosendaal on the second by 'ELECTRA'.

As well as the advertised railtours, certain other unadvertised steam specials ran. Despite many visiting enthusiasts being present, the NS kept details of these secret! One such special ran whilst your publisher was present on 19th July for the benefit of NS pensioners. One wonders what these pensioners, all of whom would have unhappy memories of the second world war, thought of the motive power – 03 1010 of the Deutsche Reichsbahn!

◄A view of the train show taken on 8th July. On the first track can be seen V200 007 with its double decker set. Next are DB 120 157 and NS double-decker stock. Also visible are NS 1000 Class loco No. 1010 and an SNCB 900 Class 'Snorkel' EMU.

Peter Harris

VISITORS – UTRECHT 1989

14/06–03/07	3440 'CITY OF TRURO'
16/06– /08	27000 'ELECTRA' (BR)
18/06–08/08	2978 (SBB)
18/06–08/08	V200 007 (DB)
19/06–10/08	CC 7107 (SNCF)
19/06–03/07	TGV-A 305 (SNCF)
19/06–03/07	156 502 (BR)
20/06–10/07	141R420 (SNCF)
23/06–19/07	120 157 (DB)
05/07–23/07	03 1010 (DR)
21/07–08/08	475.179/498.022 (CSD)
27/07–07/08	Pt47 112 (PKP)

◄This 1924 stock 2-car EMU was reinstated to work a shuttle service between Utrecht CS and the Railway Museum. It is nicknamed "De Blokkendoos". which means "box of bricks". It is seen at Utrecht CS on 23rd July awaiting departure for the Museum.   *Peter Fox*

▼One of the many visiting locos was this magnificent Czechoslovakian 4–8–2, ČSD No. 475.178, seen approaching Utrecht CS on 23rd July.   *Graham Scott-Lowe*

▼The full-size replica of the broad gauge loco 'DE AREND' is seen on its circle of track outside the Jaarbeurs Centre on 21st July.   *Peter Fox*

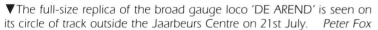

▼Two EM2s stand side by side at the train show. On the left is 1501 in NS livery owned by a group of Rotterdam Feyenoord railwaymen. On the left is 27000 'ELECTRA' in BR livery, complete with dummy vacuum pipe. Charlie Petty of the EM2 society is seen waving from the cab.   *Peter Fox*

▲One visitor to the NS150 celebrations was the joint world speed record holder for an electric locomotive, SNCF No. CC 7107. It is seen approaching Rotterdam Alexander whilst working the return leg of one of the excursions from Antwerpen on 5th August.   *David Brown*

▶The EM2 society ran four railtours during NS 150 comprising of 27000 'ELECTRA' and the set of plan E coaches which was also used on the steam specials. It is seen on 8th July at Hoek van Holland with the 'Tilburg Tommy' tour.   *Peter Harris*

▼On 19th February the NS ran the longest passenger train in the world consisting of Class 1600 electric loco No. 1607 and sixty ICR coaches. The train, which was 1601 metres long (approximately one mile) is seen near Lage Zwaluwe.   *Thom van Amsterdam*

▲Because of the problems with 3737, the NS had to press foreign locos into service to haul the steam railtours. One such loco was DR 3-cylinder pacific No. 03 1010 seen at Den Haag CS on the 'Rijnmond Express' of 20th July. *Peter Fox*

▲▶The East German crew of 03 1010 from Halle depot appeared to be enjoying the proceedings. *Peter Fox*

▶BR Class EM2 No. 27000 'ELECTRA' was used for various jobs in connection with NS 150, in addition to hauling special tours. It is seen passing through Houten on 19th July, hauling DB 120 157 plus three 'Interregio' coaches back to the German border. *Peter Fox*

▼On 23rd July, the SSN's ex-ÖBB 2–10–0 52.8179 failed at Den Bosch whilst working the 'West Betuwe Express'. The train was then electric-hauled to Nieuwersluis where the only other available loco, NS 3737, hastily commandeered out of the parade, took over for a round trip to Utrecht. It is seen at Gouda on the way to Den Haag CS. *Peter Fox*

TGV-ATLANTIQUE.

▲ Six TGV sets make an impressive sight in this line-up at Châtillon Depot, Paris, specially arranged for publicity purposes. The next development will be the double-deck TGV, a mock-up of which was displayed at the Gare du Nord. *SNCF*

THE GLASNOST EXPRESS

A scoop for a British organisation was the running of the 'Glasnost Express'. This two-day railtour of the USSR organised by Vic Allen ran on 12th/13th July and from Brest to Kovel from where diesels took over to Lvov. 0–10–0 Er 770-17 worked the special train from Lvov to the polish border station of Przemysl.

▲◄P 36-0064 is seen at Vyzhva.
Graham Scott-Lowe

◄770-17 about to leave Lvov for Przemysl.
Graham Scott-Lowe

A Railway Diary for 1989

JANUARY

01. SCOTRAIL. Smoking is banned from first class accommodation on ScotRail Express services between Edinburgh, Glasgow and Aberdeen.

05. BREL SALE. A GEC–Alsthom consortium establishes itself as rival bidders to the Asea Brown Boveri – Trafalgar House – management team in the battle to buy BREL.

06. APPOINTMENT. Network SouthEast appoints Mr Jim Vine to the newly created post of project director, Networker EMU, at its London HQ. He will be responsible for £250 million Networker EMU project.

08. WARNING. Officials of the Keighley & Worth Valley Railway warn photographers against a repetition of the trackside vandalism of fences and unruly behaviour witnessed at the Modern Traction Weekend during November 1988.

08. INDUSTRY. Andrew Barclay of Kilmarnock and Hunslet of Leeds restructure to form Hunslet Barclay Ltd and Hunslet GMT at the respective works. The former will concentrate on major locomotive work and modifications, the latter with the supply of industrial machines, including underground locomotives.

09. FARE INCREASES. In response to BR's latest round of ticket price rises the day before, John Prescott, Opposition transport spokesman, demands an independent review. The 20% increases in long-distance season tickets from places such as Grantham, Swindon & Leicester and a 10% increase in NSE short-distance fares are well above the 6% inflation rate.

09. NEW TRAINS. The first 'Anglia Electrics' – Class 321s – arrive at Southend and enter passenger service.

10. PROVINCIAL. BR advises the secretary of state for transport that it wishes to withdraw the closure proposal for the line between Mansfield Jn. and Trowell Jn. via Radford Jn. in Nottinghamshire. Provincial now plans to use the line to speed up Nottingham–Manchester/Sheffield services.

10. INQUIRY. The Clapham crash inquiry opens – BR offers to disclose details of its internal inquiry but government inspector Anthony Hidden QC says that the piecemeal release of information might affect the outcome.

11. ORDER. BR is given approval to order a further 138 Class 158 vehicles at a cost of £54 million.

11. IMPROVEMENTS. A £300,000 initial package of improvements at Leeds City station, particularly to lighting, information displays and flooring is completed.

12. CEREMONY. John Ellis, ScotRail's general manager officially opens the second phase of a £750,000 scheme to refurbish Perth station.

12. RAILFREIGHT. Michael Portillo opens a Section 8 grant-aided private rail terminal of EEC Quarries Ltd. at Wick Lane, Bow. This will enable EEC to move 250,000 tonnes of granite per year from its Croft Quarry in Leicestershire to London by rail instead of road.

12. TRANSPORT. In its new annual publication, Transport Statistics for London, the Department of Transport reveals that since 1983 the number of commuters to Central London using BR and the tube has risen by 19% and 42% respectively.

12. ACCIDENT REPORT. Broken safety rules cost the lives of four track maintenance men hit by a Leeds–Sheffield train on 8th December 1987 while using power hammers, says a Railway Inspectorate report released today.

13. BREL SALE. The BRB accepts the management (20%), Trafalgar House (40%) and ASEA

Brown Boveri (40%) buyout of BREL which employs 8,500 at York, Derby and Crewe.

13. ACCIDENT. An 11-tonne boat falls off a road transporter whilst crossing Brundall level crossing (on the Norwich–Yarmouth/ Lowestoft line). Part of the line is blocked by the boat and single line working inaugurated.

14. CHANNEL TUNNEL. Architects Ahreds, Burton and Koralek are nominated to develop proposals for the Channel Tunnel train servicing depot at 'North Pole' near Wormwood Scrubs, west London.

15. APPOINTMENT. The former chairman of London Underground, Dr. Tony Ridley – who resigned when the King's Cross fire report was published – is appointed managing director (project) of Eurotunnel.

16. NAMING. Class 89 89001 is named 'Avocet' by the Prime Minister, the Rt. Hon. Margaret Thatcher MP at King's Cross. The train travels to Sandy and back but, true to form, the PM choses not to go along.

16. SCOTRAIL. ScotRail announce that cycle capacity on Class 156 trains will be raised from two to four per two-car train from the summer in "the light of experience gained" elsewhere.

16. DISRUPTION. Bury–Manchester Victoria services are severely disrupted when a fault in an EMU causes a total power failure on the route. Diesel motive power is substituted after a lengthy delay.

19. SUPER SPRINTERS. The first Class 156 sets arrive at Inverness for driver training before service operation on Aberdeen/Kyle of Lochalsh/ Wick/Thurso lines in May.

20. CLAPHAM REMEMBRANCE. Leading politicians attend a memorial service to victims of the Clapham rail crash at Winchester Cathedral.

20. SCOTRAIL. Babcock Thorn at Rosyth Dockyard will carry out the internal refurbishment of 32 coaches used on Edinburgh–Glasgow services it is announced.

20. CHANNEL TUNNEL. A 14,000-name petition against BR's plans for a high-speed channel rail link is presented to Kent County Council.

20. CLOSURE. The four-mile freight line from East Dereham to North Elmham in Norfolk officially closes, one day after 31164 hauled the route's last freight train.

21. ACCIDENT. Single-car Class 121 unit No. 55033 fails to stop at Stourbridge Town station whilst working the 23.32 service from Stourbridge Junction. It runs through the buffer stops and adjoining wall. No-one is badly hurt.

21. PEAK RAIL. Having bought 800 metres of rail from BR, Peak Rail volunteers start to remove it from Ardwick West sidings near Manchester. It will be used for part of the Matlock–Darley Dale section of the line to Buxton.

21. WEST YORKSHIRE. A plaque is unveiled to mark the completion of Ilkley station's refurbishment (with the rest of the £3.6 million area development due to be finished in May).

23. WESTERN REGION. The Western Region introduces extra train services to relieve overcrowding, including an 09.10 Swansea–Paddington, an MO 09.20 Taunton–Paddington and a 15.22 Paddington–Bristol. Other services are extended, for example the 18.07 Paddington–Swindon is extended to Bath and Bristol.

23. RECONSTRUCTION. ScotRail announce that work will start on the £250,000 reconstruction of the Pitscottie Road bridge, near Cupar. The bridge, which crosses the main Aberdeen–Edinburgh line, was damaged when struck by a derailed freight train in June 1988.

23. SCOTRAIL. Class 156s are introduced on the Glasgow–Oban/Fort William routes. Journey time reductions on Glasgow–Fort William services are about 25 minutes.

23. CHANNEL TUNNEL. A waste train goes out of control in the service tunnel killing a construction worker, the project's first fatality.

24. MOTORAIL. The new national Motorail reservation office, transferred from London, is officially opened at Edinburgh Waverley station.

26. POLICING. It is announced that about 80 Metropolitan and City police officers are to begin duties on the London Underground it is announced. These officers will strengthen the Underground ('L') Division of the British Transport Police while extra BT police are being trained.

26. CROSSRAIL. BR chairman, Sir Robert Reid, welcomes the Central London Rail Study as an exciting opportunity to match Paris's rail system. Projects recommended for further study include fast, limited-stop underground North-South and East–West NSE/LUL lines (King's Cross/St. Pancras–Victoria, Paddington–Liverpool Street).

26. NETWORK SOUTHEAST. Options are published for the development of Waterloo–Exeter services over the next 40 years. Included is one for Salisbury–Exeter electrification (Worting Junction, Basingstoke–Salisbury electrification being under a different submission). Crewkerne, Axminster, Honiton and Exeter Central will receive much-needed refurbishments.

28. EDINBURGH. Work at Waverley station in the Calton tunnels in preparation for the introduction of electric services is completed at a cost of £700,000. The tunnels work involved partial relining following track singling, new drainage and ballasting and installation of catenary.

28. NEW COACH. The first Mark 4 coach is collected from Metro-Cammell's Washwood Heath plant.

30. TICKETING. ScotRail introduces airline-style APEX fares offering discounts on the normal Saver fare if bought at least one week in advance.

30. REORGANISATION. Salisbury, Portsmouth and Redhill area managers' areas are absorbed into new area boundaries.

31. BEST STATION. Templecombe, in Somerset, wins the 1988 'Best Station' competition, beating Dumfries, winner for the past two years and over 1,600 other BR stations. Best medium-sized station is Stratford-upon-Avon and best large station is York.

31. CUSTOMER CARE. Ipswich station staff receive the 'Best Customer Care' award. Helpfulness, quality of information given and cleanliness of the station set Ipswich above the other contenders.

31. IMPROVEMENTS. A £2 million improvement package for Blackpool North station is started.

FEBRUARY

01. BREL SALE. The director general of fair trading gives the go-ahead to BREL to operate as a privatised company. There will be no referral to the Monopolies and Mergers Commission.

03. 'PEAK' FIRE. Green-liveried Class 45 No. 45106 catches fire after failing on the 07.12 Derby–St.Pancras.

06. SAFETY. A £300 million programme to improve safety on the Underground is announced by London Regional Transport in response to the Fennell Report. Better safety training, clearer delegation of responsibilites, better communications and station modernisation are featured.

06. DOCKLANDS. London Regional Transport awards a £10 million contract for 10 more trains for the Docklands Light Railway. They will be needed when the Bank extension opens in 1990 with a full service operating in 1991. BREL Ltd. will build them.

06. STANSTED RAIL LINK. Excavation starts on the 1.8 km-long tunnel which will carry the £44

million Stansted Airport rail link beneath the airport's main runway and on to the new passenger terminal.

06. METROLINK. Workers start relocating telecommunications, sewer pipes, water, gas and electricity mains that are in the path of the new Manchester Metrolink. These services are diverted so that there is access – whether for maintenance or renewal – before on-street track is laid in the city centre. Roads are closed or made one-lane and traffic diverted.

07. RAILFREIGHT. Doncaster County Council and BR announce initial plans to develop a £5 million Channel Tunnel rail freight interchange at Doncaster Carr. It is part of a £35 million development covering 54 acres which will incorporate commercial and shopping facilities. The whole complex is close to the A1(M) and M18 and is called Fountain Park.

07. ELECTRIFICATION. The electrification of the 41-mile line between Cambridge and King's Lynn is authorised, together with the purchase of 7 x 4-car Class 321 EMUs at a cost of £20 million. West Norfolk Borough Council is supporting the project.

07. NETWORK SOUTHEAST. The purchase of 77 new Class 165 'Networker Turbo' vehicles is authorised for Marylebone services at a cost of £39 million. This is part of the 'Total Route Modernisation' of the Chiltern line from Marylebone to Aylesbury, High Wycombe and Banbury.

07. FLOOD. Following severe weather, the Waterloo Viaduct at Inverness collapses, severing the link to destinations farther north. ScotRail's general manager, John Ellis, pledges that the bridge will be rebuilt.

08. LAST TRAIN. The final freight train, hauled by 47532, operates from Tarmac's quarry at Caldon Low to Leek Brook Junction, before proceeding to Birmingham.

10. SIGNALLING ERROR. The 06.46 Penzance–Paddington HST, which normally runs via Bristol, is signalled on to the wrong track at Cogload Junction, Taunton. The driver is forced to make an emergency stop and then reverse to the correct line. Newspapers get hold of the story.

11. CLASS 442. The last 'Wessex Electric' set is delivered from Derby Litchurch Lane to Bournemouth.

12. CRIME. A gang of 'steamers' run through a Bedford–St. Pancras train robbing passengers of cash, credit cards and watches. Arrests follow quickly. 'Steaming' is yet another unwelcome American import.

12. TRACK REMODELLING. Line speeds at Chester East Junction are due to be increased following extensive work starting today to eliminate a severe speed restriction. The new layout should also improve operating flexibility.

12. CHANNEL TUNNEL. The mis-information continues: on discussing the planned high-speed link to the Tunnel the high-circulation 'Sunday Mirror' says that 12,150 square miles of Kent will be bulldozed. An artist's impression shows a Class 91 storming through Charing, Kent on single track and only feet from houses with no fence in between.

13. PUBLICITY. A five day behind-the-scenes 'Railwatch' series by the BBC begins. Eight million people watch the coverage of rail operations on the ECML and surrounding lines. Passenger, freight and station operations are covered, as is electrification, trackwork and new motive power. Today, John Prideaux, director, InterCity names HST power car 43108 'BBC Television Railwatch'.

13. CAMPAIGN. Local authorities in the East of Scotland, with the support of trade unions and chambers of commerce, launch the Campaign for Rail Electrification, Aberdeen to Edinburgh (CREATE). InterCity services to Fife, Tayside and Grampian serve 1.25 million people.

14. PRESERVATION. 'CLAN LINE' hauls the North Wales Coast Express test train.

14. ORDER. BREL wins an order worth over £12 million to build 20 DMUs for Thai railways.

▲Several landmarks were reached during the year for the £460 million electrification of the East Coast Main Line. Class 86/2 No. 86234 moves light engine at Whitehall Junction, Leeds, on its way to Doncaster after working the first electric train to Leeds, a charter from London King's Cross. The project is being funded entirely from BR's own resources. The date is the 18th February. *Les Nixon*

They will be air-conditioned and built at Derby Carriage Works.

14. NEW STATION. The new Epsom Downs station comes into use. At about 300 metres closer to London than the original terminus, the single-platform station has a shelter and will soon have a ticket office. The original 1865-built station buildings and forecourt have been sold for redevelopment.

14. FLOOD. The Reedham–Lowestoft line is flooded and damaged. Services are disrupted.

15. PRESERVATION. Netherlands Railways (NS) inspectors give official permission for EM2 27000 (ex NS1502) ELECTRA to run at main-line speed on the NS network as part of the NS150 celebrations to be held in the summer.

16. PROVINCIAL. The Monopolies and Mergers Commission report on BR's Provincial Sector is published. Concluding, the MMC says: "We find that the [BR] Board is not pursuing a course of conduct which operates against the public interest. On the contrary, we have pointed to the impressive achievement of Provincial in significantly reducing its costs while increasing its revenue and concluded that this is a clear endorsement of the Board's sectoral management of the railway."

17. LIVERIES. BR unveils its family of four liveries to be adopted for all diesel and electric locomotives by 1993. Corporate blue will be completely phased out leaving: 'InterCity', 'BR Mainline', 'Railfreight', 'BR General'.

18. VISIT. Class 86 electric locomotive No. 86234 becomes the first of its type to work to Leeds hauling the 'Thames–Eden' InterCity charter from King's Cross.

20. 'PEAK' CONDEMNED. Following serious fire damage Class 45 No. 45106 is officially condemned. The extended life of 45106 therefore lasted barely six months having been retained by the InterCity Charter Train Unit after the rest of the Class was withdrawn in August 1988.

20. ACCIDENT. 'Pacer' set 142049 is badly damaged whilst working the 19.20 Blackpool–Manchester. It struck a road crane which had been taken from a scrapyard and parked on the track near Salford Crescent, Manchester.

22. SCRAPPING. The pioneer Class 33 No. 33001 (D5600) is cut up at Eastleigh after having suffered collision damage.

23. TERRORIST ALERT. Services on the southern half of the WCML are brought to a halt for nearly five hours following a terrorist alert on the 13.40 Euston–Shrewsbury. Passengers are evacuated and services diverted.

23. CLOSURE. The Foss Islands branch in York closes after the loss of Rowntrees traffic.

25. PRESERVATION. A4 No. 2509 'SILVER LINK' alias 'BITTERN' moves to Tyne and Wear Stephenson Museum.

25. ACCIDENT. The 05.59 Sprinter from Chester to Shrewsbury is derailed after colliding with a lorry that had fallen onto the track from a bridge in Bradley, just north of Wrexham. No one is seriously hurt.

27. ACCIDENT. Two freight trains collide at Arpley Speedlink yard, Warrington. The driver of the 10.26 Dover Mossend Speedlink service and another railwayman die when it runs into the rear of the 21.15 Warrington–Doncaster Railfreight Distribution train. The loco involved is 85020.

27. AGREEMENT. A deal is struck between Humberside County Council and BR over the swing-bridge at Goole. The council will pay about £70,000 a year towards insurance cover on the bridge over the River Ouse (which carries the London–Hull line). Since the bridge was hit, London-bound trains have been diverted via Selby.

27. UNION. Mr Richard Rosser takes over as general secretary of the Transport Salaried Staffs Association.

27. STATION CONSTRUCTION. Work starts on Oxford's new £3.5 million station.

28. RAILFREIGHT. After being repaired at BRML Doncaster following its serious derailment at Copyhold Junction, Heywards Heath in 1988, 56062 is handed over to Railfreight in pristine condition.

28. AIRPORT LINK. The London Paddington–Heathrow airport high-speed rail link Bill is given an unopposed second reading in the House of Lords.

MARCH

01. CRIME PREVENTION. 'Station Watch', a new crime-prevention programme is initiated by British Transport Police. It is based on Neighbourhood Watch and Business Watch schemes. Based initially at Victoria, London, the scheme involves police lectures and a communication system between shops and to the police.

01. UNDERGROUND. New measures to speed up Victoria line trains and reduce both train and platform crowding begin at Victoria Underground station, the busiest on the system with 73 million passengers annually. New automatic station announcements – giving details of train crowdedness – and chimes to let passengers know that train doors are about to close should improve passenger flow.

02. MERSEYSIDE. Government grant (£316,000) and capital allocations (£1.1 million) for the Merseyside PTA to help with their programme of works to improve fire safety on the Merseyrail Underground are announced by the minister of transport.

03. NETWORK SOUTHEAST. It is announced that, as from 15th May, there will be no 'last trains' on the London Euston–Northampton line. All night services and new Class 321 EMUs from July are promised.

03. CLASS 91. The first revenue-earning operation of a Class 91 takes place. 91001 operates the 17.36 King's Cross–Peterborough commuter service with help from adapted HST power car No. 43083 'County of Derbyshire'.

04. PRESERVATION. The Swanage Railway's two-mile extension from Herston to Harman's Cross is officially opened by Gordon Pettit, Southern Region general manager.

04. DISRUPTION. Services out of Euston are disrupted at 17.00 when 85 013 catches fire while taking stock to Watford. Power is cut off for nearly two hours, but firemen cannot prevent the locomotive from burning out.

04. PURLEY TRAIN CRASH. Six die and more than 80 are injured when the 12.17 Littlehampton–Victoria EMU, travelling at 60 mph, crashes into the rear of the 12.50 Horsham–Victoria at Purley. The former consisted of Class 421 sets 1280 and 1295, the latter of Class 423 set 3441.

05. UNDERGROUND. Northern Line trains start to serve King's Cross Underground station again for the first time since the fire in November 1987. £10 million has been spent on the station which includes installation of new escalators fitted with a host of safety features.

06. GLASGOW TRAIN CRASH. Two die and 52 are injured when the 12.20 Milngavie–Springburn service collides with the 12.39 Springburn–Milngavie on a single track section by the junction east of Bellgrove station.

06. NETWORK SOUTHEAST. NSE orders 792 more 'Quickfare' self-service ticket machines bringing the total ordered to 1,200 at a combined cost of £21 million.

06. REFURBISHMENT. Work starts on the £600,000 modernisation of Twyford station, between Paddington and Reading.

08. HOLD-UP. The 18.00 Brighton to London Bridge mail train is held up by armed gunmen at Merstham. The gunmen take a bag of what turns out to be Polish newspapers.

08. DISRUPTION. For the second time in three weeks, InterCity and local services are severely disrupted for about four hours whilst police deal with bomb threats at Darlington station; again, it turns out to be a hoax.

08. IRELAND. The first set of Mark 3 push-pull coaching stock enters service when a single-cab GM 130, four TSOs and DTSO 6101 works the 12.55 Dublin (Pearse)–Drogheda.

09. RAILFREIGHT. Peter Walker MP, secretary of state for Wales, opens a Section 8 grant – assisted rail siding for Kronospan, chipboard manufacturers, at Chirk, Clwyd. The £900,000 siding will eventually handle 135,000 tonnes of timber per year.

09. SETTLE & CARLISLE. The minister for public transport, Michael Portillo announces the Settle & Carlisle line will stay open until mid-October 1989 to ease hardship on local businesses and tourist centres.

09. INQUIRY. An internal inquiry blames human error for the Glasgow train crash. This is a prelude to the public inquiry findings.

09. LAST SHUNTERS. The last three BR Class 03 shunters operating on the British mainland finish work at Birkenhead Docks: 03162/70 and 03073. Only the two Class 03s on the Isle of Wight remain.

09. FLOOD. Flooding results in the eight-day closure of the railway bridge over the River Rhondda at Trehafod. A Treherbert–Porth shuttle serves the north-western part of the route whilst a bus shuttle operates between Dinas and Trehafod (for trains to Pontypridd and south).

10. WEST HIGHLAND LINE. Disruption to passenger and freight services follows the derailment (caused by flooding) of the 23.18 Mossend New Yard–Fort William British Alcan Company freight train; eleven alumina wagons are derailed four miles south of Gorton. One particularly strange result is that Oban gains a sleeper service for three days until the line is cleared!

11. ELECTRIFICATION PROGRESS. A nine-day closure of the route between Newcastle and Darlington permits electrification of Durham Viaduct, a 135-year old Grade II listed building, and track realignment at Durham station. The electrification masts on the viaduct are of a special low-profile design to minimise environmental impact.

11. NEW ERA. 91 008 operates the first scheduled Class 91-hauled train to Leeds, the 06.50 from King's Cross. Until today, Class 91s had not ventured north of Grantham.

12. STUPIDITY. Vandals drop a shopping trolley with debris down a ventilation shaft in one of Sunderland's tunnels. A Middlesbrough–Newcastle Pacer DMU is damaged in the resulting collision.

13. APPOINTMENT. Mr Mike Rayner is appointed quality manager for the Provincial Sector.

13. DISRUPTION. An empty stock train leaving Brighton carriage sidings becomes derailed, blocking the Up main line to London and tripping out the electric current supply on all routes into Brighton station. Services are severely disrupted until late evening.

15. LIGHT RAIL. Three consortia are chosen to bid for Greater Manchester's LRT scheme – 'Metrolink'. They are: GMA Group (GEC, Mowlem, Amec); Hawker Siddeley/Norwest Holst/ Rosehaugh; Trafalgar House/BREL.

15. PROVINCIAL. Work starts on a £66,000 package of improvements for stations at Devonport, Dockyard, Keyham, St. Budeaux Ferry Road, St. Budeaux Victoria Road, Bere Ferrers and Bere Alston. The scheme is jointly funded by BR, Devon County Council and Plymouth City Council.

15. DAMAGE. Class 150/2 unit No. 150236 is damaged near Pontefract Baghill station when missiles are thrown off an overbridge. The unit was operating the 21.22 York–Sheffield. This stretch of line has gained a reputation for such mindless attacks.

15. TESTS. Class 50 No. 50024 hauls a high speed track test special from Penzance to Reading West with a view to increasing line speeds to, and in, the West Country.

15. RAILFREIGHT. Class 37 No. 37674 hauls the first Caledonian Paper Company china slurry train from Burngullow, Cornwall to Irvine, Strathclyde. At first the new service is Wednesdays only.

16. LAST FREIGHT TRAIN. Class 31 No. 31 217 with two barrier wagons and two ammunition wagons, with loco headboard 'The Last Trip', runs along the Warcop branch, the only branch line off the Settle–Carlisle line.

16. ENVIRONMENT. Mrs Virginia Bottomley praises a £5 million scheme to clean up a rail corridor on Merseyside. The route from Liverpool to Southport will be cleared of debris and stations cleaned. The Merseyside scheme is one of three pilot schemes: the two others are London Bridge–Sevenoaks and Glasgow–Motherwell.

16. NETWORK SOUTHEAST. NSE reveals its £500,000 snowblowing machine. The self-propelled, 34-tonne machine can be readily converted to work as a mobile inspection platform, a shrub-cutting unit and a shunting loco.

16. TELEVISION. The BBC screens 'By Steam to Sennar Junction' as one of its '40 Minutes' presentations. The rehabilitation of Sudan's railways including British-built steam locomotives and rail-cars is featured. The programme is produced by Paul Fabricius, respected for his coverage of railway matters.

17. CHANNEL TUNNEL. Paul Channon, transport secretary, switches on one of the two 1,350 tonne boring machines used to bore the main tunnels to France at a ceremony in Dover. Markham of Chesterfield built the £7.5 million machine.

17. DERAILMENT. The 05.00 empty stock train from Slade Green to Dartford is derailed at Slade Green sidings causing cancellations and diversions to passenger services until 12.30.

17. BOMB ALERT. A suspicious package is found on board the 13.05 Holyhead–Euston. The train is held at Nuneaton, passengers evacuated and some other services diverted via Birmingham.

18. CHANNEL TUNNEL. About a thousand protestors meet outside Maidstone town hall to complain about BR's plans for a high-speed rail link and its consultations with local councillors and pressure groups.

19. PRESERVATION. The first service train to use the North Norfolk Railway's 4-km extension from Weybourne arrives at Holt with a five-coach train from Sheringham.

20. RAILFREIGHT. The new £750,000 Millerhill signal box, near Edinburgh is officially opened. The first of its kind in Scotland, it is wholly owned by Railfreight and features solid state interlocking.

20. NEWSPAPERS. The 16.52 Weston-super-Mare–Bristol Temple Meads service makes several national papers when it overruns a red signal at Worle Junction, but manages to stop just short of the main Taunton–Bristol line.

21. ANNIVERSARY. Today marks the 150th anniversary of the opening in 1839 of both the Newcastle Upon Tyne and North Shields Railway and the Brandling Junction Railway. Two Metrocars, Nos. 4044 and 4051 are repainted in the coach livery of the 1839-formed companies.

21. UNUSUAL VISITOR. Class 309/2 'Clacton' unit No. 309624 leads units Nos. 309618 and 309627 into Birmingham New Street whilst operating a return Willesden–New Street overhead line and pantograph test train.

21. CLASS 83. No. 83012 is withdrawn from its Euston empty stock workings marking the demise of the class introduced in 1960.

22. INSTRUCTIONS. Paul Channon announces the remit he has given Mr Wilfrid Newton on taking up his new post as chairman of LRT: act on Fennell Report safety recommendations; provide greater capacity to cater for rising demand; improve quality and security.

22. WORST STATION. Clapham, south London, and Hunt's Cross in Liverpool beat more than 120 other contestants by being awarded joint winners of the Daily Telegraph's 'Best of the Worst' station (created in response to BR's annual Best Station award announced in February.

22. ORDER. A further 31 Class 321 units, costing £43.4 million are approved for purchase by Paul Channon, secretary of state for transport. Thirty-one sets, each of four cars, are destined for services out of King's Cross, Liverpool Street and Fenchurch Street. A total of 102 units are now on order.

22. INQUIRY. The public inquiry into the collision between two freight trains at Warrington (on

27th February) opens in Crewe.

23. PUBLIC INQUIRY. Even though the Wortley curve (between Wortley West Jn. and Wortley South Jn., Leeds, has been 'closed' for five years, a public inquiry is held into its closure. BR's methods in avoiding using the line (with echoes of Settle and Carlisle) had been declared illegal under the terms of the Transport Act 1962 by the High Court in an action brought by Bradford Council.

23. NEW TRAINS. Most Manchester–Buxton services are greatly improved with the introduction of Class 150/2 Sprinters on the line. They are replacing Class 108s.

24. DEATH. The driver of the 04.40 Treherbert–Cardiff dies at the controls but the brakes apply automatically.

25. EXPANSION. The Forth Valley line opens the extension to Birkhill.

26. OBSTRUCTION. The 11.28 Leeds–St Pancras HST hits a metal object placed on the track at Luton North Junction rupturing the front power car's fuel tanks.

27. IMPROVEMENTS. Engineers complete a four-day remodelling of the approaches to Liverpool Street station. A total of 1,000 metres of new switch and crossing rail is relaid as is over 1 km of new track. No trains run west of Stratford or south of Hackney Downs. Meanwhile, signals and telecommunications engineers commission the new £2.5 million Liverpool Street Integrated Electronic Control Centre which features solid state interlocking and automatic route setting.

27. SETTLE & CARLISLE. Due to planned permanent way work on the West Coast Main Line between Carnforth and Carlisle, services are again diverted over the S & C during the weekend. By today a total of 116 diversions have operated over the three-day Easter weekend.

27. RATIONALISATION. Cramlington station, between Newcastle and Morpeth, becomes an unstaffed halt from today.

28. NEW VIADUCT. ScotRail announces detailed plans to invest £3 million in a new single-track viaduct over the River Ness to replace the Waterloo Viaduct destroyed by flooding.

28. DISRUPTION. Serious signal failures start in the morning peak in the Liverpool Street area. Great Eastern and NE London lines are seriously affected. The next day, about one in three trains are terminated short of Liverpool Street. (The only time this technology has been used before has been at Leamington Spa). Problems concern interference to trackside micro-processors resulting in signals returning to red.

28. LAST TRAIN. The final official train runs along the Appleby–Warcop branch, a railtour, the 'Eden Vale Creamer' from London.

29. INQUIRY. The Purley rail disaster public inquiry opens in Croydon.

29. PROVINCIAL. A 'road lift' starts at Inverness to transport five 2-car Class 156 sets to Dingwall. These will operate Dingwall–Wick/Thurso services until the severed link is repaired. Seven InterCity charter coaches for 'The Orcadian' (and eventually nine 'Hebridean Heritage' carriages) are also being moved north. Ten BP tank wagons, two Class 37s and 10 coaches will be moved south to Inverness. Work has already started on the £250,000 temporary maintenance depot at Muir of Ord.

29. FRANCE. The TGV Sud–Est services cross the point of carrying 100 million passengers since they began in September 1981. The 108 sets of the PSE fleet have covered 238 million km.

29. TRANSFER. B1 4–6–0 No. 61306 is moved to Hull Dairycoates from the Great Central Railway.

29. NETWORK SOUTHEAST. After two weeks of complete closures of the Waterloo and City line during peak hours due to the appalling reliability of Class 487 trains, services are returned to normal. The line was closed because it was deemed that overcrowding on the two available units would be dangerous.

31. RAILFREIGHT. The 9 km freight-only Appleby–Warcop line is closed. The line, used by army ammunition trains, earned BR over £50,000 per year. The army was one of the last two freight customers on the Settle–Carlisle line.

31. WEST YORKSHIRE. The West Yorkshire PTA orders 10 x 2-car Class 158 Sprinter Express units to ease overcrowding in advance of plans being drawn up to electrify certain lines in West Yorkshire.

31. SETTLE & CARLISLE. Over the last year (1st April 1988 to today) no less than 495 diverted WCML trains have used the Settle–Carlisle line, 408 of those during March 1989 when diversions occurred every weekend.

31. SALE COMPLETE. The Vale of Rheidol Railway passes into private ownership. The Brecon Mountain Railway paid £306,500 for the narrow gauge line.

31. NEW SUB-CLASS. The first two members of a new privately-owned sub-class of locomotive leaves Hunslet-Barclay's Kilmarnock works for Horsham. Class 20/9 locomotives 20901/4 (formerly 20041/101) will initially operate the Chipman weedkilling train.

APRIL

03. COSTLY LIVING. Pullman breakfasts on InterCity trains go up from £9 to £9.95, one of 100 increases on food and drink charges averaging 10%, another above-inflation rise.

03. GOOD INVESTMENT. The BR Pension Fund sells 25 works of art for £38 million: it bought them in the mid-1970's for £3.5 million, a real rate (i.e. above inflation) of return of 12% p.a.

03. NEW STATION. Tutbury and Hatton station on the Crewe–Derby line re-opens. Tutbury station closed in November 1966. Derbyshire and Staffordshire County Councils (£20,000 each), South Derbyshire and East Staffordshire District Councils (£5,000 each), the Rural Development Commission (£25,000) and the Nestle Company (£2,500) have supported BR with its re-opening. By May a more intensive hourly service in each direction will operate from the unstaffed station.

03. RAIL STRIKE. After increasing its 6.7% pay offer, BR offers the unions a 'final unconditional' 7% pay offer.

03. BOMB SCARE. Services are disrupted when a bomb is reported on the 08.40 Euston–Wolverhampton; it turns out to be a hoax.

03. ESSEX. Class 310 units are introduced on Clacton/ Walton-on-Naze–Colchester workings releasing Class 313 units to the Great Northern.

04. ORDER. BREL (1988) wins an order for 58 more Class 158 DMU vehicles.

05. CRITICISM. The North West branch of the Town & Country Planning Association criticises Network North West's plans for the region as "little more than cosmetic." The association demands electrification of trans-Pennine routes as a start.

05. POLICY. The chief secretary to the Treasury, John Major, says in a written answer that the required rate of return for nationalised industrial and public sector trading organisations will be raised from 7% to 8%.

05. ASLEF/LUL DISPUTE. ASLEF drivers hold the first unofficial strike on the London Underground.

06. CHANNEL TUNNEL. The value of orders placed by Transmanche-Link to British companies for the Channel Tunnel Project hits £500 million.

06. SAFETY. It is revealed that all 129,000 BR staff are to be given training in fire safety in a two-year training programme starting next month. This is a response to the King's Cross disaster.

06. BREL. The European Commission agrees to BREL writing off debts of £64 million which now clears the way for a management buy-out. The last week in March sees £107 million worth of business attracted.

06. DERAILMENT. The 10.36 Waterloo–Southampton is derailed near Wimbledon. Services are disrupted but nobody hurt. The unit involved is 4 Cig No. 1822.

07. NAMING. The first Class 442 'Wessex Electric' to be named is No. 2402 'COUNTY OF HAMPSHIRE' at Eastleigh station.

07. CARLISLE. HRH the Duchess of York officially opens Carlisle station's new £700,000 ticket-office complex.

07. MIDLINE. The Walsall–Hednesford line is formally re-opened. Ceremonies are held at Landywood, Cannock and Hednesford, with other new stations at Bloxwich and Broad Lane to be completed later. The line last saw regular passenger trains in 1965. West Midlands PTE (£230,000), Staffordshire County Council (£200,000), South Staffordshire District Council (£25,000) and Cannock and Chase District Council (£76,000) have all supported the project.

08. VALLEYS LINES. Two youths park a stolen dumper truck across the track at Treorchy on the Pontypridd–Treherbert line. They are caught and charged later.

09. SCOTRAIL. One month after work started on the £300,000 temporary maintenance depot at Muir of Ord, engineers discover a 5-metre under-water scour in the central pier of the Conon viaduct (between the depot and Dingwall, temporary terminus for Far North/Kyle services) and it is closed to all traffic for repairs to be effected.

10. INVESTMENT PLEA. John Banham, director-general of the CBI, calls for a faster planning framework and greater public and private sector investment in infrastructure to counteract the transport thrombosis caused by congestion.

10. CRIME. The first passenger train on the re-opened line between Walsall and Hednesford is taken out of service after hitting concrete blocks thrown on to the track by vandals.

10. PRESERVATION. 'Schools' 4–4–0 'REPTON' arrives at Felixstowe.

10. ACCIDENT. Portsmouth–Cardiff services are delayed when a Class 156 DMU hits a dumper truck which had fallen onto the line after a platform coping stone gave way during construction work at Swanwick associated with the 'Solent Link' electrification and improvements.

11. SETTLE & CARLISLE VICTORY. In the first unsuccessful application by BR to shut a line since Mrs Thatcher took office, Paul Channon rejects plans to close the 72-mile Settle & Carlisle line. He says that "a number of factors" had changed since last year. The threat to the Blackburn–Hellifield line is also lifted.

11. ACCIDENT. Six people are hurt when the 07.25 Tattenham Corner to London Bridge train hits the buffers at its destination.

11. VANDALISM. Two miles of overhead line are brought down causing 24 hours of disruption to services on the Great Eastern line when vandals dangle an obstruction in front of the 15.56 from Witham. The cab sustains damage.

11. STUDY. Tyne & Wear PTA commissions consultants to investigate the feasibility of a Metro link to Washington and Wearside.

11. BIRMINGHAM. Main-line and local services in the Birmingham area are cancelled, diverted or delayed when high winds blow down a wall of Duddeston carriage sheds during demolition work. Cross-city and Walsall services are worst affected.

12. RAILFREIGHT. Peter Bottomley, parliamentary under secretary of state for transport announces a grant of £750,000 to British Coal towards new facilities and track at Blyth, Northumberland. This will allow 1.5 million tonnes of coal at present transported by road to be switched to rail.

12. EXHIBITION. Today marks the opening of a three-day exhibition Rail Freight 89 at Cricklewood, north London, the largest freight exhibition since 1981.

12. NEW ROUTE. Class 155 No. 155 314 travels on the Swindon–Oxford–Bicester–Bedford–Corby–Peterborough route to evaluate a possible future service.

14. SERVICE QUALITY. Mr Michael Portillo, in a Commons written reply, says BR's InterCity trains failed to meet Government punctuality and

▲The most important railway event of 1989 was the reprieve of the Settle & Carlisle line. 47291 heads the King's Cross–Carlisle 'Thames-Eden' InterCity excursion train at Garsdale on 7th.   *Les Nixon*

reliability targets during 1988. The network, which was expected to get 90% of its trains within 10 minutes of its timetable, managed only 87.3%. The reliability target of 99.5% of services to run was missed by 0.5% NSE fared better on punctuality, with 91.3% of services within 5 minutes Provincial had 90% within 5 minutes. NSE and Provincial fell short on reliability.

14. UNION. Mr Jimmy Knapp, general secretary of the NUR since 1983 (then replacing Sid Weighell) is re-elected unopposed.

15. DISASTER. Sheffield station manager Richard Sworoski praises staff at Sheffield and Wadsley Bridge stations who helped distressed supporters following the Hillsborough football disaster in which 95 died. They offered free use of the emergency 'phones and arranged tickets for those who had lost them in the confusion. Only one football special was run to Wadsley Bridge.

17. DERAILMENT. Part of the Milford Haven–Theale Murco tanker train becomes derailed on the curve between Hawkeridge and Heywood Junctions (Westbury), spilling some of their load. The two wagons involved are righted and track repaired.

18. BREL SALE COMPLETED. The sale of the BRB's engineering subsidiary BREL (1988) Ltd. to a consortium comprising the management and employees of BREL, Trafalgar House PLC, and Asea Brown Boveri Ltd. is completed. BREL will now consist of a New Construction Group and a Manufacture and Repair Group.

18. INVESTIGATION. Transmark Worldwide is commissioned jointly by the London Regional Passengers Committee, Essex County Council and London Underground Ltd. to undertake a study of the existing and potential future use of the Epping–Ongar branch of the Central Line.

18. WORKS STATION. Toyota announce plans to build a £700 million car plant at Burnaston, near Derby, in preference to sites in South Wales and Humberside. Dr Toyoda, the company president, had chosen the site after a careful review of infrastructure. Derbyshire County Council has pledged to improve roads, with funding from the DTp. Other promises include a railway station nearby at Willington. Enhanced rail services from Peartree are also in prospect.

18. REDEDICATION. Sir Robert Reid, BR chairman, rededicates LNER K4 2–6–0 No. 3442 THE GREAT MARQUESS at the Severn Valley

Railway.

18. WEST YORKSHIRE. The PTA's campaign to make public transport more accessible to people with mobility problems continues with a braille guide to local and longer-distance public transport opportunities and facilities.

19. RECORD. For the second year running, Andrew Kendall of Moreton in the Wirral, Merseyside, wins BR's Young Super Traveller of the Year Competition with 116,224 miles in 1988, an increase on his 1987 mileage.

19. ACCIDENT. The driver is killed after leaping from his locomotive before it crashes into the rear of a slow moving freight train, the 13.32 Wareham–Eastleigh, at Holton Heath, Dorset, on the Bournemouth–Weymouth line. The locomotive involved is 33107.

19. INVESTIGATION. The public inquiry into the Bellgrove, Glasgow, accident, which occurred on 6th March, opens.

20. TRAVEL GUIDE. Provincial and the Automobile Association produces a new book 'See Britain by Train', an important and surprising departure for the huge motoring organisation.

21. OPENING. The Swansea Vale Railway Centre is formally opened.

22. RAILTOUR. Class 5 No. 44932 hauls the first Midland Counties 150 Lincolnshire Poacher tour.

22. CHARTER. A Class 91 No. 91003 works InterCity's 'Thames Eden Ltd' Settle and Carlisle charter train between King's Cross and Leeds. This is the first time a Class 91 is used on a charter special.

22. TRACK LIFTED. The last of the remaining sidings and up side platform are removed after two weeks' work at the once expansive Seaton Junction station between Yeovil Junction and Exeter.

22. END OF AN ERA. The last Class 45 'Peak' locomotive, the re-instated 45128, is written off. This is 30 years and one day after the first, D1 'Scafell Pike', was displayed to the public. All 193 'Peaks' (Classes 44,45 & 46) built are now withdrawn from capital stock.

24. DEATH. Inspector Jack Street dies on the footplate of No. 6201 'PRINCESS ELIZABETH' working a 'Wye–Dee Express' special train.

24. SCOTRAIL. ScotRail announced that Haymarket South Tunnel in Edinburgh will close

between 15th May and 1st October for fitting of concrete slab track.

24. ELECTRIFICATION. The last 'open country' Scottish electrification mast is 'capped' at Dunbar station on the East Coast Main Line.

24. TRAINING TRAIN. A Class 305/302 hybrid EMU, now converted to a mobile training unit is handed over to InterCity. It will be used for training staff on electrification matters. The ancient unit is in InterCity livery and carries departmental numbers: ADB 977639/640/641.

24. CLASS 91. No. 91009 starts a week of acceptance trials on the West Coast Main Line.

25. PRESERVATION. Return to steam and rededication of King No. 6023 'KING EDWARD I.'

26. BORDERS. Senior girls at Moreton Hall School near Oswestry, Shropshire, are praised for their efforts at the official opening of the school's travel centre. All profits will go towards their long-term campaign to re-open Whittington station, now scheduled for 1991.

27. SIGNALLING. BR orders signalmen to be extra vigilant following faults which have caused some Sprinters to disappear momentarily from track control panels. Faults have occurred at Diss, Annan and Swindon.

27. UNDERGROUND. "We want to move away from the cold greys and blues of the 1960s and 70s and introduce warmer colours," said Mr Bill Clarke, development director, after announcing that brighter colours are to be introduced on the interior of LUL trains to cheer up passengers and staff.

27. DERAILMENT. The rear five coaches of the 18.14 London Euston–Northampton 'Cobbler', hauled by 85012, become derailed just south of its destination.

28. CLOSURE. The secretary of state for transport gives his consent to the withdrawal of passenger service between Mexborough East Jn. and Aldwarke Jn. near Sheffield. This is subject to the new Swinton curve being open in May 1990.

28. REFURBISHMENT. The refurbished Gobowen station on the Chester–Shrewsbury line is officially re-opened. The £300,000 scheme has been shared between BR, the Rural Development Commission, the Railway Heritage Trust, English Estates and local councils.

28. FIRST RUN. The Travelling College makes a successful Cardiff Cathays–Swansea return test trip hauled by 47537.

MAY

01. DIESEL DAY. The National Railway Museum diesel day is held.

01. VANDALISM. Train services between Rugby and Coventry are severely disrupted by repeated vandal attacks at various locations along the notorious stretch of line.

01. SCOTRAIL. After the asbestos-infested 1960s station building at Elgin, between Aberdeen and Inverness, is demolished, work starts on a £380,000 replacement.

02. TRAVELLING COLLEGE. HRH Princess of Wales unveils The Travelling College at Cardiff. The 13-carriage train, converted at a cost of £500,000, and is owned by Mr Barrie Masterton, a Welsh businessman.

02. SCOTRAIL. A ceremony is held to mark the completion of the £425,000 refurbishment of Dundee station.

03. LIGHT RAIL. The first Avon Metro Bill receives an unopposed third reading in Parliament. It provides for a £28 million, 16 km link between Bristol and Portishead.

03. BRITISH TRANSPORT POLICE. London Underground and the British Transport Police open a £1.2 million satellite police station at Finsbury Park Underground station. This will compliment similar bases at East Ham, Heathrow and Stockwell and is part of a £15 million programme to reduce crime on the Underground.

03. NUR/LUL DISPUTE. London Underground is granted a High Court injunction outlawing the planned strike on 7th May. The NUR complains that it has had no time to prepare a defence after LUL's last-minute legal challenge.

04. CANADA. After a C$500 million investment in the line CP Rail (part of Canadian Pacific) opens the new Roger's Pass Tunnel. The line now features 34 km of new track of which 14 km is new tunnel. Gentler gradients will reduce operating costs.

04. NUR/LUL DISPUTE. The NUR's April ballot is ruled invalid by the High Court. The issues mainly revolve around LUL's 'Action Stations' programme. This includes promotion based on merit rather than seniority and changes to transfer arrangements. There are 10,000 NUR members on LUL including stations staff, drivers, guards, track and signalling staff.

05. UNION. Mr Derrick Fullick will be the next general secretary of ASLEF it is announced. He will be general secretary elect until the end of 1989 and will replace Mr Neil Milligan who has held the post since Mr Ray Buckton left on 20th October 1987.

05. RAIL STRIKE. The National Union of Railwaymen calls a strike ballot of its 75,000 BR members over BR's 7% pay offer and changes to pay bargaining. Members are asked if they would support an overtime ban and/or 24-hour strikes.

07. HOPE VALLEY LINE. The last steam excursion runs on the route, hauled by Class 8F No. 48151. The line is now deemed too busy for steam excursions.

08. ACCIDENT. Class 156 No. 156491 on the 21.30 Manchester–Leeds hits the buffer stops at Bradford Interchange and is badly damaged. Brake failure at Bowling Junction was the cause.

08. RAIL STRIKE. On the Southern Region, ASLEF drivers begin an unofficial overtime ban.

09. RAIL STRIKE. BR imposes its 'final offer with no strings attached' on the rail unions.

09. REPRIEVE. The British Railways Board advises the secretary of state for transport that it wishes to withdraw the closure proposal for the 7 km stretch of line from Henley in Arden to Bearley Junction and Wootton Wawen station, Warwickshire. The closure had been proposed in 1984.

09. NORFOLK. With BR's imminent closure of the East Dereham–Wymondham freight-only branch, a meeting of the Mid-Norfolk Railway Project group attracts many supporters of a re-introduction of passenger services.

10. HOLIDAYS. BR's Gold Star Holiday business, formerly known as Golden Rail, is sold to Superbreak Mini-Holidays, a London-based business owned by BR until 1983.

11. YORK. After a warning about severe disruption to passengers, BR starts a four-day signalling commissioning and platform renumbering at York. The number of platforms is reduced from 16 to 11.

11. NEW STATION. Yate station on the Bristol–Gloucester line re-opens. Trains last served Yate in 1966. The £140,000 station includes parking space for 65 cars.

11. NEWSPAPERS. 'The Guardian' reports that breaking up BR by selling shares in its current operating divisions has emerged as the government's favourite option for if the railways are privatised.

11. RAIL STRIKE. In Network SouthEast, the sector with the greatest staff retention problems, BR offers additional allowances to selected staff groups including locations further from central London. This represents another 2% on the offer for these employees.

12. GRAFFITI REMOVAL. The last graffiti-covered train on the New York subway is taken to the scrapyard. It marks the end of a £66 million four-year campaign to wipe the scrawl from trains by The New York City Transit Authority. Now LUL is under pressure to start a similar campaign, although £500,000 a year is already spent and £2.5 million is budgeted to improve security around depots where most vandals 'hit' trains.

12. KING'S CROSS. The architect Norman Foster formally submits a revised design for the international concourse of King's Cross to Camden

◄107746 is at Miliken Park for the official opening ceremony on 15th May. 318 250 pauses with a Largs–Glasgow Central service. *Tom Noble*

▼156 473 stands at Yate, Avon, on 11th May at the end of the opening ceremony. The platforms are staggered, each side of the overbridge. *Mike Goodfield*

Council. The whole scheme involving four international platforms, two more for Thameslink, ticket halls, customs and passenger lounges are dealt with in King's Cross Railway Bill which passes its second reading in Parliament.

12. GUARDIAN ANGELS. The 'Guardian Angels' stage a 'passing out' parade of 30 recruits. Each has had 120 hours of training in law, martial arts and first aid.

12. FAVERSHAM, KENT. The last mixed-traction driver's duty takes place. From tomorrow drivers are restricted to EMUs and no longer take turns on Class 33 and 73 locomotives on freight, engineering ot parcels trains; Network SouthEast therefore now has full use of Faversham drivers.

13. SUPER SPRINTERS. The first Class 155s start running again after lengthy safety modifications. Last November, all 42 were withdrawn for door modifications. Seven Class 155s owned by the West Yorkshire PTE were also withdrawn. From today, the WYPTE units work the Calder Valley route.

13. NEW ARRIVAL. A Class 321 works on the West Coast Main Line for the first time, operating on a Rugby–Northampton service.

13. OPENING. Islip station, re-opens on the Oxford–Bicester line. Trains last served Islip in 1967.

13. MORECAMBE. Bare Lane station, the only

intermediate station on the branch to the Lancashire resort, becomes unstaffed. A ticket issuing machine is to be installed.

14. CLASS 50. After a reign of 12 years, Class 50s work their last schedule weekend Hereford–Paddington services. Class 47s will take over.

15. INTERCITY. The biggest speed improvements in the new timetable are on the West Coast Main Line with the fastest London–Glasgow service covering 401 miles in 4 hours and 53 minutes.

15. SCOTRAIL. ScotRail inaugurates its new Edinburgh–Dunfermline–Thornton–Kirkcaldy–Edinburgh service, improving travel opportunities in Fife. Meanwhile, Aberdeen–Inverness services change to Class 156 operation.

15. RESERVATIONS. BR-appointed travel agents will get direct access to European railways' computer reservation systems for the first time this summer, it is announced today. Using the separate facility on BR's Railtrak system, agents can book and confirm through the Fastrak Viewdata link.

15. NEW STATION. Dodworth station, near Barnsley, re-opens exactly 30 years after BR closed it.

15. NSE TIMETABLE. Despite industrial problems, NSE's new timetable features several improvements. The frequency of off-peak Hastings–

Charing Cross services is doubled to half-hourly. Also in Kent, Maidstone East is served by a new weekday non-stop service each hour to London Bridge, Waterloo and Charing Cross.

15. NETWORK SOUTHEAST. Chris Green launches 'Project 89' on NSE, just over three years after the sector's launch. "We really do want the customer to be a guest on the railway, not just a face in the crowd." With the launch of 19 brand names for individual lines, the whole emphasis will be on making lines more individual and personal. Specially-branded routes will all have their own route managers. There will be 'surgeries' with commuters. 'Excellence Vouchers' worth £25 are to be introduced to reward staff who show extra customer service.

15. DIVERSION. Manchester Victoria loses its remaining InterCity services and most long-distance Provincial services to Manchester Piccadilly.

15. SUPER SPRINTERS. West Yorkshire PTE's Class 155s are withdrawn from service again due to more problems with doors.

15. RAIL STRIKE. The white-collar union the Transport Salaried Staffs Association (TSSA) conference decides to refer the pay issue to the Railway Staffs' National Tribunal (RSNT) an independent body consisting of three members. The ASLEF conference postpones plans for a strike ballot by 33:13; it would concentrate on the bargaining procedure dispute. The NUR is on its own regarding the pay offer.

15. WEST YORKSHIRE. Whilst calling for more government support to increase capacity and so reduce overcrowding, the PTE adopts Network SouthEast's target of not expecting passengers to stand for more than 20 minutes, or allow a train to be loaded to more than 135% seating capacity. This implies greater capacity on 11 specified services.

15. NEW STATIONS. ScotRail and Strathclyde PTE open five new stations: Drumgelloch, Greenfaulds, Stepps, Airbles and Milliken Park. Total cost is £1.7 million.

15. PARCELS. From today the Parcels Sector no longer has a requirement for the Class 127 DPU sets based at Longsight.

15. RENAMING. Clapham station becomes Clapham High Street.

15. SWANSEA DOCKS. The end of an era occurs with the arrival of the last train of vacuumbraked MDV wagons.

16. DERAILMENT. An ammunition train becomes derailed at Cambuslang, Glasgow whilst carrying smoke mortar shells from the Royal Ordnance factory at Bishopton, Renfrewshire, to an ammunition store at Longtown, near Carlisle.

16. GUARDIAN ANGELS. British Guardian Angels begin patrolling the London Underground for the first time. Under the suprvision of Mr Curtis Sliwa, their leader, they are told to be "courteous and vigilant."

16. WITHDRAWAL. The Class 33 locomotive, No. 33107, involved in the accident at Holton Heath on 19th April, is withdrawn.

17. CATERING. NSE announces privately-run refreshment trolleys on seven more routes. It brings to 11 the number of Network services with on-train trolleys that are privately-run.

17. STATIONS. Carnforth station, Lancashire, becomes an unstaffed halt from today.

18. SETTLE & CARLISLE. Thirty-seven days after its surprise reprieve, BR forms a Joint Line Liaison Group to plan the future of the Settle–Carlisle line, including the new timetable.

18. VANDALISM. Vandals armed with rifles shoot out signal lights at Temple Mills with the result that the Sizewell–Sellafield nuclear flask train is derailed.

18. ACCIDENT. A railman is killed and his driver injured when their coupled locomotives ram into a line of empty coal wagons at Worksop depot in the small hours. The crushed loco is 20134.

18. APOLOGY. BR Anglia Region staff hand out 100,000 leaflets to commuters at Liverpool Street during the evening rush hour. Headed 'Sorry' and including a free travel voucher, it says BR wants to offer a "tangible apology for the appalling delays that occurred in the two weeks after Easter." Up to two adults and two children can take a standard class trip at BR's expense anywhere on NSE and parts of the InterCity area before 30th June.

18. DELAY. The introduction of £166 million fleet of Class 158 Express units is postponed. Construction problems at BREL partly revolve around working in welded aluminium instead of steel, and difficulties over the supply of some components. BR Provincial is reportedly unhappy with BREL's performance.

18. CLAPHAM INQUIRY. On the 51st day of the public inquiry into the Clapham rail crash, Sir Robert Reid says that the victims did not die in vain: "We have learned lessons that will save lives and make rail transport even safer." He gives his commitment to three innovations: the Automatic Train Protection system; cab radios; tachographs. The main problem is to combat human error. He reveals that Paul Channon had told him that the government would give "sympathetic consideration" to major investment in safety measures.

18. ELECTRIFICATION. BR dismisses the idea of onward electrification from Edinburgh to Aberdeen at a cost of about £80 million. Sir Robert Reid, in a letter to an Aberdeen MP, says the "InterCity 125 can offer most of the benefits of speed and comfort ... traditionally thought of as being available only with electrification." Only an oil price rise and/or a cut in electricity prices would alter the equation.

19. STEAM. Jubilee Class 4–6–0 No. 45596 'BAHAMAS' hauls the first BR load test between Derby and Sheffield as a prelude to being passed for main-line running.

20. OPEN DAY. Network SouthEast's Ilford open day attracts 10,000 visitors. Locomotives from A4 Pacific No. 4498 'SIR NIGEL GRESLEY' to EM2 No. 27000 'ELECTRA' to 'Deltic' D9000 'ROYAL SCOTS GREY' to brand new Class 91 No. 91010 are among those present.

20. SWITZERLAND. The metre-gauge Rhaetishe Bahn celebrates its centenary this year with the first event taking place at Chur today. The first train ran from Landquart to Klosters in October 1889.

20. SUMMER EXTRAS. The first summer Saturday trains of 1989 run with BR declaring its determination to improve the lot for InterCity holiday travellers; more widespread use of HSTs and, on certain routes, compulsory seat reservations are the means.

21. DIESEL DAY. The InterCity diesel day is held at St. Pancras with a variety of diesel-hauled trains working to Leicester and back, mostly via Corby. Classes 20, 33, 37, 47, 56 and 58 operate, the less powerful locos running double-headed.

22. ASLEF/LUL DISPUTE. After the fourth unofficial strike by ASLEF drivers on the Underground, management say that the strike is being led by "shadowy figures." Denis Tunnicliffe, managing director of the Underground says: "To accede to demands which have never been put to us formally ... and in defiance of union instructions would be to allow industrial anarchy."

22. ASLEF/BR DISPUTE. The unofficial overtime ban by ASLEF drivers on Southern Region ends.

22. WATERLOO. The main pedestrian entrance to Waterloo station, the Victory Arch, and adjoining facade are floodlit for the first time during a ceremony to mark the occasion.

22. TERM STARTS. The world's first purpose-built Travelling College starts a four-day London–Oxenholme–Edinburgh–York–London inaugural excursion.

23. FENNELL AFTERMATH. Recommendation 131 in the report by Desmond Fennell QC called for the Railway Inspectorate under review. The RI's report, out today, makes 71 recommendations. Mr Channon calls for decisive action by London Re-

gional Transport's chairman, Mr Wilfrid Newton. Priority areas for improvement listed are leadership in health and safety management, job evaluation, organisational rules, and emergency preparedness.

23. NAMING. As part of the Midland Counties 150 events, BR Research Division locomotive 97561 is named 'Midland Counties Railway 150 1839–1989'. The locomotive is repainted in Midland maroon livery, lined in yellow with mid-grey roof and wrap-round yellow warning ends.

24. PROFIT. InterCity becomes the only national passenger railway network in the world to operate profitably. John Prideaux, InterCity director, confirms a provisional profit figure for 1988/9 of £24 million, a year earlier than government targets.

26. SALE. Laird sells Metro-Cammell to GEC–Alsthom for about £35 million, with a condition that a further £9.5 million is paid if Metro-Cammell win certain other contracts.

27. PRESERVATION. Today marks the first main line revenue-earning trip for Jubliee Class 4–6–0 No. 45596 'BAHAMAS'.

29. FIRE. The third floor of the former Midland Grand Hotel at St. Pancras is gutted by fire. It is a Grade II listed building.

29. PRESERVATION. Following the commissioning of the rebuilt Llangollen Goods Junction signal box earlier in May, two-train operation on the Llangollen Railway begins for the first time by means of the associated loop.

29. STRATHCLYDE. The first Strathclyde PTE-liveried Class 156s Nos. 156501/3 arrive at Corkerhill for crew training.

30. RAIL STRIKE. The NUR holds its strike ballot on pay and bargaining.

31. ORDER. Associated Roadstone Company (ARC) order four Class 59 locomotives from General Motors EMD and sign the contract today. The locos will be designated Class 59/1. All will be based at Whatley Quarry.

JUNE

04. ANNIVERSARY. The Midland Counties Railway 150 celebrations reach their height on the anniversary date of the Nottingham–Derby line in 1839. Platform 5 publishes 'Midland Railway Portrait' to celebrate the occasion.

04. SOVIET UNION. The world's worst rail tragedy for eight years occurs in the Urals. A gas pipeline leak, sparked off by a train, causes an explosion wrecking two passenger trains. 650 people are killed. The disaster occurs on the Trans-Siberian railway, 8 miles from Asha, 750 miles east of Moscow.

04. ARRIVAL. Foster Yeoman's fifth Class 59, number 59005 arrives from the USA at Felixstowe docks.

05. ROADS. Britain agrees to let 40-tonne lorries operate on its roads from 1999 under EEC rule changes.

05. CENTRAL WALES. From today, loco-hauled trains over the Swansea–Shrewsbury route can traverse it at 45 mph instead of 30 mph, back to the situation before autumn 1980.

06. CLAPHAM INQUIRY. The last submissions for the Clapham Junction Accident Investigation are made.

06. BELFAST–DUBLIN LINE. A £50 million upgrading of the line is announced by Northern Ireland Railways and Irish Rail. Relaying continuous welded rail and installation of multi-aspect signalling will increase the maximum line speed to 100 mph. Some new air-conditioned coaches will operate with existing 071/111 Class General Motors locomotives.

07. DEATH. Celebrated photographer and S&D expert Ivo Peters dies.

08. OPENING. North Tyneside Railway opens at North Shields.

08. UNDERGROUND. The five-year £19.5 million remodernisation of Piccadilly Circus Underground station is completed. The station serves over 36 million passengers annually.

09. DERAILMENT. A Bidston–Wrexham

DMU is derailed south of Bidston at 40 mph when it strikes debris left on the line by vandals.

10. BIRTHDAY. On the third anniversary of the launch of Network SouthEast, another Network Day is held. Passenger demand is now 12% up on 1986.

11. IMMIGRATION. Turkish Stanier 8F arrives at Immingham bound for Swanage.

12. EXTRA COACHES. Transport secretary Paul Channon gives BR approval to buy 31 new standard class Mark 4 carriages for London–Scotland services. They will permit nine-coach formations, as originally envisaged. The order is worth about £8.7 million.

12. RAIL STRIKE. The NUR ballot favours strike action over pay and bargaining by a margin of 3:2. The Advisory Conciliation and Arbitration Service (ACAS), independent arbitrators not connected with the railway, or any other industry, calls both parties in dispute to talks.

13. RAIL STRIKE. ASLEF recommends a ban on overtime and rest-day working in a ballot of its 17,500 BR members over the 7% pay offer after a month's postponement of a decision.

14. IMPROVEMENTS. A jointly-funded BR/Welsh Development Agency improvement scheme at Neath station, east of Swansea, is completed.

16. RAILFREIGHT DISTRIBUTION. Paul Channon opens the £2.25 million Wilton Railfreight Distribution depot at Middlesbrough. It is one of the British 'hub' centres for European freight traffic and the first new intermodal freight terminal to be built by BR for 17 years.

16. NETWORK SOUTHEAST. The refurbished station at Faversham, Kent, is officially re-opened. Total cost of the work was £300,000.

16. RAIL STRIKE. After half-an-hour of talks at ACAS, BR says it is seeking a High Court injunction to stop the strike. BR claims to have received 'hundreds' of complaints that union members did not get ballot papers. Commentators see this attempted legal block as BR's first major mistake of the dispute. The unions leave the talks and BR say that the offer would have risen had they stayed. The unions know more money is available: mistake number two.

17. BARNSTAPLE. Class 50 No. 50042 hauls a ballast train from Exeter Riverside to Barnstaple, the first member of its class to visit the town. This is a week after Cowley Bridge Junction–Barnstaple was passed for Class 50s and Class 47s, excluding the heavier Class 47/4s with twin tanks.

18. OUTPOST. Three years after the formation of Network SouthEast and 172 miles west of London Waterloo, NSE station signs are erected at the cavernous Exeter Central station. Revenue taken at this station has more than doubled since 1985 and a £200,000 refurbishment is almost complete.

19. PRESERVATION. The East Lancashire Railway's new station at Ramsbottom, present terminus of the line from Bury is formally opened at a civic ceremony.

19. CHANNEL TUNNEL. Farthinglow Construction Village at Dover is formally opened. It was operational from January 1989 and houses up to 1,150 employees. A strange sight, it is visible from the A20.

19. UNDERGROUND. Paul Channon approves the preparation of detailed plans to build a Jubilee line extension from central London to Docklands.

19. RAIL STRIKE. The High Court finds that BR's evidence does not justify the injunction. The decision is upheld on appeal. In a press statement the NUR says: "In contrast to BR's misguided excursion to the courts, London Underground and the NUR's negotiators are now down at ACAS trying to find a way out of our problems." The appeal judge describes the NUR as "a highly responsible union."

20. AWARD. BR's newly-formed Architectural Services Group wins an international commendation for the £475,000 refurbishment of Scarborough station funded by BR Provincial, Scar-

borough Council and the Railway Heritage Trust.

21. RAIL STRIKE. The first 24-hour strike is held by NUR members bringing the BR and LUL rail networks to a halt. This is the first major NUR rail strike since 1982, before that the 1926 General Strike. Meanwhile BR chairman is criticised for being in Utrecht to attend the 150th anniversary of the start of Dutch railways.

22. RAIL STRIKE. The NUR decides to call their members on BR and LUL out on strike on Wednesday 28th June and Wednesday 5th July. The NUR attacks BR's apparant plans to use the industry's arbitration service, the RSNT, to settle the dispute because of the time needed to come to a conclusion and the irony involved: in the proposed bargaining machinery changes the Board intends to abandon the RSNT.

22. UNDERGROUND. A study into Northern Line-modernisation is started. The study concentrates on the purchase of about 115 trains and increasing the line's capacity. A new computer-based automatic train control system called Transmission Based Signalling (TBS) is being considered. Paris's RER Line A and the Vancouver and Toronto metro systems already use forms of TBS.

22. RAILFREIGHT. A 10-year contract to transport domestic refuse by rail is signed in Edinburgh. The first of its kind in Scotland, Railfreight will arrange 5 trains a week, each carrying up to 550 tonnes of waste, from Edinburgh District Council's compaction depot at Powderhall to a private siding at Kaimes, near Kirknewton.

22. PRESERVATION. Wales Railway Centre at Bute Road station, Cardiff, is officially 'launched' when delivery is taken of a diesel shunter from British Coal's Maesteg Washeries to be used for shunting the ten ex-BR steam locomotives being restored.

22. NETHERLANDS. The 'Trains through Time' exhibition opens in Utrecht as part of the NS 150 celebrations.

22. SEVERN-DEE LINE. Rossett station, between Wrexham and Chester re-opens for the day when a school party joins a Shrewsbury–York special organised by the Moreton Hall School travel centre. The last use of the station was in 1964.

24. AUCTION. The nameplate of ex-LMS Jubilee Class 4–6–0 No. 5595 'SOUTHERN RHODESIA' fetches £16,800 at the Myers Grove School, Sheffield Railwayana auction – a record price.

25. WALES. Sugar Loaf Halt is re-opened for 11 weeks from today to serve Heart of Wales Rambler trains.

27. PRESERVATION. First public North Wales Coast Express runs.

28. NEWSPAPERS. The national newspapers make the most of photographs of the Queen in a traffic jam on the way to a function in the City, caused by the rail strike.

28. ASLEF/LUL DISPUTE. ASLEF drivers on the Underground vote 13:1 in favour of official one-day strikes over their pay claim which centres around additional payments for operation of one-man-operated (OMO) trains. LUL insist that drivers already receive £6 out of every £10 saved from OMO operation. The NUR's 2,000 LUL drivers are in dispute over the same issue.

28. RAIL STRIKE. The second NUR 24-hour strike is held. Trevor Toolan, director, employee relations at BR attacks the NUR over their entrenched attitudes.

29. RAIL STRIKE. BR press advertisements urges the NUR to take the pay dispute to the RSNT, a procedure established since 1956.

30. RAILFREIGHT. Colin Driver, BR's director, freight, accepts 60001 'Steadfast' from Brush Electrical Machines' at their premises in Loughborough, the first of 100 Class 60s in a £120 million contract. The main bulk businesses of Coal, Construction, Metals and Petroleum should benefit from lower operating costs, partly due to the locomotives' better rail adhesion.

30. CLOSURE. The freight-only line between Wymondham Junction and Dereham, Norfolk,

closes.

JULY

01. ANNIVERSARY. Celebrations of the centenary of the Chesham Metropolitan branch commence. The first of 28 special trains between Chesham and Watford are operated by GW 0–6–0 pannier tank 9466 and, at the other end, ex-Metropolitan electric locomotive No. 12 'Sarah Siddons'.

01. RAIL STRIKE. After BR invites the NUR for talks, the union dismisses the offer as a "public relations exercise." Michael Meacher, shadow employment secretary, meanwhile gives his support to win the NUR. They are, he says, "in a position to win the dispute and deserve to win it."

03. NETWORK SOUTHEAST. Dr Robert Runcie, archbishop of Canterbury, re-opens renovated Canterbury East, following a £400,000 station facelift.

03. ELECTRIFICATION. BR engineers energise the wires between Arksey (north of Doncaster) and Copmanthorpe (south of York).

03. RAIL STRIKE. Amalgamated Engineering Union (AEU) workers, mainly at BR depots decide to join the NUR's 24-hour strikes. Meanwhile the NUR dismisses BR's offer for pay talks.

03. NORTHAMPTON LINE. Chris Green, director of Network SouthEast takes delivery of the first Class 321 No. 321 401 for the Northampton Line.

03. LIVERY. A Class 321 in the proposed Class 322 Stansted Express livery appears at York Works. Five Class 322s are being built, essentially 321s with more spacious seating and extra room for luggage.

04. RAIL STRIKE. Despite BR's attempts to split the pay and bargaining issues, NUR advertisements say that only ACAS can deal with them both. Also, from now on Union leaders have the power to call strikes on two days per week.

04. PRIME MINISTER. Mrs Thatcher attacks the rail unions for breaking a 1956 agreement to go to the RSNT before taking industrial action and who were now setting pre-conditions for further talks.

05. DOVER. Plans for a £70,000 investment in a new passenger information system at Dover Western Docks are announced.

05. NETWORK SOUTHEAST. In a jointly-funded programme, Network SouthEast and the Thurrock Training Association announce plans for environmental improvements to stations between Shenfield and Southend Victoria. Shenfield, Billericay, Wickford, Rayleigh, Hockley, Rochford and Prittlewell stations will benefit.

05. RAIL STRIKE. The third NUR 24-hour strike is held and is as solid as the first two. The general public, whilst often inconvenienced seem generally sympathetic to the rail workers' frustration over low pay.

05. MEETING. The RSNT meets regarding the TSSA's referral of the BR pay offer.

05. ASLEF/LUL DISPUTE. Today marks the first official 24-hour ASLEF strike on the LUL network. Congestion in London in particular is severe with BR and LUL networks not in operation. ASLEF say that two more stoppages will occur on Wednesday 12th July and Tuesday 18th July.

05. BAD TIMING. BR's annual report is released for 1988/9. On the day of the third national rail stoppage, BR reveals that a profit of £304 million is the best result since nationalisation 40 years before. This figure has been achieved after a £549 million subsidy, a reduction of 5,090 jobs, fare rises of up to 21% and income from property sales and rents of £335 million.

05. CARDIFF. The director of Cardiff airport urges the need for a new rail link to Rhoose. Until then, he says, road congestion on routes to Cardiff means that some passengers risk missing their flights.

06. RAIL STRIKE. ASLEF ballot results are announced: an 8:1 call for industrial action over pay on BR consisting of a ban on overtime and rest-day working.

07. RAIL STRIKE. The RSNT recommends an 8.8% pay award for TSSA members, with no conditions, and notes the high productivity of rail workers. BR invites the unions back to ACAS. This is the watershed in the strike. The award applies to the TSSA but in reality would have to be paid to all workers.

08. PRESERVATION. Class K4 2–6–0 No. 3442 'THE GREAT MARQUESS' begins the long journey back to Scotland.

10. ACCIDENT. The 08.56 Liverpool–Kirkby collides with buffers and is derailed at its destination. It lodges under the bridge situated between the two dead-end lines from Liverpool and Wigan.

10. DERAILMENT. Class 47 number 47488 'Rail Riders' plus four carriages are derailed when a tyre on the locomotive is shed. The 14.20 Newcastle–Liverpool is derailed just south of Darlington station and the accident causes major disruption on the East Coast Main Line.

10. NETWORK SOUTHEAST. Driver-only operation on the London Euston–Watford suburban lines starts today. Also, Class 321s begin operation on Euston–Northampton (–Birmingham) services.

11. BOMB ALERT. Newcastle station is sealed off by police for two hours when a suspected bomb is found in a left-luggage locker on the concourse. Train services are severely disrupted until the all-clear is given.

11. CLOSURES. In a review to 'improve housekeeping', two lines are now identified by BR for closure: the 18-mile Doncaster–Gainsborough line and the 20-mile Gainsborough–Barnetby line, previously proposed for closure.

11. RAIL STRIKE. BR and the unions meet to discuss the RSNT award. BR offers 8.8% with pre-conditions: an end of industrial action, no additional payment for cashless pay or working in the South East. BR refuses to backdate pay to April; the unions walk out.

11. MODERNISATION. The rebuilt Brondesbury Park station is officially re-opened as part of the modernisation of NSE's North London Lines. £174,000 has been spent on the station with Kew Gardens and Gospel Oak to follow.

12. RAIL STRIKE. On the day of the NUR's fourth national 24-hour rail strike, BR drops the previous day's pre-conditions. It does, however, make the offer subject to progress on new bargaining machinery on which the new deadline is February 1990; basic pay, hours and conditions will still be negotiated nationally.

12. NETWORK NORTHWEST. Wall posters blame delays and cancellations since the new May timetable was introduced on staff shortages and the withdrawal of Class 155s (used on Manchester/Liverpool–Cardiff and York/Leeds–Manchester/Blackpool services). Continued vandalism is also blamed.

13. 'NEW' TRAINS. At a ceremony at Ryde Pier, IOW, the first of the 'Island Line's' 'new' (ex-1938 LUL stock) Class 483 trains is shown off to the civil dignitaries.

13. ASLEF/LUL DISPUTE. The 2,500 ASLEF drivers on the Underground accept a £42 rise, more than the £30 per week originally offered by LUL but less than the £64 per week demanded for OMO. 'Strings' are attached though and talks at ACAS continue.

14. OPENING. John Cameron, owner of A4 No. 60009 'UNION OF SOUTH AFRICA' opens the boiler shop at Bridgnorth.

14. RAIL STRIKE. The TSSA accepts BR's 8.8% pay offer.

14. DISPOSAL. The last 36 milk tank wagons are taken from storage sidings to Vic Berry's for disposal.

15. INVESTMENT. BR receives £19.5 million in European Regional Development Fund grant from the EEC today. Representing the most recent award, it is specifically for the Newcastle Area Resignalling scheme which in total costs £31 million. ECML electrification has now attracted grants worth £47 million.

15. SWINDON. Five years after BREL closed its Works with 2,000 redundancies, Honda announces plans for a £300 million car assembly plant providing 1,300 jobs. A sign of the times?

17. UNDERGROUND. Sixty changes to new automatic gates at 63 LUL stations are recommended by independent experts called in by London Regional Transport. Last week the gates were branded 'mechanical rottweilers' in demonstrations by pensioners. London Regional Transport accepts the recommendations which cover certain changes to the design, layout, maintenance and staff operation.

17. RAIL STRIKE. ASLEF accepts BR's pay offer and their ban on overtime and rest-day working is lifted. The NUR executive votes 12:8 not to accept it to many observers' surprise. The NUR say that they want to return to ACAS. Robert Reid, BR chairman says no more cash is available. Jimmy Knapp urges members to resist the "threats and blandishments" of management.

17. SURPRISE VISITOR. Four months after the last 'official' freight and charter trains worked the line, No. 20902/903 haul the Schering weedkilling train from Appleby to Warcop and back.

18. RAIL STRIKE. On the day of the fifth national rail strike some Waterloo–City and Ashford–Rye services operate. There are reports of splits in the NUR executive.

19. EXTRA CAPACITY. The capacity of the DLR will have doubled by early 1990, Michael Portillo says, due to the introduction of two-car trains. A further increase is planned for early 1991 with the delivery of new trains, bringing capacity to some 6,500 passengers per hour compared with 1,750 at present.

19. DOCKLANDS EXTENSION. Two years after first opening, it is announced that the Docklands Light Railway will be extended from Poplar to Beckton with intermediate stations initially at Blackwall, Brunswick Wharf, Canning Town, Victoria Docks, Custom House, Prince Regent, Royal Albert Dock, Beckton Park, Cyprus and Gallions Reach.

19. RAIL STRIKE. In announcing a sixth national strike on the following Wednesday, the NUR continues to urge BR to meet at ACAS over pay and bargaining. On the Underground, pay and the Action Stations proposals are still to be resolved. The NUR begins to lose public and political support.

20. DERAILMENT. The 14.00 Glasgow Central–Euston, hauled by 85023, is derailed at Harrow. Travelling at 100 mph the train splits into two, sending two carriages hurtling along the track on their sides. Services on the West Coast Main Line are seriously disrupted with trains being diverted to Paddington or terminated at Watford. Over 300 people were on board with a total of five coaches being derailed.

20. VALLEYS SERVICES. Two 7-year-olds start a fire at Stormstown Sidings near Abercynon that severely damages three Class 118 vehicles, a Class 116 DMBS and a Class 110 TSL. This compounds problems caused by life-expired first-generation DMUs failing in the July temperatures. Sprinters normally on the line are on cross-country services, until the 155s return.

20. RAIL STRIKE. Neil Kinnock, leader of the Opposition, indicates that the NUR should accept BR's offer.

20. INQUIRY. The inquiry into the two-train collision at Holton Heath on 19th April is opened. It is promptly adjourned to allow unions to try to indemnify rail staff involved from criminal prosecution.

21. NETWORK SOUTHEAST. Completion of a £62,000 refurbishment of Oakleigh Park station, which is situated between King's Cross and Potters Bar, is marked at a ceremony.

21. ROYAL ASSENT. The Bill for the 8 km Poplar–Beckton DLR extension gains Royal Assent.

21. DERAILMENT. The 08.40 Wolverhampton–Pwllheli, operated by 150 138 becomes derailed at Barmouth, another incident

during a year of poor reliability and punctuality on the line.

22. NEW STATION BUILDINGS. Ingrow West station on the Keighley and Worth Valley Railway is formally opened.

23. PROVINCIAL. The summer-only Blaenau Ffestiniog–Trawsfynydd service starts operation. The CEGB provides onward bus services for tourists to the power station.

▲ Cecil Parkinson, MP, the new secretary of state for transport. *Department of Transport*

24. GOVERNMENT RESHUFFLE. In the prime minister's reshuffle, Paul Channon is sacked and Cecil Parkinson, 57, is appointed secretary of state for transport. Nicholas Ridley is moved from environment to trade and industry, Chris Patten becomes secretary of state for the environment. Cecil Parkinson follows Messrs. Channon, Moore, Ridley, King, Howell and Fowler, holders of the post since 1979.

25. REPORT. The Central Transport Consultative Committee publishes its annual report. Major-General Lennox Napier says that passengers are being robbed of the quality of service they expect. Cancellations are up, fare rises "outrageous", overcrowding worse and reliability of trains and catering facilities poor. There was a strong link between cuts in government grant and the quality of service being provided. About 10% of InterCity trains arrived more than 10 minutes late. Network SouthEast showed a slight improvement with more than 90% of trains arriving within 5 minutes of the advertised time. 10% of Provincial trains arrived more than 5 minutes late.

25. APPOINTMENTS. Mrs Thatcher puts the finishing touches to her reshuffle with appointments to the lower ranks of the Department of Transport.

25. LIGHT RAIL. The last three competing consortia to build and run Greater Manchester's Metrolink LRT system submit their final bids today: GMA Group; Hawker Siddeley/Norwest Holst; Trafalgar House/BREL.

25. ANGLIA REGION. £3 million will be spent upgrading overhead electric lines to improve the reliability of services to Liverpool Street it is announced. Non-standard catenary will be renewed between Chelmsford and Colchester and modifications made to the pantograph dampers on Class 86 locomotives to reduce damage to the carbon strip and catenary.

25. TELECOMMUNCATIONS. Peter Borer is appointed director, commercial telecommunications unit of BR. The Board wants to exploit its telecommunications assets in the new liberalised market.

26. EAST LONDON. Cecil Parkinson announces the conclusions of the East London Rail Study launched in January. Consultants recommend that the best option for a second line to the

Docklands is a Jubilee-line extension: Green Park–Waterloo–London Bridge–Canary Wharf–Stratford. The cost will be over £900 million. The Department of Transport wants "sufficient contributions" from private sector developers.

26. RAIL STRIKE. On the day of the sixth NUR 24-hour strike between 6,000 and 12,500 NUR members turn up for work. BR claims success. When over 2% of services run, Jimmy Knapp accuses the Board of "double-counting ghost trains." London's traffic is still heavy – ASLEF drivers on the Underground are holding their 13th strike–but commuters are adapting.

26. FIRE. Erdington station, between Birmingham New Street and Sutton Coldfield on the Cross City Line, is badly damaged after vandals set it alight. It is decided to demolish the Victorian buildings as a result.

26. CHANNEL TUNNEL TRAINS. A £600 million contract is placed for the supply of shuttle trains to carry cars, coaches and HGVs.

27. COMMONS. The Commons Select Committee on Welsh Affairs says that Wales could gain from tourism and business investment from the Channel Tunnel but would require a major improvement in road and rail links.

27. LEEDS. Leeds City Council unveils plans for a £150 million overhead rapid segregated transport system.

27. RAIL STRIKE. The NUR accepts BR's offer and suspends industrial action pending negotiations on bargaining machinery. It warns that a long-term campaign of eradicating low pay will continue. Workers in the South East will be paid the 8.8% plus an improved regional allowance.

27. NUR/LUL DISPUTE. The NUR executive calls for a further 24-hour strike on the Underground on Wednesday 2nd August. Action Stations proposals and payments for OMO trains are still the sticking points.

28. CLOSURE WITHDRAWAL. BR withdraws its plans to close the Doncaster–Gainsborough Line. Gainsborough–Barnetby will still go ahead for closure.

28. PROVINCIAL. New 'quality targets' are set by the government. Long-distance provincial trains now have the same target as InterCity trains – 90% of services must arrive within 10 minutes of the scheduled time. Short-distance Provincial trains will have the same targets as NSE: 90% of trains to arrive within 5 minutes of scheduled time.

28. NEW TEAM. Cecil Parkinson announces the responsibilities of his ministerial team. Michael Portillo will be second in command and continue as minister for (public) transport. His brief includes responsibility for the Channel Tunnel fixed link and for promoting private sector finance in all modes of transport. Responsibilities are also detailed for the two parliamentary uder secretary of states Robert Atkins and Patrick McLoughlin. The former is minister for roads and traffic, the latter the minister for aviation and shipping.

28. CONTRACT. The contract for the construction of the new railway bridge over the River Ness at Inverness is awarded to Fairclough Scotland Ltd.

29. ACCIDENT. One freight train runs into the back of another near West Brompton station on the West London line between Clapham Junction and Kensington Olympia. The driver and an engineer in the locomotive are killed and the second man is seriously injured. It occurred during an engineers' possession of the line. The loco is 215.

). NEW STATION. Llanrwst station, nearer the town centre, is opened. The existing station the Llandudno Junction–Blaenau Ffestiniog e is renamed Llanrwst North.

BIRMINGHAM. The 06.25 Bradford Forster Square–Paignton HST, headed by 43040 hits a BR van that had run out of control onto the k at Barnt Green. Southbound services are rted via Stourbridge Junction and Worcester ub Hill.

DEATH. David Garnock, the Earl of dsay, owner of the LNER K4 No. 3442 'THE GREAT MARQUESS' dies. His wish to see the engine back on the West Highland Extension was fulfilled just 16 days before his death.

31. APPOINTMENT. John Edmonds, Anglia Region general manager since its formation in 1987, becomes a full-time executive member of the British Railways Board. As managing director, group services, he is now responsible for self-accounting services such as architecture, Transmark and information systems. His replacement at Anglia is Mr David Burton.

31. KENT. Class 205 DEMU No. 205101 hits a van on the open crossing at Appledore whilst working the 07.31 Ashford–Hastings. No-one is hurt.

AUGUST

01. DOCKLANDS. Cecil Parkinson gives consent for a £240 million extension of the DLR. Opening in 1992, it will extend the railway from Poplar to Beckton, passing close by London City Airport. Trains being ordered (from BN Constructions of Belgium) would run from the city to Beckton every four minutes during rush hour, giving the DLR a capacity of 14,000 people an hour-eight times the present level. Chippenham-based Hawker-Siddeley Rail Projects is a major sub-contractor.

02. GRANT. It is revealed that the EEC will provide the bulk of grants totalling £430,000 for the Ffestiniog Railway to promote tourism in North Wales. The Welsh Tourist Board will also contribute towards construction of a two-road carriage shed at Glanymor, station improvements and three coaches.

02. TYNESIDE. Vandals derail a Metro train carrying 150 passengers near Heworth, Gateshead. They had thrown steel beer kegs onto the line. This act receives national coverage four days later when general analyses are made of vandalism against the railways.

02. RAILFREIGHT. Cerestar, starch and glucose processors, opens new sidings to the main Trafford Park sidings. Until then Cerestar had solely been using contract road distribution.

03. LITTER. InterCity says that it is investing £500,000 in 3,500 new-style litter bins to be fitted in all InterCity coaches over the next three years. They will replace those already fitted. £143 per bin?

04. TEST TRAIN. The first testing of a full Mark 4 coaching stock train takes place on the East Coast Main Line; it comprises DVT 82200, coaches 11201, 10300/1/2, 10202, 11200 and Class 91, 91010.

05. LIGHT RAIL. It is announced that six groups will bid to build the £100 million 'Supertram' system in Sheffield with submissions in mid-September. They are Mowlem-GEC; Balfour Beatty Power; Hawker Siddeley Norwest Holst; Alfred McAlpine; Henry Boot-Gleeson; CIE Consult.

05. TRANSFER. Rebuilt Royal Scot No. 6115 'SCOTS GUARDMAN' is moved by rail from Dinting to Tyseley.

06. DERAILMENT. The 21.15 Oxford–Paddington train is derailed at West Ealing station. Two of the nine coaches roll on to their sides. Class 50 No. 50025 and one of the coaches catch fire. The accident blocks all lines out of Paddington to Bristol, Wales and the West. The loco and coaches 5165 and 5205 come off worst.

07. ORDER. One hundred years after Charles Brush started his factory in Loughborough, the company wins a large order to supply Moroccan National Railways with 19 Bo–Bo diesel-electric shunting locomotives, each with a Cummins engine.

07. VISIT. Cecil Parkinson, secretary of state for transport, makes his first official visit to BR in his new role when he tours NSE's Great Northern Line. He says that future applications for railway investment can expect a sympathetic hearing.

07. REWARD. BR offer a £10,000 reward to catch vandals who derailed the previous day's 21.15 Oxford–Paddington. More facts emerge: 74 minutes earlier the 20.45 Paddington–Reading train hit an object on the same stretch of line. The fated 21.15 train hit the object at Hanwell at 70 mph, possibly chosen to be next to a viaduct for maximum casualties. The locomotive pushed the object along the line for a mile before hitting points and jamming. The last 280 yards of track were ripped up. Another down train passed close by the wreckage.

07. SCOTRAIL. New Class 156s enter service on the Glasgow (Queen Street)–Cumbernauld line. Station stops include the two new stations at Stepps and Greenfaulds opened in May and which now attract about 550 passengers a day each. The new trains replace Class 101 DMUs.

08. FINE. The driver of last December's King's Cross–Aberdeen train involved in the accident at Newcastle is fined £60 for driving through a red light. Fifteen people were injured in the crash on the King Edward Bridge. The driver had claimed that the signal was on yellow.

08. AUSTRALIA. No. 4472 'FLYING SCOTSMAN' beats the world record by the longest non-stop journey by a steam locomotive completing 422.1 miles between Parkes and Broken Hill in Australia. It is touring Australia as part of the country's bicentenary celebrations.

08. MIDLINE. Nearly one km of track between Barnt Green and Redditch is closed until 11th August for the installation of continuous welded rail. For the first time in the area steel sleepers are used instead of concrete. Replacement bus services operate.

09. WATERLOO. Sixty people are affected by CS gas at Waterloo station. Police say opponents to the Channel Tunnel are "prime suspects." The gas was sprayed near the Lost Property Offices and telephone exchange. Security will be stepped up after this, the latest of a series of incidents. Work is about to start at Waterloo on alterations to accommodate the new trains.

09. CHANNEL TUNNEL LINK. BR announces its changes to the preferred route of the proposed high-speed link. Kent County Council reject them as "not good enough." The changes – introduced to overcome fierce environmental objections – meet only a few of the 60 demands put to BR in public.

09. REPAIRED. InterCity services are restored to normality between Paddington and Reading following the repair of damage after Sunday's derailment.

09. MEXICO. Over 100 passengers are killed when the 'El Burro' train from Mazatlan (on Mexico's Pacific coast) to Mexicali (on the Californian border) plunges off a railway bridge into the rail-swollen Bamoa river in the north west.The locomotive and two carriages end up in the river. About one hundred more people are reported missing.

09. BIRTHDAY. Pembroke Dock station celebrates its 125th anniversary.

09. PROVINCIAL. Yate, Avon's newest station is proving highly successful. Opened on 11th May 1989, nearly 300 passengers use the station daily. Seven trains a day run to Bristol, six head north to Gloucester.

09. NUR/LUL DISPUTE. The NUR accepts ACAS's proposals for settling the dispute. For the 2,000 train operators and guards, an average 11.5% rise on basic wages is agreed, the extra in recognition of the productivity gains from OMO operations. The Action Stations scheme is withdrawn.

09. ASLEF/LUL DISPUTE. ASLEF accept LUL's 8.75% pay offer back-dated to April (also awarded to LUL's NUR employees). This is in addition to concessions from LUL to OMO payments agreed in July. Several other issues are resolved.

09. COMMUNICATION PROBLEMS.The new public address system for stations between Lockwood and Denby Dale on the Penistone line,installed in July, is rendered silent after cabling is stolen.

12. DOCUMENTARY. Channel 4 screens

Equinox: 'Fatal Attraction' comparing public transport provision in Birmingham and Cologne. Light rail schemes are evaluated.

12. NORTHERN IRELAND. Great Northern Railway (I) V Class compound 4–4–0 No. 85 'Merlin' hauls a special train from Belfast Central to Lisburn to commemorate, to the day, the running of the first train between the towns. The celebrations also mark the 21st anniversary of the formation of Northern Ireland Railways.

13. OPINION POLL. According to a BR public opinion survey only 20% of people are in favour of the railways being denationalised. Around 41% said BR should definitely remain publicly-owned. 19% said it probably should not be sold off. If privatisation was inevitable, 50% thought BR should be broken up into a series of operating companies, 35% thought it should remain a unified national network.

13. PRESERVATION. First public passenger service occurs for the newly-restored Isle of Wight Central Railway No. 11.

13. NEWCASTLE. The north face of the new island platform 15 is brought into use as part of the station's remodelling before catenary is installed.

13. LEEDS. The same gang attempts to derail Class 156 490 on the 17.48 Scarborough–Liverpool service and also drops ballast collected in a blanket on 47423 at the head of the by then stationary 12.17 Poole–Newcastle. The incidents occur in the eastern suburbs at Cross Gates.

14. ELECTRIFICATION. Work starts on electrifying the King's Lynn–Ely line. Train services will be suspended between 09.00 and 16.00 Monday–Friday until 1st October for work to take place. The whole programme will cost £20.1 million.

14. UNDERGROUND. One of the prototype Underground trains becomes derailed at Neasden station on the Jubilee Line. A bracket holding one of the electric motors snapped, fell onto the track jamming the points mechanism. The incident delays announcment of which firm will win the huge contract to build a fleet of new trains as part of the £750 million Central Line modernisation.

14. PHOTO CALL. One of the fastest steam locomotives in the world meets one of the slowest at Lubcke Siding between Tarcoola and Alice Springs in Central Australia. In a publicity photograph that makes the national newspapers, the now superceded 3 ft 6 in gauge Old Ghan stands alongside No. 4472 'FLYING SCOTSMAN' on the new line. The A3 hauls a 712-ton tare weight train on the 490-mile route.

14. MISNOMER. The West Ealing crash locomotive No.50025 'Invincible' is officially condemned after 21 years' service and vincible only at the hands of vandals.

14. ASLEF/LUL DISPUTE. After four months of one-day official and one-day unofficial strikes, the last unofficial 'wildcat' strikes are called off with London Underground ASLEF drivers' pay rise pay (agreed on 13th July) now being backdated to 10th April.

15. MEMORANDUM. A confidential memo from David Rayner, joint managing director (railways) to Maurice Holmes, safety director, is leaked to the press. It urges a tightening of safety standards and mentions "shades of Clapham installation practice." It follows the findings of an internal inquiry into the derailment at Harrow on 20th July. A heavy alternator cradle had fallen off the carriage underside of 12061 becoming entangled in the wheels. It had been insecurely fastened. After checks, alternator cradle faults were found on another 16 Mark 3 coaches.

15. VERDICT. Accidental death verdicts are returned by a jury at Warrington of two rail workers who died after an accident on 27th February. Two goods trains collided at Warrington. The loco in which the two men were killed ran into the back of the stationery goods train. Tests reveal an intermittent fault in the wiring of the lamp battery on the freight train's tail light.

16. BRAKING PROBLEMS. Thirty Class 90 locomotives are withdrawn due to deterioration in part of the valve seating which supplies air to the braking system, a fault discovered during routine examinations.

16. TOXIC WASTE. Stourton freight depot staff refuse to work near toxic waste stored there and only yards from the Leeds–Normanton line. A dispute over whose responsibility the waste is has gone on for several months between three companies, BR not included.

16. INDUSTRY. Tiphook, the huge wagon and trailer rental group, buy Railease, the leasing side of Standard Wagon of Heywood, Lancashire.

16. NEW BUSINESS. A new company, Charterflow, is formed from the previous operational side of Standard Wagon. It aims to act as an intermediary between BR Railfreight and private firms interested in transferring traffic to rail.

17. DERAILMENT. Vandals derail two tankers on a goods train just outside Hebden Bridge, West Yorkshire.

17. PORTUGAL. Seventeen people are injured when an Express train bound for Porto collides with a locomotive near the Portugese pilgrimage town of Fatima.

17. DEATH. Richard Levick, Midland Railway Centre workshop manager, dies in an accident at Butterley.

17. INDUSTRY. Powell Duffryn takeover Standard Wagon's manufacturing operations.

18. LONG-DISTANCE COMMUTING. Due to the withdrawal of Class 90s, Class 321 units 321 401/8 provide a London Euston–Manchester Piccadilly return service.

18. TAUNTON. To match the northbound one, a new £100,000 car park is opened alongside the southbound platform. It can accommodate up to 150 cars.

19. TRANSPORT SAFETY. After the M1 air crash and Purley and Glasgow rail crashes earlier in the year, 63 people die when a barge hits a small pleasure boat, the 'Marchioness', on the Thames. MPs criticise seemingly poor transport safety in Britain. Over the last two years, 651 people have died in transport disasters, including King's Cross (1987) and Clapham (1988).

19. LOCOS RETURN. After two days of disruption to West Coast Main Line services, Class 90s are returned to traffic following modification to braking systems.

21. SWEDEN. Swedish train drivers hold a 24 hour strike over pay and pension rules. Swedish Railways say only 10% of trains operate normally.

21. DRIVER-ONLY OPERATION. A late-night Aylesbury–Marylebone service is halted after 10 km at Wendover when the driver discovers the guard is in fact a passenger. The real guard has been left behind at Aylesbury.

22. TELECOMMUNICATIONS. Mercury Callpoint announces a national agreement with BR which allow Mercury Callpoint to install Callpoints at every station at more than 2,400 sites nationwide.

22. CHANNEL TUNNEL LINK. Chris Green, director of NSE, promises east Kent commuters a halving of journey times if the high speed rail link to the Tunnel is constructed.

22. NETHERLANDS. NS orders 118 new double-deck coaches and 38 new electric locomotives. The latter will be similar to the current Class 1600 but will be designated Class 1700.

23. CHANNEL TUNNEL. Eurotunnel admits that progress is being hampered on the British side by problems getting spoil out of the workings. Batteries on locos are running down too quickly. The trains run on batteries when deep in the tunnels, but pick up power from overhead wires nearer the entrance. Spoil is taken to the foot of Shakespeare Cliff.

23. PROVINCIAL. BR tells councillors that it intends to spend a further £4 million on Cambrian line improvements, most of this being spent on new Class 155/156 trains. Following the success of a test train the day before, substantial journey time reductions are promised.

23. SCOTRAIL. Construction work starts in Inverness to replace the collapsed Waterloo Viaduct. Its cost, at £1.8 million, is lower than first predicted.

23. CLOSURE. The freight yard at Dufftown, Grampion Region, is lifted.

25. NETHERLANDS. NS announces a doubling of capacity on the Amsterdam Central–Schipol airport rail link by 1994. Platforms at the stations will be extended and Schipol station fully integrated with the airport.

25. BOARDING CARDS. Boarding cards are used to reduce overcrowding on busy trains over this August Bank Holiday weekend. They are used on the Euston–Holyhead and Euston–Glasgow routes. The cards are a back-up to seat reservations.

25. RAILFREIGHT. The 1.6 km Cornish freight branch from Bugle to Carbis Wharf closes.

27. ATTEMPTED DERAILMENT. Vandals place an eight-foot trolley on the rails at Balcombe tunnel just south of Gatwick Airport. The 16.15 Victoria–Portsmouth strikes it, travelling at 80 mph with around 150 passengers on board.

27. CRIME. The driver of the 19.25 Waterloo–Portsmouth Network Express is almost blinded after an object is thrown through his cab window. The train was travelling at 90 mph at the time and was between Hersham and Walton-on-Thames. He undergoes a successful eye operation.

28. FIRST RUN. The first revenue-earning service occurs of BR Class 4MT 2–6–0 No. 76079 on the East Lancashire Railway.

28. ANNIVERSARY. Centenary celebrations at Southend commemorate the opening of the line to Shenfield.

28. OPENING. The Mangapps Farm Railway opens at Burnham on Crouch, Essex.

28. PRESERVATION. Only three days after being steamed for the first time since 1962, Great Eastern N7 0–6–2T NO. 69621 operates return trips at BR's Southend open day.

28. ELECTRIFICATION. Special composite third rail to be used on the 7.2 km stretch of line being electrified between Fareham and Botley is delivered to site, for installation over the next eight weeks. It is part of the £16.4 million electrification of the Portsmouth–Southampton/Eastleigh lines covering a total of 98.2 km of track.

28. CAMBRIAN LINES. The 15.00 Pwllheli–Machynlleth hits a van at an ungated crossing at Tygwyn, the scene of a fatal accident in 1987.

29. UNDERGROUND. It is reported that the proportion of escalators in use on the London Underground has dropped from 80% to 68% in a year. The escalators are switched off whenever a fault emerges following the King's Cross disaster. The problem is aggravated by a shortage of experienced engineers.

29. NETHERLANDS. The first 'International Gourmet Express' train runs as part of the Dutch Railways 150 celebrations. EM2 No. 27000 hauls restaurant cars from the Netherlands, France, Hungary, Belgium, Poland, Austria, Switzerland and Czechoslovakia. Specialist menus are offered in each car.

30. VANDALISM. The 05.40 Norwich–London, travelling at 40 mph smashes into a greenhouse left by vandals on the track at Trowse, Norwich. No-one is hurt.

30. STAFF SAFETY. In the light of a wave of well-publicised attacks on, or attempted derailments of trains ASLEF calls for bullet-proof glass to be fitted to cab windows. Mr Derrick Fullick, general secretary designate says: "Anybody throwing things at trains or putting anything on the track should be charged with attempted murder."

30. CHANNEL TUNNEL. The Channel Tunnel service tunnel reaches halfway stage, with 24 km cut by four boring machines working simultaneously from Britain and France, both under land and under sea.

30. ACCIDENT. Two freight trains collide at Worksop. Each train was pulling 36 laden coal wagons on British Coal property at Shireoaks. A train pulling coal from Barrow Hill to Toton near Long Eaton failed to give way on an approach to the main line. A fail-safe device derailed the locomotive and first two wagons, one of which collided with a truck on the second train – travelling from Shirebrook, Derbyshire, to Cottam power station, derailing 14 more trucks.

30. AUSTRIA. One person is killed when a locomotive crashes head-on with an express train near Bregenz, western Austria; 27 are injured.

30. TURKEY. Two freight trains collide in central Turkey killing 7 people.

30. FINLAND. At least 50 people are hurt when an express collides with a freight train carrying butane near Riihimaki, 30 miles from Helsinki. This is Finnish Railways' third accident in less than a week.

30. UNDERGROUND. As part of the Central Line's modernisation, a £300 million order for 85 new trains is placed with BREL Ltd. of Derby. Traction equipment supplied by Brush/ABB is included in the order.

30. ELECTRIFICATION. The first of 1,825 overhead power line supports for the Cambridge–King's Lynn electrification project is planted at an official ceremony at the Norfolk terminus.

31. INVESTMENT. The government sanctions £257 million spending on new trains in NSE. Cecil Parkinson gives approval in detail for the construction of 400 Class 465 Networker vehicles for North Kent routes and approval in principle for a further 276 vehicles. Mr Parkinson says: "NSE plan well over £1 billion of invesment over the next 5 years; that is the equivalent of at least £400 a year for every rail commuter into London."

31. PRESERVATION. A light railway order is granted to the Bodmin and Wenford Railway.

31. TOXIC WASTE. BR launches an inquiry into the handling and storage of toxic waste at Stourton freight depot. The manager of the depot is suspended pending the outcome of the inquiry.

31. MINISTERIAL APPROVAL. The prime minister makes a rare journey by train, this time on the InterCity charter train between King's Cross to Sandy behind 89001 'Avocet', the loco she named in January.

31. NETWORK SOUTHEAST. Cecil Parkinson approves the purchase of 400 Networker coaches at a cost of £257 million. They will be used to replace archiac EPB trains on Cannon Street/Charing Cross/Victoria–south east London/North Kent services. The order is divided evenly between BREL Ltd. and Metro Cammell. The trains will feature ac traction motors, swing-plug doors and alumunium construction.

31. CHANNEL TUNNEL. The value of the 60,000 orders placed to UK firms now stands at £750 million.

SEPTEMBER

01. UNIFORMS. British Rail announces its intention to spend £30 million on redesigned uniforms for station staff and train crews, the first restyling since the 1960s.

01. SOUTHAMPTON PARKWAY. It is announced that work to upgrade Southampton Parkway and its interchange with roads and Southampton Airport will start shortly as part of the latter's expansion programme.

01. FIRST RUN. The first train runs on the Bodmin and Wenford Railway after receiving its Light Railway Order award.

03. ACCIDENT. 'Wessex Electric' unit No. 2407 runs away from Bournemouth Depot, travels without a driver for almost half a mile ending up in Wharfedale Road, Bournemouth.

04. SOUTHERN REGION. Pay-trains are introduced on the Paddock Wood–Maidstone West–Strood line. Only Maidstone West, New Hythe and Snodland remain staffed.

04. RATIONALISATION. Batley near Leeds, Ferriby, and Hessle stations near Hull become unstaffed from today.

04. RECORD. The Snowdon Mountain Railway welcomes its 100,000th passenger of the year – a month before the end of the season.

04. ELECTRIFICATION. Current to the overhead wires between Copmanthorpe and Skelton Junction, York, on the East Coast Main Line is switched on marking the completion of electrification between King's Cross and York.

04. NEWCASTLE. The 16.50 Wisbech–Deanside animal food train becomes derailed at Manors causing considerable track damage.

05. RAILFREIGHT DISTRIBUTION. Doncaster Council appoints a Railfreight expert, Mr Neil Worthington, a former BR commercial development officer, to oversee development of Doncaster rail-road interchange over the next three years. This is the first such appointment by a local authority. The terminal – aimed at Channel Tunnel traffic – will be called Doncaster International Railport, to be completed by 1992. In response to the 65-acre Railport, Leeds City Council continues to back its Stourton scheme. The council's assistant director of planning says: "Doncaster may be well-placed on the railway network but the commercial heartland is around Leeds."

05. MERSEYSIDE. Merseyside PTE threatens to withdraw some of its £35 million subsidy to BR's Merseyrail system following chaos on services due to staff shortages. Cyril Bleasdale, LMR general manager admits that it is the worst timetable in the country with services on the Northern line being particularly bad.

05. DECISION. The Director of Public Prosecutions decides not to bring criminal charges against BR over the deaths of a driver and three passengers when a Swansea–Shrewsbury train fell into a flooded river at Glanryhd Bridge, near Llandeilo, west Wales, in October 1987.

06. CRIME PREVENTION. With funding from Strathclyde Regional Council, British Transport Police set up a five-man team of officers to patrol two crime-troubled Strathclyde lines: Paisley–Gourock/Wemyss Bay; North Clyde service between Dalmuir and Helensburgh, Balloch, Milngavie and Hyndland.

07. CHARGE. The driver of a train that crashed at Purley killing five people and injuring 87 others is charged with manslaughter. The office of the director of public prosecutions discloses that the driver has also been accused of endangering the safety of passengers.

07. CHANNEL TUNNEL. The total weight of reinforced concrete tunnel linings moved by rail from the plant at the Isle of Grain to Shakespeare Cliff exceeds 250,000 tons.

10. SIGNALLING. The 20-lever ex-Midland Railway signalbox at Bamford on the Hope Valley Line is closed and semaphore signals abandoned. Peak Rail have bought it.

11. TRAVEL AGENTS. The British Railways Board introduces a flat rate of 9% commission for travel agents on tickets, railcards, reservations and other commissionable products.

11. SCOTRAIL. The Ayr–Stranraer line is closed for urgent repairs after masonry is seen falling off the viaduct over the River Girvan.

11. SMOKING BAN. As part of a three-month experiment, Class 315s operating out of Liverpool Street provide only no-smoking accommodation from today.

12. ASHFORD. Following an invitation to tender on 15th September 1988, Eurotunnel Developments Ltd., Ashford Borough Council and Mountleigh Group plc sign a sale agreement to create a 100-acre business park in Ashford. It is next to the planned Ashford International station and is close to the M20 motorway and the Inland Freight Clearance Depot. The land is currently owned by the BRB and the council.

13. EUROPE. The Community of European Railways (EEC countries plus Austria and Switzerland) disclose that last year 198 billion tonnes/km were transported by rail, up 2.7% on 1987. On the passenger side, 248 billion passenger/km, is up 5% on 1987.

13. NEW LOOK. Denis Tunnicliffe, managing director of London Underground, and Dr Eric Midwinter, chairman of the London Regional Passengers' Committee unveil seven completely

modernised Underground vehicles of 1967/A/C design. Brighter interiors, flame-retardent materials and graffiti-resistant paints are used. Some fittings, including flooring and stanchion poles are in the appropriate line's colours.

13. ANNIVERSARY. The Central Transport Consultative Committee holds its 200th quorate meeting at Charing Cross; the first was 40 years before.

14. ELECTRIFICATION. Dr John Prideaux announces that electrification of the 27-mile Edinburgh–Carstairs line will proceed. The approval of the scheme gives continuation of employment to the 150 BR and contractors' staff working from the Millerhill depot in Edinburgh. It will also mean more jobs for the BR engineering works at Polmadie in Glasgow and Craigentinny in Edinburgh. The scheme will cost £12.25 million and has a completion date of spring 1991 matching the introduction of electric ECML services. The electrification will permit direct Anglo–Scottish services from the ECML to run to Glasgow Central and from the WCML to Edinburgh Waverley.

14. DEATH. A Royal Mail train driver dies at the controls two minutes after pulling out of Peterborough station. The driver is found slumped over the 'dead man's handle', the latter having brought the Liverpool Street-bound train to a halt.

14. STRIKE STATISTICS. The Department of Employment reveals that the number of days lost through strikes in July was the highest since the height of the miners' strike of 1984. Stoppages by workers in local government, on the railways and in the docks led to a total of 2,317,000 days lost, 158,000 of which were on BR.

15. FACELIFT. A £250,000 refurbishment of Ealing Broadway station, between Paddington and Slough, is celebrated at a ceremony.

16. RAILFREIGHT. Trials begin with Class 59 locomotives on the Southern Region.

17. RENDEZVOUS. 'FLYING SCOTSMAN' and 'PENDENNIS CASTLE' meet in Perth, Australia for first time since 1974.

17. ACCIDENT. The 14.50 Hull–Scarborough DMU smashes into a car straddled across an unmanned level crossing near the village of Thorneholme, 10 miles from Bridlington. The car driver is killed. BR starts an inquiry into the accident – a few miles along the line where 9 people died at Lockington in 1987 when a train hit a van on a level crossing. Crossings on the line had been modernised following that accident but the Thorneholme crossing was excluded, being used as access to only one cottage along an unclassified road.

17. SAFETY. Strict fire safety regulations aimed at preventing a repeat of the King's Cross disaster come into force on the London Underground, MerseyRail, Tyne and Wear Metro, the Glasgow Underground and BR stations with underground sections. Regulations cover sprinkler systems, heat detectors, staff training, staffing levels, fire drills, cleaning and escalators. Local fire brigades now have the power to enforce fire prevention measures.

17. SPEED RECORD. The InterCity 225 reaches a speed of 260 km/h (162 mph) between Grantham and Peterborough. The loco is 'governed' to 162 mph, tantalising 1 mph below the 163 mph record set by the APT in 1979. The train consists of 91010, six Mark 4 coaches and a Mark 4 DVT. Today, 91010 also visits York.

17. SMOKING BAN. After a smoking ban was introduced on the Glasgow Underground in 1980 and following the King's Cross fire, Strathclyde local train services are declared a 'no smoking zone'. The six sub-surface stations in Glasgow are included in the ban: Queen Street Low Level, Central Low Level, Charing Cross, Anderston, Argyle Street and Dalmarnock.

19. ACCIDENT. The 21.32 Hull–Leeds service, operated by 156 476 hits debris that had fallen on to the line at Bar Lane bridge near Garforth following a road accident and is derailed. The line is blocked until 03.00 the next morning.

20. SIGNALLING. Rush-hour chaos follows the

theft of signalling cables near Liverpool Street, this example being one of a growing number.

20. INTERCITY. The last cast nameplate to be fitted to an InterCity locomotive is to 47586 'Northamptonshire', named at Kettering today. Black lettering on a silver background is the sector's replacement specification.

20. PRESS LAUNCH. InterCity 225 is launched to the press after Class 91 loco No. 91001 is named 'Swallow'. The train runs from King's Cross to Leeds and back, it being featured on national TV news later in the day. By May 1991, 31 Class 91s and 314 Mark 4 coaches should be operating King's Cross–Leeds/Edinburgh services.

21. THROUGH TRAIN. Passengers at three Yorkshire railway stations are left standing when the train they should have caught sped through without stopping due to it being overcrowded. The Leeds–Bradford–Blackpool train is so full that stops at Mytholmroyd, Sowerby Bridge and Hebden Bridge are eliminated. BR blames a shortage of Pacer railbuses.

21. APPOINTMENT. Cecil Parkinson announces that John Welsby, 51, will become chief executive of railways from 1st January 1990, with responsibility for the whole railway business.

22. OPENING. The modernised station at Epsom Downs is officially opened by Leslie Crowther. Services started operating from the (now complete) station six months before.

22. ACADEMIA. Railfreight sponsors two appointments at the University College of Swansea – to the newly-created BR chair of marketing and the Railfreight research fellowship. The two academics will initially study industrial relocation and restructuring with reference to the effects of the opening of the Channel Tunnel. The marketing of recent Railfreight technical innovations will also be examined.

23. DEATH. The death occurs of the celebrated railway photographer W.J.V. Anderson. His most favoured, and famous, railway photographs were taken in the Scottish Highlands.

23. PRESERVATION. 'Castle' Class 4-6-0 No. 4079 'PENDENNIS CASTLE' and A3 No. 4472 'FLYING SCOTSMAN' double-head a Perth–Northam return excursion train in Australia.

23. YORK. Class 91 No. 91003 hauls the 09.31 York–King's Cross special, the first electric out of the city on public service.

24. FRANCE. TGV Atlantique services start between Paris and Brittany. With 187 mph running between Paris and Le Mans, journey times to cities such as Rennes and Nantes are cut dramatically. With the other half of the fork to Tours due to open in September 1990, the 17 billion-franc capital cost of the TGV A service will be fully recovered within a decade.

24. IRELAND. Seventy people are injured when a special train collides with a herd of cows that had strayed on to the line near Claremorris. Seven out of the 11 coaches are derailed. The train had been carrying pilgrims from Balbriggan, Co. Dublin, to Knock, Co. Mayo.

25. ACCIDENT. A misunderstanding of hand-signals causes a collision between two stone freight trains in Mountsorrel Sidings, near Loughborough. Four wagons are derailed and five damaged.

26. DOCUMENTARY. ITV broadcasts 'M40 – The Road Ahead' analysing the effects of the M40, to be completed in 1990. Damage to countryside four miles south of Banbury, where the River Cherwell meanders through flood meadows, is highlighted. Similar destruction will follow from some 'Roads to Prosperity' road schemes it is alleged.

26. CHANNEL TUNNEL. The North of England Consortium urges the government to provide extra funding for better rail links between the North and the Channel Tunnel. Mr John Gunnell, chairman of the consortium, says: "The nation will only be able to exploit the single market if the whole nation benefits and the correct rail links are in place."

27. PAY DISCLOSURE. The Transport Salaried Staffs Association discloses that some of BR's 10,000 managers have had pay rises of up to 19%, but others have had nothing under a new 'payment by results' scheme. The association says that rises averaged 11.8% which is 3% more than the deal which ended the dispute with the NUR in the summer. ASLEF announce that they want 19% next year.

27. METROLINK. Greater Manchester PTA and PTE choose the GMA Group, comprising GEC, Mowlem, AMEC and GM Buses Ltd. to design, build and operate the new LRT system.

28. CHAOS. It is reported that new fire safety precautions introduced the previous week are causing havoc on the Underground. New rules following the King's Cross fire stipulate minimum numbers of staff to be on duty to help with evacuation during an emergency. Staff shortages have caused key central London stations such as Euston and Westminster to be closed for 15-60 minutes.

28. EMBARRASSMENT. Class 91 No. 91008's pantograph becomes entangled in York station's platform canopy after being signalled onto a non-electrified line. The train it was due to haul south from York was a special carrying Institution of Electrical Engineers delegates.

29. INTERCITY. Nottingham station's new £70,000 InterCity lounge is officially opened, as is the expanded CCTV-protected car-park.

29. NETWORK SOUTHEAST. A commemorative plaque is unveiled to mark the completion of a £500,000 restoration of Langley station, between Paddington and Slough.

29. DOCKLANDS LIGHT RAILWAY. A mock-up of one of the DLR's third batch of trains is put on show to invite comments from the public. These BN-built units have more standing room and extra grab rails. Two types of seat are fitted for evaluation.

30. STATION RENAMED. Magdalen Road, between King's Lynn and Downham Market becomes Watlington again after 114 years!

30. GALA DAY. Routes radiating from Cambridge are branded with a 'West Anglia' heron symbol to coincide with the gala day. As well as rolling stock exhibits at Cambridge, Class 73 No. 73003 hauls an excursion train to Fen Drayton to St. Ives and Class 56 No. 56062 hauls Class 312 EMUs to King's Lynn, for shuttle services to Middleton Towers.

OCTOBER

01. SWEDEN. Four people are killed when the Hamburg–Oslo night train collides with a lorry near Varburg, Sweden.

02. PROVINCIAL. Gilberdyke station, between Hull and Selby, becomes unstaffed from today.

02. WEST YORKSHIRE. The new MetroTrain winter timetable is launched. Included in the changes is a new hourly Leeds–Skipton service.

02. SCOTRAIL. Class 156 'Super Sprinters' replace conventional DMUs between Glasgow and East Kilbride and between Glasgow and Barrhead/ Kilmarnock.

02. INTERCITY. Six months ahead of schedule, an hourly Sheffield–London service is started, facilitated by the transfer of one HST set from the ECML.

02. CLASS 313. Thirteen-year-old Class 313 sets take over North London Line workings replacing Class 416 units up to 35 years old, a considerable improvement.

02. GOOLE. The Ouse bridge is re-opened after £2 million of repairs are completed. Hull–London through services have not operated over it since it was hit by a Swedish freighter in November 1988.

03. MARKETING INITIATIVE. In a joint initiative with the local authorities in Devon and the Countryside Commission, BR relaunches the Exeter–Barnstaple line as the 'Tarka line'. Service improvements and marketing will be closely tied in with Devon County Council's 'Tarka Project', a walking and cycle route along the valleys of the rivers Taw and Torridge.

03. LOWESTOFT. British Rail announces plans to demolish the present decrepit station to make way for a redevelopment.

04. ACCIDENT. One man is killed and another injured when Class 155 No. 155 343 hits a car on an unmanned level crossing at Duckett's Lane, Laisterdyke, West Yorkshire. No-one on the train, the 16.23 Halifax–York, is injured. The impact does, however, derail the Sprinter. An inquiry is launched.

05. KING'S CROSS. After St, Bartholomew's Hospital demanded £15 million to surrender its claim to 20 acres of the 120-acre King's Cross redevelopment site, BR makes a final offer of £12 million. BR is overseeing the site on behalf of the

▲*Electro-diesel Class 73 No. 73003 is seen at Swavesey with the return leg of one of the 'West Anglian Enterprise' excursions of 30th September. Note the platforms!*　　　　　*Les Nixon*

London Regeneration Consortium.

05. EUROPEAN FORUM. The leaders of the railway administrations that make up the Community of European Railways agree to establish a European Railway forum. Its aim is to broaden the debate on the role and place of the railways in the forthcoming single market.

05. GRANT. The Scottish Office grants Strathclyde Regional Council (SRC) £562,000 towards the re-opening of the Paisley Canal Line. This follows the decision made in March to re-open the line and is a result of a recommendation of the 1987 joint ScotRail/SRC review of local rail services.

05. FIRE. The Goole swing bridge is closed for a day following fire damage, another setback in its troubled existence.

08. OPEN DAY. Didcot Railway Centre is forced to turn some visitors away after more than 20,000 people arrive during the 'Thomas the Tank Engine' Weekend. Nene Valley Railway Hudswell Clarke 0–6–0ST 'Thomas' is hired for the starring role. Faces and names are given to 10 other attendant steam locomotives.

08. STATION RESTORATION. Wymondham station's restoration is marked by the unveiling of a plaque by Bill Pertwee, actor and railway enthusiast. The station is a Grade II listed building.

09. DELEGATION. A joint parliamentary and local authority delegation meets transport minister Michael Portillo to persuade him to consider a £130 million extension of the Docklands Light Railway to Greenwich, Deptford and Lewisham.

09. CANADA. It is reported that the 'Canadian', one of two trans-continental trains will be scrapped as part of the Canadian government's efforts to reduce subsidies to the passenger system of $645 million a year by half. The 'Canadian', serves a southern route through Winnipeg, Regina and Calgary. The more notherly 'Transcontinental' service is cut to three services a week. Train services in the Maritimes and Western Provinces will also be cut. Subsidies will be diverted towards the more heavily-travelled Quebec City–Toronto route. Via Rail's network and services will be halved within 3 years.

09. NEW STATION. Berry Brow station, on the Sheffield–Huddersfield line is officially re-opened. Thirty two trains a day will serve the station on weekdays, with a reduced service operating at weekends. The station was closed in 1966.

09. PROVINCIAL. The first Class 158 'Express' DMU No. 158 701 is launched to the press at the Railway Technical Centre, Derby, some four months behind schedule.

10. MODERNISATION. Nairn station, situated on the Inverness–Aberdeen line, is officially re-opened following a £50,000 refurbishment of the station.

12. CRIME. The 13.38 Balloch–Drumgelloch service is attacked at Dalreoch station by a gang of youths. The train's driver and guard are assaulted and the train withdrawn as a result of damage. The line has gained a bad reputation for crime.

12. SIGNALLING. British Rail invites tenders from twelve firms for the first of two pilot systems of Automatic Train Protection.

13. COMMUTER SIT-IN. When the 17.18 Waterloo–Alton terminates at Woking due to staff shortages, commuters stage a well-publicised sit-in. Commuters say that the train often terminates at Farnham but this is the final straw.

13. CATERING. After a competitive tendering exercise, Network SouthEast awards three-year contracts for train buffet services on London–Sussex coast services (InterCity On Board Services, (ICOBS)), London–Portsmouth (ICOBS), London Weymouth (ICOBS) and London–Salisbury–Exeter (Trailfare).

16. FIRST RUN. First revenue-earning service occurs of 2–6–2T No. 4561 on the West Somerset Railway.

16. SIGNALLING. Westinghouse Brake and Signal Ltd. is awarded the £50 million contract to resignal the Underground's Central Line. A total

of 49 stations and 72 km of track will be equipped with the new automatic-train control system.

18. VALLEYS. The first phase of a joint BR/Welsh Development Agency programme to improve all stations in Mid-Glamorgan – at a cost of £298,000 – is marked at a ceremony at Treherbert; stations as far south as Dinas have been facelifted so far.

20. SCOTRAIL. Banavie swing bridge, on the Fort William–Mallaig line, is closed for urgent repairs. The bridge carries the line over the Caledonian Canal.

20. NEW PRESIDENT. Drs Leo F Ploeger, chairman of the board of Netherlands Railways, is elected president of the Community of European Railways. He will succeed BR chairman Sir Robert Reid whose term ends on 31st December.

20. WARRINGTON. Class 156 No. 156 418 is badly damaged near Central station after hitting a large obstruction placed on the track.

22. MODERNISATION. The refurbished station building is re-opened at Berwick-upon-Tweed.

23. STANSTED RAIL LINK. An official breakthrough ceremony is held to mark the completion of the £11 million, 1.8 km-long tunnel beneath Stansted Airport's main runway. Sir Robert Reid also accepts the handover, by a private construction firm, of the £3 million, 5.4 km-long trackbed which extends from the London–Cambridge main line to the tunnel portal.

23. PRESERVATION. Class 5 No. 5305 hauls the centenary special from Fort William to Crianlarich.

23. SERVICES WITHDRAWN. Some Chiltern Line services are withdrawn in an effort to provide a reliable timetable. Gearbox failures, a poor supply of spare parts and the age of the DMUs are blamed. The withdrawn services will be reinstated as soon as possible, NSE promises.

23. CENTENARY. One hundred years after the West Highland Line was started from Craigendoran, Helensburgh, a plaque is unveiled at Fort William and a special train runs to Crianlarich. The centenary of the granting of Royal Assent to the Act of Parliament was marked on 14th August.

24. LIGHT RAIL. Michael Portillo approves Phase One of Manchester's Metrolink LRT system. A grant under Section 56 of the Transport Act 1968 of up to 50% of the scheme's £110 million capital cost would be available.

24. RENAMING. Surrey Docks on the East London section of the Metropolitan Line is re-named Surrey Quays, not, as 'Private Eye' magazine quips, at the request of the new secretary of state for transport. The station was originally called Deptford Road.

26. ACCIDENT. The 01.30 Paddington–Reading single-car DMU No. 55023 is derailed and overturns after hitting a derailed Whatley–Ripple Lane stone quarry train near Maidenhead. Three of the four tracks are blocked with the result that trains from the West Country and Wales terminate at Reading the following day. From Reading, BR operates a 20-minute shuttle service to Paddington. Vandalism is ruled out.

26. ACCIDENT. A lorry hits the parapet of a bridge at Box. The 08.10 Paddington–Penzance hits the resulting debris. The line is closed for three hours.

28. DEMONSTRATION. A thousand anti-terrorist campaigners travel on two charter trains between Dublin and Belfast in protest against continued disruption of the line, the IRA having bombed and threatened the line more than 60 times so far this year.

29. RAILFREIGHT. The Powderhall branch, Edinburgh, is re-opened in readiness for a new flow of refuse by rail.

29. NORTHERN IRELAND. A £93 million 5-year investment package for transport improvements in the province from the European Regional Development Fund is announced. On the railways, upgrading of the Belfast–Dublin line is top priority.

30. ORDER. A £59.3 million contract to supply 103 Networker Turbo coaches for NSE's Thames and Chiltern line services is awarded to BREL Ltd. This brings the total number of vehicles on order for these services to 180, an earlier order being placed in February.

30. VALLEYS. A £200,000 improvement project starts at Caerphilly station. This project is in addition to the programme marked on the 18th.

30. OVERGROUND. Seven years after the proposed closure of the line, LRT re-introduces an all-day service on the Epping–Ongar branch of the Central Line on a one-year experimental basis.

30. DEARNE VALLEY. Ten services daily on the Sheffield–Leeds via the Dearne Valley route become locomotive-hauled due to a shortage of DMUs.

31. DEPARTURE. 'FLYING SCOTSMAN' leaves Sydney for home.

NOVEMBER

01. STEAMING. A successful steam test is held for the 'DUKE OF GLOUCESTER' at Didcot.

01. STATION REFURBISHMENT. Barrow station's £88,000 refurbishment is commemorated today. Cumbria County Council has contributed £10,000 to the project. Rolling stock on the Cumbrian line consists almost entirely of first-generation DMUs.

01. SIGNALLING. At a ceremony, the new colour-light signalling on the Abercynon–Aberdare line is officially inaugurated. Mid Glamorgan County Council has paid the £700,000 cost with assistance from the European Regional Development Fund.

02. INDIA. Thirty six people are killed and 78 injured when a Delhi–Calcutta passenger train, the Toofan express, is derailed near Moghulsarai in northern India.

02. FARES. Next year's fare rises will average 9%, the British Railways Board announces, above inflation again. Long-distance commuters will be hit harder.

03. NEW COMPANY. Eurorail is formed to develop and operate the planned high speed line from London to the Channel Tunnel, in conjunction with BR. Eurorail is a consortium of Trafalgar House and BICC Ltd. Meanwhile, Swanley residents are upset about plans for an international station there on the high speed line.

04. SETTLE & CARLISLE. The first service train aimed at attracting the modern traction enthusiast is run headed by 56104 piloting 47503.

05. PRESERVATION. It is reported that the Snowdon Mountain Railway has had the busiest season in its 94-year history. A total of 120,826 passengers were carried, 21% more than the previous record of 99,695 in 1976.

05. EXTENSION. The first train on the extension to Rawtenstall is operated on the East Lancs Railway.

05. CHANNEL TUNNEL LINK. PEARL (Peckham against the Rail Link) members stage a torchlit march from Waterloo to King's Cross as a mark of continued opposition to the high speed link and the reduction in the value of their houses during the period of uncertainty over the Swanley–Waterloo/King's Cross section.

06. LORDS. In the Lords, Liberal Democrat Lord Grimond suggests that army engineers should be brought in to repair London Underground's 275 escalators.

06. ACCIDENT. The late-running 21.26 Huddersfield–Wakefield Westgate, operated by 141104, runs into the 19.48 Scarborough–Liverpool, operated by 156476 at Huddersfield. Eighteen people are injured both units seriously damaged.

07. CLAPHAM REPORT. The Clapham Inquiry report is published. A total of 93 recommendations are made by its author, Sir Anthony Hidden, of which 71 apply directly to BR. Faulty wiring caused the crash the report concludes. The report is highly critical of "dangerous" work standards, bad management and communications between staff and excessive hours worked by some staff.

08. ACCIDENT. The 12.29 Cliffe to Sevington stone train stops at Swiss Green between Headcorn and Pluckley following the failure of 33022, the train's other locomotive being 33055. 47455 is sent from Ashford 'wrong line' to assist but collides with the disabled train causing serious damage and disruption to train services. By the following day, both lines are cleared.

08. NETWORK SOUTHEAST. An investment package, including 20 new coaches and resignalling is announced for the archaic Waterloo and City Line. The new trains will enable the frequency of service to be increased by 20%.

09. END OF AN ERA. GW 2–8–0 No. 3845 is the last locomotive to leave Barry, destined for Brighton Railway Museum. Most of the 300 or so steam locomotives at the site until today have been preserved over the years.

10. UNDERGROUND. The £55 million expansion and modernisation of Angel station is started by Cecil Parkinson in an official ceremony.

11. HUMBERSIDE. Hull City Council, Beverley Council and Humberside County Council commission a study on the feasibility of a light rapid transit system.

12. PRIVATISATION STUDIES. Latest figures indicate that about £1 million has been spent by the government on different consultants to find the best way of eventually privatising BR.

13. PRESERVATION. ScotRail hires Class 5 No. 5305 for crew training in order to protect its successful Fort William–Mallaig tourist steam operation.

13. LIGHT RAIL. Legislation allowing Sheffield's 'Supertram' system to go ahead is held up by a procedural dispute in the Commons. Two Conservative MPs block the private Bill saying that they will lift their block on the Bill only if a Labour MP removes his blocks on other private Bills, in particular one which would expand port facilities at Immingham and possibly increase coal imports.

13. CRAZED. A youth trying to copy the new craze of 'train surfing' is killed when trying to get on the roof of a moving train at Plaistow, east London, after losing his grip. The craze is widespread in South America.

14. ATMOSPHERIC RAILWAY. The Atmospheric Railway Museum at Starcross the last surviving atmospheric pumphouse built by Brunel in 1845 is put up for sale. 20,000 people visit the museum each year. After spending more than £100,000 on restoration and seeing one grant application after another be turned down, the owners decide to sell up after 8 years' work. Market interest is focused on potential for conversion to flats.

14. EXHIBITION. Light Rail 89 starts in Bristol, the comprehensive exhibition being held alongside the 4th International Conference on Electrifying Urban Public Transport.

14. IRELAND. An early-morning Tralee–Dublin train hits a tractor passing over a level crossing at Cuddagh, between Ballybrophy and Portlaois in County Laois. The farmer is killed.

15. HOLIDAY PLANS. InterCity unveils its Christmas travel arrangements. 320 extra train services will operate on the busiest days of the Christmas period. On very busy services particularly from Euston, King's Cross and Paddington, only passengers who have reserved a seat or obtained a boarding card will be allowed to travel. Standard class reservations and boarding cards will be free of charge.

15. SUPERTRAM. South Yorkshire PTA is advised that the funding provided in the government's Autumn Statement would not be sufficient to fund the Supertram project in 1990/1. Funding at a later date is not ruled out.

15. NAMING. Class 90 No. 90010 is named as '275 Railway Squadron (Volunteers)' in recognition of the part played within the Territorial Army, most members being recruited from BR.

16. ROYAL ASSENT. The Parliamentary Bill for the first Midland Metro light rapid transit line between Birmingham Snow Hill and Wolverhampton receives Royal Assent. Line 1 will cost £60 million to build. Elsewhere, Tyne and Wear PTE's Bill to extend the Metro system to Newcastle International Airport also receives Royal Assent. The £1 million link involves construction of 3.5 km of track and two new stations.

16. RAILFREIGHT. The government grant £1.75 million towards Section 8 freight facilities at the Bardon Group plc's Angerstein Wharf, Greenwich. The grant will enable the quarry company to transport by rail about 300,000 tonnes of aggregate each year to the new terminal, relieving London's roads of about 50 lorries a day.

16. ITALY. At least 12 die when two passenger trains collide head-on just south of Crotone on a single-line section of track.

16. LONDON. Cecil Parkinson gives LRT permission to deposit a Bill for the extension of the Jubilee Line to Docklands at a cost of £1 billion. Developers will contribute £400 million. The route is: Green Park–Westminster–Waterloo–London Bridge–Surrey Docks–Canary Wharf–Canning Town–Stratford. Mr Parkinson delays a decision on even one of the new crossrail lines proposed in the Central London Rail Study until 1990.

16. UNDERGROUND. LUL announces plans to spend £1 billion on safety improvements over the next decade – by reducing congestion through an expansion of capacity, better communications, procedures, management and less dangerous construction materials.

17. CRITICISM. The London Regional Passengers' Committee responds to the Jubilee Line extension news by saying that it is a second-best improvement. An East-West crossrail project should be higher priority. The fear is that "the lure of private capital has led to a misjudging of priorities."

17. FRANCE. Paris Metro staff go on strike in a protest over a gun and machete battle between drug gangs at a central station. Several stations were shut on Line Nine, which links the wealthy western suburb of Pont de Sevres in the west with the run-down area of Mairie de Montreuil in the east.

20. CLAMP-DOWN. Network SouthEast introduces wheel-clamping at pay and display station car parks on the King's Cross–Huntingdon line.

22. RESTORATION. Europe's largest brick restoration project – the 'Stockport Viaduct Venture' – is completed. After a £3 million, two-year programme the 27-arch viaduct is both cleaned and illuminated at night.

22. UNDERGROUND. The first two cars of the refurbished 'C' stock unveiled to the press on 13th September start passenger reaction trials. Cars 5585 and 6585 will spend most time on the Circle and District Lines.

22. EUROPE. The transport commissioner of the European Community Commission, Mr Karel van Miert presents his strategy after months of speculation about its contents. A greater division between infrastructure and operations, the latter open to new companies, is proposed. EEC financial support for piggy-back road/rail transport is proposed as is greater harmonisation of track gauge, already under way, and signalling systems.

23. UNDERGROUND. A new £3 million ticket hall for Tower Hill station is officially opened, one of the first projects aimed specifically at relieving congestion to be completed. About 31,000 people use the station each day, a figure that has more than doubled in the last 5 years.

23. RESIGNALLING. A £21 million contract to resignal the main line from Chislehurst, south east London, to Orpington and Folkestone is awarded. Signalling will be controlled from Ashford. Another £59 million is to be spent upgrading the line in readiness for Channel Tunnel traffic.

24. ACCIDENT. The Vale of Rheidol Railway's only diesel locomotive, No. 10 collides with a car at the unguarded Glan-yr-Afon level crossing, Aberystwyth. No-one is seriously injured but a Railway Inspectorate report is ordered.

24. WESTERN REGION. A £347,000 scheme is started to install digital clocks at key stations between Paddington and Swansea and Plymouth. Like the clocks used on NSE's stations, they are controlled by the Rugby Master Clock System for complete accuracy.

24. ELECTRIFICATION. Two weeks ahead of schedule installation is completed of the 7.2 km of composite third rail between Fareham and Botley. The aluminium third rail's main advantage is that it conducts electricity better than normal steel third rail, so reducing substation requirements.

25. RAILFREIGHT. Today marks the last day of Speedlink operations at Tyne and Millerhill marshalling yards.

26. CHANNEL TUNNEL. It is announced that the Ancient Council of the North is to be convened for only the second time in 348 years, this time in order to campaign for a high-speed channel tunnel link.

27. DEADLINE. Today marks deadline given to BR by West Yorkshire PTA to improve train service reliability. The PTA has threatened to withhold money.

27. LIGHT RAIL. West Midlands PTE deposits a parliamentary Bill for Lines 2 and 3 of its light rail programme, of a construction cost of £238 million and £120 million respectively.

27. LIVERPOOL. After the success of 'Station Watch' at London Victoria, the scheme spreads to Liverpool's Central station.

28. POLICING. Cecil Parkinson opens the new £2 million divisional British Transport Police headquarters at Victoria. High-profile police stations such as this plus a continuing "battle against the public transport thug" would check and even reverse rising crime. Mr Parkinson stresses recent successes in catching graffiti vandals and ticket fraudsters and forgers.

29. INTER-RAIL EXPANSION. BR announces that the 1990 Inter-Rail card will offer unlimited rail travel to people under 26 for one month in 22 countries – to include, for the first time, Czechoslovakia and Asiatic Turkey.

29. ACCIDENT. The 21.30 St. Pancras–Sheffield HST ploughs into a herd of cows at Wingfield, near Alfreton, Derbyshire. Although less serious than the Polmont disaster (in which an Edinburgh–Glasgow push-pull train was derailed in similar circumstances), the train is delayed by more than two hours after the fuel tank is ruptured.

29. ESSEX. The £177,000 refurbishment of Ingatestone station, between Romford and Chelmsford, is completed.

30. ROADS. The death toll on the roads in 1988 was the lowest since 1953 according to statistics published by the Department of Transport today. There were 5,052 road deaths in 1988, 63,000 serious injuries and 254,000 slight injuries.

30. BIRTHDAY. Collectors' Corner, the shop near Euston station devoted to selling railway memorabilia celebrates its 20th Anniversary today.

DECEMBER

02. NEW TRAFFIC. Freight haulage commences on the Bodmin Steam Railway.

03. WARRINGTON. Central station is closed to Manchester-bound trains for one week to enable the eastern approach to be remodelled.

04. SOUTHERN REGION. An Eastbourne-Victoria commuter who travelled to work for three months on his expired First Class season ticket "to expose British Rail's appalling service", is ordered to pay fines, costs and compensation totalling nearly £1,000. He had complained about malfunctioning heaters but said that he was simply ignored by BR. As BR refused to accept part-payment of his £2,500 annual season ticket as compensation for this poor service he decided to openly evade payment.

04. ADVERTISING. InterCity's latest advert in the newspapers shows a Peterborough–Edinburgh ticket alongside a Summons Notice with the captions underneath contrasting a high-speed rail ticket with a high-speed road ticket. Curiously, the rail ticket has no price written on it!

04. FRANCE. The SNCF announces a tenfold increase in the number of security staff to be employed on Paris commuter trains to combat an increase in violent crime. The plain-clothes security force is to be increased from 100 to 500 by late 1990.

05. SOVIET RAILWAYS. The Soviet Union's prime minister Nikolai Ryzhkov criticises Soviet railway management for the 12 billion rouble (£12 billion) cost of running the system. During the first 11 months of 1989, the railway network failed, he says, to deliver 10 million tonnes of fertiliser, 9 million tonnes of coal and 7 million tonnes of crude oil.

05. WORLD RECORD. A TGV Atlantique unit set No. 325 sets a new world record of 482.4 km/h. A 2 + 4 formation and 1,050 mm-diameter wheels are used to reach the speed which equates with 300 mph. The speed was reached near Vendôme.

05. DERAILMENT. In an incident similar to that on 10th March, a Speedlink freight train becomes derailed between Gorton and Rannoch, seriously damaging track.

▲ Sir Robert Reid, CBE, departing chairman of BR, has been the driving force behind sectorisation and the movement from a production-led railway to a business-led one. He departs after a 7-year extended tenure of the post. *BR Board*

▲ Mr Bob Reid, the incoming chairman of BR and widely-respected in industry. *Shell UK*

06. NEW CHAIRMAN. Robert Reid is chosen as the next chairman of British Rail. Currently chairman of Shell UK, he will become BR chairman-designate on 1st January 1990. After the present chairman Sir Robert Reid's retirement in March, Robert Reid will become part-time non-executive chairman. In October 1990 he will become chairman at a salary of £200,000 a year.

06. MOCK-UP. Transport minister Michael Portillo inspects a mock-up of the new Class 471 Net-

worker Express at Victoria station. After public consultation and their construction the trains will be used mainly on Charing Cross–Dover and Victoria–Ramsgate services.

07. RETIREMENT. After 27 years singing and telling jokes to passengers, a Ramsgate guard Mr Leslie Basset, retires; passengers have mixed feelings. On his last run from Charing Cross Mr Basset sings 'Wish Me Luck as You Wave Me Goodbye' over the train's public address system.

07. STRATHCLYDE. The PTE unveils its public transport proposals following its two-year Transport Development Study.

08. MODERNISATION. The rebuilt Guildford station is opened after an £8 million transformation.

08. INTERCITY. The Class 91-hauled 17.50 'Yorkshire Pullman' from London King's Cross brings down the wires south of Newark. Single-line-working and diversions via Lincoln follow a lengthy delay.

09. CHANNEL TUNNEL. The 17-month construction of the loop tunnel at the Cheriton (Folkestone) terminal is completed. It carries the three shuttle tracks under and round the west end of the terminal and into the platforms.

09. WARCOP. Class 26 No. 26032 and Class 47 47819 propel a charter train down the Warcop branch – a hopeful sign?

09. CLASS 442. The entire fleet of 'Wessex Electrics' is grounded when Bournemouth depot staff believe that a consignment of brake blocks contains asbestos; their fears prove unfounded.

09. TICKETING. The last Edmondson-style card tickets are sold at Pembrey and Burry Port, west Wales.

11. REPAIRS COMPLETE. Following the accident on the 5th December and almost a week of service disruption and diversions the West Highland Line reverts to normal.

11. CHANNEL TUNNEL TRAINS. Cecil Parkinson approves expenditure by BR of £356 million on new high-speed trains for 'Three Capitals' services – BR's share of the fleet.

11. VALLEYS. BR stops issuing cheap day returns on services to Cardiff for the next three weeks to reduce expected overcrowding.

11. CLASS 60. Class 60 No. 60005 works a Mountsorrel–Radlett stone train, the first of the class to earn revenue for Railfreight.

12. CHARING CROSS. The Lord Mayor of Westminster unveils a plaque to commemorate the official opening of the modernised Charing Cross station. Concourse improvements and restoration of the exterior courtyard have cost £3 million. A £130 million 14-storey office block is currently being built over the station by Laing for developers Greycoats.

13. PAY DEAL. BREL's 6,500 workers at Crewe, Derby and York accept a 13% basic pay rise and a commitment to a 37 hour week in return for more flexible working practices.

13. STUDY. British Rail, Merseytravel and the Merseyside Development Corporation start a £30,000 joint study of the feasibility of new stations at Brunswick Dock and Vauxhall on Merseyrail's Northern Line and Conway Park in Birkenhead.

14. PRESERVATION. 'FLYING SCOTSMAN' returns from Australia to Tilbury.

14. BULGARIA. Ten die when a train derails as it approaches the town of Roman at 60 mph, four times the speed limit.

14. INQUEST. After returning a verdict of accidental death on the driver of a car who was killed on a level crossing after being hit by a train near Pudsey on 4th October, the inquest jury urges BR to carry out a review of level crossing safety. A man is due to appear before magistrates next week charged with leaving the crossing gates open.

14. CHANNEL TUNNEL FREIGHT. Cecil Parkinson officially welcomes the British Railways Board's plans for international passenger, freight and parcels traffic to use the Tunnel. Speaking about non-bulk freight, in which road transport is dominant, particularly in Britain, he

says that he has "asked the Board to consider how they might improve the financial performance ... to maximise the involvement of the private sector."

15. EXPANSION PLANS. West Yorkshire PTA agrees to proceed with plans to relay part of the Leeds–Wetherby line. A 20-minute interval service would operate into Leeds, serving Scholes, Stanks and Cross Gates. The transport authority also agrees to buy land at six potential station sites along the freight-only Wakefield–Pontefract line. Forecasts indicate that the proposed stations at places such as Streethouse, Sharlston, Featherstone and Tanshelf could attract about 1200 passengers a day.

17. ASHFORD DEVELOPMENT. Proposals for a £1 billion mixed commercial development of industry, housing, shops and open space at Ashford Great Park are rejected by Chris Patten, environment secretary. The 2,000 acre 'park' was designed to take advantage of Ashford's position on the Channel Tunnel rail link. This scheme is separate from the Ashford Business Park.

18. TUNNELLING PROGRESS. Channel Tunnel boring machine 'Pascaline' (or T5) completes the 3.25 km south running tunnel between Sangatte and the Coquelles terminal site in France. T5 will now be turned around to bore the north running tunnel. The service tunnel was completed in April.

18. CHANNEL TUNNEL. The Maître d'Oeuvre independent review of Channel Tunnel construction costs "supports in general terms" the figures put forward by Eurotunnel.

18. CHANNEL TUNNEL TRAINS. A £500 million-plus order is placed with the Transmanche Super Train Group for the supply of 30 'Three Capitals' high-speed trains.

19. CRIME REDUCTION. It is reported that every passenger using the Victoria line of the London Underground is to be filmed in order to reduce crime. This follows the success of a trial with closed-circuit TV cameras at Victoria station. Cameras will now be installed at the other 15 stations on the line from Brixton to Walthamstow. Also, East London line trains from Whitechapel to New Cross will be fitted with interior cameras for use by police.

20. COURT CASE. Three directors of Fleetcare, a former subsidiary of the National Freight Consortium, are cleared of deliberately overcharging BR for the maintenance of its fleet of 7,000 vehicles. BR responds by saying that it intends to pursue a civil claim against the National Freight Consortium, now NFC.

20. REPORT. The Railway Inspectorate's annual report, 'Railway Safety', covering accidents in 1988, is published. The number of train accidents increased by 14% compared with 1987, to a total of 1,330. More than 300 accidents were due to malicious acts (mainly vandalism) and the number of passengers killed in accidents was 97.

20. RAILFREIGHT. The last coal train runs from Princes Risborough to Chinnor, Oxfordshire, the 07.10 Alexandra Dock Junction–Chinnor hauled by 47258.

21. ROADS. The London Traffic Monitoring Report, published by the Department of Transport, finds that average traffic speeds in inner London areas during the morning peak period has fallen from 13.9 mph in 1968 to 11.3 mph in 1988.

22. NEW BOGIE. A collaborative agreement worth £500,00 is signed by British Rail and Specialist Rail Products Ltd. for the design, development and prototype manufacture of a new, lightweight, Advanced Suburban Bogie. Future builds of Network SouthEast and Provincial multiple units will benefit from the lighter and more aerodynamically-efficient bogies. The company is a subsidiary of Doncaster-based RFS Industries.

30. WEYMOUTH. The Weymouth Quay branch celebrates its centenary with the operation of four special train services during the day.

31. EXHIBITION. At year's end almost 500,000 people have visited the Eurotunnel Exhibition Centre at Folkestone, opened in September 1988.